DISTANCING ENGLISH

Distancing English
A Chapter in the History of the Inexpressible

PAGE RICHARDS

THE OHIO STATE UNIVERSITY PRESS | COLUMBUS

Copyright © 2009 by The Ohio State University Press.
All rights reserved.

Library of Congress Cataloging-in-Publication Data
Richards, Page.
  Distancing English : a chapter in the history of the inexpressible / Page Richards.
    p. cm.
  Includes bibliographical references and index.
  ISBN-13: 978-0-8142-0741-3 (cloth : alk. paper)
  ISBN-10: 0-8142-0741-3 (cloth : alk. paper)
  1. English language—United States—History. 2. American literature—Foreign influences. 3. Literature and society—United States—History. I. Title.
  PE2809.R53 2009
  427'.973—dc22
                            2008039125

This book is available in the following editions:
Cloth (ISBN 978-0-8142-0741-3)
CD-ROM (ISBN 978-0-8142-9187-0)
Paper (ISBN: 978-0-8142-5680-0)
Cover design by Laurence J. Nozik
Type set in Adobe Granjon
Text design by Juliet Williams

ONTENTS

ACKNOWLEDGMENTS vii

INTRODUCTION 1
CHAPTER 1 A Tale of Two Languages and Whitman's Preface 9
CHAPTER 2 The Inexpressible 32
CHAPTER 3 Framing 49
CHAPTER 4 Translating English into English and "Damned Serious *Humour*" 72
CHAPTER 5 The Inexpressible and the Thing Itself 103

Notes 121
Selected Bibliography 153
Index 169

Acknowledgments

A book on the inexpressible is the work of many. To think and talk with scholars, teachers, students, friends and family for years on something both quiet and vivid has been a gift for me, a privilege, and a way of life. I thank my parents especially. My father gave wonder, his precision, and tireless care. He inhabits every sentence of *Distancing English*. My mother's openness, principles, and insights are close and present everywhere. In these years I have traveled distances and in place with my kind husband. My sister has kept her home open to us all, as has her family, Steve and Bonnie. Alice L. Wolper, Michaele Whelan, Christine Gross-Loh, Rita Mall, Giah Rosenthal, Suhlle Ahn, and my parents-in-law have stayed with me through the course. I am in spirit and days indebted to them.

I am grateful for the generous support and assistance that I have received in many ways. I hope this work may in some measure live up to the company of those who have made it possible. I owe special appreciation and debt for this book to Barbara Johnson, Helen Vendler, and Rosanna Warren. I thank the Woodrow Wilson National Fellowship Foundation for early support, and in particular Robert F. Goheen of the Andrew W.

Mellon Fellowships in the Humanities, who encouraged and supported early phases of research. Grants and fellowships from Harvard University and The University of Hong Kong made research and travel to libraries possible at crucial points. Scholars and librarians helped locally and overseas at many institutions, including the Rare Book & Manuscript Library at The University of Pennsylvania; Widener Library and Houghton Library of Harvard University; The University of Hong Kong Libraries; and The Poetry Collection at the University of Buffalo. Work in progress has also appeared earlier: I am thankful to the editors of *Wascana Review, The Dalhousie Review, ARIEL: A Review of International English Literature* and *"After Thirty Falls": New Essays on John Berryman*. My ideas and research on a subject so vast and specific grew only with the spirit and suggestions of those who took time in the midst of enormous demands: Margreta de Grazia, James Engell, David Ferry, Marjorie Garber, Mark Halliday, Anthony Kubiak, David McWhirter, Derek Pearsall, Robert Pinsky, and Derek Walcott. I am fortunate to work with generous and welcoming colleagues in the School of English: Wendy Gan, Otto Heim, Elaine Ho, Christopher Hutton, Douglas Kerr, Q. S. Tong, and all in the School who have given me support and encouragement in research, teaching, and projects. Shirley Geok-lin Lim offered attentive and continuous guidance in research and plans from my first day on campus, and I am sincerely thankful. I also thank the Officers of The University of Hong Kong and the many contributing members of the university for their continuing and strong support of research and scholarship. For years, research assistants and coordinators, locally and overseas, including Sonal Srivastava and Mônica Zionede Hall, have given their energy, patience, and expertise to growing proposals and plans, and I am grateful to them. To Marina Ma and Fiona Chung, longstanding companions in research, projects, and poetry, I am each day grateful for continuing conversations and their remarkable visions. I warmly thank Senior Editor Sandy Crooms of The Ohio State University Press for her sustained support, fellowship, and guidance. I also sincerely thank Managing Editor Eugene O'Connor, as well as everyone at the press.

*I*NTRODUCTION

This book is a chapter in the history of the inexpressible. My interest in the subject emerged in poetics. As a poetic topos, the inexpressible comes up, for the most part, in the context of forces considered to be at the very edge of representation, such as God, transcendence, suffering, evil. I found myself drawn in its long history to one node in particular: an exaggerated and overstated conundrum in nineteenth-century America, a perceived overlapping English language. Walter Channing is known for his blunt statement in 1815 about a perceived inadequacy in expression and writing: "If then we are now asked, why is this country deficient in literature? I would answer, in the first place, because it possesses the same language with a nation, totally unlike it in almost every relation."[1]

In postrevolutionary America, and peaking after the War of 1812, this node of language, bound in its articulation to the people and nation of England, found itself at the edge of its own seat of representation. The perceived impasse of speaking and writing in a language inextricably joined to itself with each utterance was a new chapter in the inexpressible. For me, there was a great deal to learn and ask. How does this perception of English overlapping English come about? Who is most concerned with the perceived impasse? How does the rhetoric of the inexpressible intersect the already fervent political and social discourse of the period? How does it intersect the history of rhetoric and the inexpressible? How does it gain footing? Where does it *not* gain footing? How is it perceived to matter or to resolve itself?

I did learn, early, its scope. The rhetoric of the inexpressible in the nineteenth century regarding a "doubled" language had a long reach in which to take root. Inexpressibility, as I will show, is traditionally founded in a combination of perfection and inadequacy: the human speaker falls forever short of meeting expectations demanded by the perfection of his or her chosen subject, whether God or a saint or inexplicable beauty. The pivot for the rhetoric of the inexpressible, therefore, is not human inadequacy. It is first a determination of the subject of praise or perfection. From discovery to settlement, the colonies were concerned, as researchers have shown, with expectations of perfection, whether of a New Golden Age, the trope of Eden, or a City upon a Hill. Of course, expectations of explorers and emigrants fell short. Where imperfection or inadequacy of land or natural commodities was detected, hyperbole of self-persuasion, poetic encomium, not to mention propaganda of investors, were at hand. Though the combined currents of expectations and disappointment competed, the rhetoric of promotion, as David Cressy explains, by far outweighed, and frequently suppressed, the "negative impressions."[2] Spreading the word of perfection by commercial entrepreneurs practically snowballed. "According to the favoured interpretation, New England promised wholesome air and brimming larders for the settlers, and enormous profits for the merchants and investors," Cressy writes. "Doubts about the barrenness of the soil or the harshness of the winters were overshadowed by the general confidence and enthusiasm" (9). The degree to which this practically formed the earliest tall tales of inexpressible and miraculous occurrences can be heard in the occasional rebuttals. Mixed in with Chistopher Levett's observations of bounty in 1624, as Cressy points to, are these concerns: "Upon these Ilands, I neither could see one good timber tree, nor so much good ground as to make a garden,"[3] he begins. He later adds,

> And to say something of the Countrey: I will not doe therein as some have done, to my knowledge speake more then is true: I will not tell you that you may smell the corne fields before you see the Land ... nor will the *Deare* come when they are called ... nor the fish leape into the kettle, nor on the drie land, neither are they so plentifull, that you may dipp them up in baskets. ... But certainly their is fowle, *Deare,* and Fish enough for the

taking if men be diligent, there be also Vines, Plume trees, Cherey trees, Strawberies, Goosberies, and Raspes, Walnutts, chestnut, and small nuts, of each great plenty.... (22)

The propensity for hyperbole of discovery, as well as the fertile land with which to ground and commercialize it, offered rich soil for inexpressibility in a continuing discourse of high expectation (along with its undercurrent of apology). Religious idealism and, particularly, new developments of inexpressibility in English Puritanism at the time of settlement traveled and intersected this node of high expectation; indeed, the rhetoric of the inexpressible, as I will show, has primary historical and fundamental ties to religious discourse. More, the turnaround and separation of the colonies from England in advancing commercial and political enterprise put new pressure on hyperbole. So did the always tailing anxieties of underachievement, which were transformed into often surprising successes (as in the *nondefeat* in the War of 1812).

Along with these acts of rhetorical self-persuasion—from discovery, to advertisement for emigration, to settlement, to political severance—an inordinate focus fell for a moment in time, cresting in the nineteenth century, on the perfection (or lack of it) in language, here, English. With every utterance, the English language and literature could be a perceived inexpressibility, potentially perfect (at best) but ultimately and hugely inhibited by its *own* expression of English and its link to England. The scope of the project, therefore, includes among many perspectives the history of the inexpressible; the delivery and style of its rhetoric in framing, even its rhetorical links to promotional rhetoric and shaggy dog stories; its intersection with commercial and religious discourse; the politics and periodicals of the period; and reference to settlement and self-persuasion. It is not a survey of the many modes or literary manifestations of the inexpressible or allied forms of frame narratives, but a look especially at extraliterary texts and contexts for this topos.

I pause at the limits of this study. This book of distancing English from English, focusing on rhetoric—not just persuasion but specifically *self*-persuasion—clearly follows lines of *choice*. As Stephen Fender says clearly, "Rhetoric may have had nothing to do with getting the African slave or the transported criminal to Virginia, but most of the anglophone emigrants to the United States up to the end of the nineteenth century ... had the *choice* whether to go or stay, or go somewhere else."[4] As we know all too well, choice involves commercial and political lines of *power*. Following the rhetoric of inexpressibility as it presumes the privilege of its nineteenth-century English speakers in the first instance, this study focuses on perfection and, in particular, poetics itself: the aesthetics of self-expression. The act of self-persuasion, to find for instance the English language a possible instrument of expression and not an impediment to it, is a matter of *perception* and opportunism based in actual economic and political options that slaves, women, Native Americans, and many others, including the English- and non-English-speaking lower class, had removed from them in their fight for basic freedoms and opportunities. Those interested in the English language as a searing source of impediment to national character (grounded in their sense that it still might lend itself to a perfect instrument) already have ties, directly or indirectly, to England, its privilege, inherited or earned, and its language; they already have ties to ancestors, real or imagined, who by choice of emigration and settlement left a country that often seemed still to set the standard of perfection in culture, literature, and poetry. Thus, this study follows the rhetoric and topos of inexpressibility, knowing that the topos suppresses and truly misses those who actually cannot speak or be heard in horrific acts of political and social oppression.

Perceptions of perfection, to which the rhetoric of the inexpressible is anchored, may be considered degrees by which potential improvement is measured, and steps of inadequacy are marked along the way. Thus, while the rhetoric of a perfect English for Americans is tied in general to privileged Americans of the expansionist period of the nineteenth century, it is worth mentioning that these privileged speakers are anything but sure of the success in the English language, literature, or aesthetics that they put forth. Many of those most concerned with this question, such as Walter Channing, George Tucker, or Fisher Ames, return to this subject and give it succinct delivery. This is important only to the degree that we recognize that *inadequacy* and *loss* are just as prevalent and valuable to those who, seeking perfection, are wrapped up in trying to express it or achieve it in the first place.

In the quest for the "re-formation of the structure of public authority" in the early republic, as Bernard Bailyn points out, there is great loss of sight: failures, as we know, of "racism, sexism, compromises, and violations of principle."[5] Combined with this quest of re-formation and its blindnesses, there is also the underpinning of extreme uncertainty: "the possibility, indeed the probability, that their creative enterprise ... would fail: would collapse into chaos or autocracy" (4). This uncertainty extends experiences of settlers in their separation from a more designed, more cultured land, and its perceived standard. This anxiety of separation, based on anything but the "newness" of the New World, and instead founded in continuities with the Old World, has now been discussed at length by scholars and historians such as Stephen Fender, David Cressy, and Andrew Delbanco, revisiting the outdated notions of American exceptionalism and indefatigable Adamic beginnings. Many emigrants' homesickness and even their return to England, landing back on grounds of familiarity and perceived certainty, are only part of the continuing story of uncertainties and fears, blindnesses and anxieties, that ideas of perfection and resettlement typically engender.

The topos of the inexpressible, therefore, is a rhetoric that is deeply concerned with uncertainty and loss in the face of high expectations. The Middle Ages were a heyday of the inexpressible, with Christianity offering high expectations of salvation in the face of earthly uncertainties: illness, plagues, and war. In the twentieth century the topos has come to be closely allied with responses to the Holocaust, where writers like Elie Wiesel and George Steiner have rediscovered the staggering gap between what can be said and what can never be said. Even in modern hands, the inexpressible is a tool of uncertainty, the stuff of ungraspable forces or events, lined up staunchly with missed opportunities. When in the nineteenth century the inexpressible comes up against language itself, it intersects postcolonial studies. The same language distribution of English in the United States at the time of independence, along with its emerging political position, put the perception of English into the category of inexpressibility as one minor but important mark of its growing influence, as well as a mark of its felt dependencies and continuities with England. A felt Englishness persisted. In 1776 an American general told his troops to behave in battle "like Englishmen,"[6] and in 1802 a report from *The American Review* also registers the problems with an overlap of language and origins with the English: "The strong resemblance which prevails in this respect among the States, is to be ascribed to the sameness of their origin, and language, and to the similarity of manners and situations."[7] The writer has to be close enough to that English to care that much. The distance achieved can appear to us to be minimal or exaggerated in its aims. We know from H. L. Mencken's *The American Language* the litany of minimal differences between American and British English.[8] Yet, for just this reason, the problem of distancing English from itself is at its most acute because of the *closeness* of American and British English, a comparison drawn by settlers and their descendants in the nineteenth century. Thus Whitman begins his Preface of 1855, not with a declaration of newness and independence, but with a funeral of the past *descending* into the future that simultaneously approaches: America "perceives that the corpse is slowly borne from the eating and sleeping rooms of the house . . . that its action is descended to the stalwart and wellshaped heir who approaches. . . ."[9] *Distancing English* is not, therefore, about the actual differences between American and British English but about the need to create distance politically and culturally and what was done about it in language.

I have now circled back to the scope of the book, which is based in poetics as it brings to bear instruments of the topos of the inexpressible, in which people reach traditionally an impasse in language and think that they cannot say anything more. Melville puts it well: "it is hard to be finite upon an infinite subject."[10] *Distancing English* maintains, therefore, a narrow focus on the subjects and objects of a specifically rhetorical discourse of those looking back to England and former privilege and reaching a perceived impasse of language itself. "[I]t is hardly to be hoped, that we shall ever make our language conform to our situation, our intellectual vigour and originality" (308) writes Channing, finishing his thought on the overlapping language. There are many causes articulated concerning a deficiency of expression and "originality" after independence, lack of leisure, improper climate, laziness of mind, along with attacks on actual copyright issues, importation laws, and curriculum decisions in the schools. But the rhetorical center of a felt inadequacy after independence looked straight at itself for a root cause of inexpressibility: language. Thus *Distancing English* begins with this impasse in the nineteenth century. It magnifies the strand of inexpressibility not to distort its proportion in the larger conversations of inadequacy, but to see its influences on literary discourse. This study, then, examines the topos of the inexpressible, explores strategies of framing associated with inexpressibility in the nineteenth century, follows the qualities of adaptation and humor in its rhetoric, and ends in modern speculations of its travels. Since the width and breadth of any of these issues, whether the topos of the inexpressible, or framing, or humor, are extremely large, I have maintained a focus on the topos and, in particular, its important intersection in the nineteenth century with Walt Whitman's 1855 Preface to *Leaves of Grass*. In examining this Preface, most of my arguments and observations regarding the inexpressibility of English overlapping English can be distilled and reconsidered from many perspectives.

Distancing English, with a special emphasis on the 1855 Preface, can be considered through genre, showing how the topos of inexpressibility works, where it comes from, and how it unfolds as a balance of literary forms. The topos of the inexpressible is not easy, nor is its context of articulation. What happens when a rhetorical strategy is aimed not only at an unbelieving audience but also at a speaker *as yet unpersuaded* of what is being said? Things are difficult to pin down with exactness. In such a text, how do we separate sincerity from insincerity, belief from unbelief, self-understanding from self-deception if the very aim of rhetoric itself is to blur the boundaries between these things? We enter the realm of rhetoric combined with speech acts trying to bring about something, with the added complication of a felt uncertainty about whether the thing being brought about is actually the "right" or "perfect" thing. Where do we draw the line? The truth is we cannot. Ambiguities are everywhere, and intention is notoriously hard to plumb. As listeners we sort this out as best we can, depending on context, but in history all the nuances of context may not be fully available to us.

My aim has been to recover the context of a rhetoric of self-persuasion within which writers seek to distance one kind of English from another. *Distancing English* may be said to be both formal and historical, formal in that the topos of the inexpressible emerges from these writers who feel they are trying to say something they are not quite able to say, historical in that formal rhetoric does not remain stable over time and must always be seen in the context of its articulation and altered conventions. But this understanding of structure and history needs to be unfolded further. The topos of the inexpressible is difficult to see, first, because of its own complex guises. It often appears when loss is great, and words fall short of the pain. Even when the topos concerns inexpressible grief, however, its foundations in the rhetoric of praise inextricably remain in its desire for unity of the body and words, the perfection of self-expression, failed expectations. The topos, moreover, has often served the body politic, where it proffers unity, a political manifestation of perfection. Under varying historical situations, moreover, its migration is not always apparent. It can be dormant, subject to disappearance, revival, and transformation. Its formal study, thus, can be misperceived as ahistorical. Poetic forms, such as the topos of the inexpressible, although persisting, appear irregularly and migrate to different politics and purposes, often appearing not to be part of the same lineage. This is the case with the topos of the inexpressible, concerned with bewilderment, uncertainty, and finally the very inadequacy of language in the face of high expectations for it.

My interest is the topos of the inexpressible's formal and historical migrations to the English language in nineteenth-century America. This migration can be said to be structural in its inception and historical in its practice; but both of these signposts can at first mislead. More accurately, it is political in its practice. The oldest form of political discourse *is* rhetoric; rhetoric is a common root of politics and poetry. Put the other way around, poetic structure and history are tied to politics. In the early nineteenth century, the topos reappears in the high expectations and dreams of perfection and consolidation concerning the language of the United States, but has been overlooked. A moment in history always looks both ways, and often the direction of poetics and *its* history can vanish in political history. *Distancing English,* therefore, explores the unexpected intersecting of histories: the contact of the inexpressible's often ignored literary history and the largely explored political history of a decolonizing United States.

It occurs with great force in early-nineteenth-century America with Walter Channing, Fisher Ames, and Charles Brockden Brown, who, for example, can host dreams of perfection in language; the structure of the inexpressible will lend itself, again, to rhetoric and the privilege of self-persuasion. Focusing on high expectations and language's inadequacy, the topos therefore can serve to consolidate self-legitimation from perceived under-recognition or insecurity. (Even when the topos depicts inexpressible pain rather than inexpressible praise, it sees personal unity and political legitimation from perspectives of loss, not insecurity.) Thus, we will see Whitman emblemizing the efforts to forge a language from itself. And in further adaptations, the topos services those who forge ahead through the trial of one's own language, dislocated and relocated, as in John Berryman's retrieval of poet-ancestor Anne Bradstreet or Wallace Stevens's formalizing the frame, "The the."[11] Framed practices of written language, as I will show, draw on humor in dead seriousness.

In new shapes, dreams of self-unity and self-expression, rooted in the history of praise and high expectations, keep alive questions concerning the politics of privilege itself. In many nineteenth-century American hands, the form of the topos with its shaggy dog pointlessness, opens its margins, theoretically, for the wider inclusion of a democracy, though within its political limitations of privilege and consolidation. The topos of the inexpressible is patterned and political wherever it occurs. This book is but one chapter in its poetic and political history.

Thus, in *Distancing English,* I have tried to see how large historical questions can often be embedded in fine-gauge adjustments of rhetoric. Indeed, I will go to some length to show that, under the pressure of two languages in one, the topos of the inexpressible comes to be temporal and practical in its usage and application at a moment of a perceived impasse of distancing English from English between 1812 and 1855. Seen in this way, a topos as seemingly otherworldly as the topos of the inexpressible can actually be minutely responsive to time.

CHAPTER I

 TALE OF TWO LANGUAGES AND
WHITMAN'S PREFACE

Most of those settlers who had elected to come to America, and their descendants, spoke English at the time of separation. Observing that "there were no 'Americans' amongst the founders of New England," Norman Pettit asks, "How, then, did the colonists think of themselves in the period leading up to Independence? By the close of the seventeenth century those who had been born in New England clearly did not think of themselves as aliens. Nor did they think of themselves as Americans."[1] "Indeed, there is every reason to believe that they thought of themselves as Englishmen," he points out, "with the rights and privileges thereof, for they referred to themselves as such" (30).[2] This self-regarding, of course, extends to language.[3] Yet the desire of distancing the colonizer's language from the settlers' self-same language is far from simple. Notwithstanding their ties to a native language, their desire to distance English in the new country suggests their need for an uneasy separation from both themselves and England.[4]

My look at self-distancing ends in this chapter with Walt Whitman's Preface of 1855. A carryover of this English self-perception into the language peaks both after the War of Independence and again after the War of 1812 (in the so-called "paper war," which heightens the growing schism of self-separation concerning the land's suitability for emigrants). Mixed in with a new-found foreignness toward the English and the language after political separation are kinship and residual loyalty. At times, the loyalty crimps; as one reviewer in 1838 writes, "We are too much in letters the province as well as colony of Britain."[5] The fear of having "no national existence" in language or literature[6] leads to the widely famous sting: "[i]n the four quarters of the globe, who reads an American book?"[7] Yet pride in American literature waxes in Theodore Roosevelt's end-of-the-century denunciation of writers who even appear to prefer English literature. The biographer Edmund Morris notes Roosevelt singling out Henry James, "whose preference for English society and English literature drove Roosevelt to near frenzy." For Roosevelt, James is an "undersized man of letters," who "finds the conditions of life on this side of the water crude and raw . . . finds that he cannot play a man's part among men, and so goes where he will be sheltered from the winds that harden stouter souls."[8] Thus, side by side with a kinship is its near relative, a bullying defensiveness.

There is, then, a built-in "civil war" of language, a perceived problem of an overlapping English language (I will from now on refer to this "perceived problem" as a "problem" to avoid the repetition of "perceived"). The impasse can seem unavoidable. The felt doubling of the English language becomes an increasingly urgent matter following the War of 1812. Walter Channing explains in 1815: "peculiarities of country, especially the great distinctive characteristick ones, and manners likewise, can be perfectly rendered only by the language which they themselves have given use to. I mean a peculiar language."[9] Yet avoiding the companion language is as difficult as losing a shadow. John Pickering's book in 1816 is titled straightforwardly, *A Vocabulary, or Collection of Words and Phrases Which Have Been Supposed to Be Peculiar to the United States of America*. But the review of it in the *North American Review* is far from simple. The review acknowledges and conservatively praises "efforts [that] have been made to preserve the English language in its purity."[10] The reviewer Sidney Willard singles out "one of the principal excellencies" of Pickering—his "enabl[ing] us to see what words are peculiarly our own" (358) while continuing to admonish that there remains the opportunity "to adopt what is necessary and useful, however new, and to guard against needless or pernicious innovations, which many, perhaps unconsciously, had before been promoting" (359). This self-debate regarding the English language, with roots in England,[11] can also seem to reflect the "want of fixity of national character"[12] (later a strategy of turning this "want of fixity" from a disadvantage to an advantage would become a trademark). Inside efforts to domesticate it, the English language can appear to remain both foreign and all too familiar. As late as 1850 a reviewer in *Harper's* is able to say that the "true secret seems to be, that the Americans, as a people, have not received that education which enables a people to produce poets," in part because "[w]riting English verses, indeed, is as much a part of an American's education, as writing Latin verses is of an Englishman's."[13] Seventy years into independence, English can still be seen as an uneasy tool for articulation.

As such, it is often seen as leading to a historical dead end: "America is an independent empire, and ought to assume a national character. Nothing can be more ridiculous, than a servile imitation of the manners, the language, and the vices of foreigners," writes Noah Webster, echoing concerns toward the English after the War of Independence.[14] Webster begins his dictionary in 1828 with a note toward redefining words as one way to approach the problem of sameness of expression:

> No person in this country will be satisfied with the English definitions of the words *congress, senate* and *assembly, court,* &c. for although these are words used in England, yet they are applied in this country to express ideas which they do not express in that country. With our present constitutions of government, *escheat* can never have its feudal sense in the United States.
>
> But this is not all. In many cases, the nature of our governments, and of our civil institutions, requires an appropriate language in the definition of words, even when the words express the same thing, as in England.[15]

More simply put, he suggests that English is a perfectly adequate language for those living in England. As David Simpson says, it is impossible after Webster "to be unaware of the argument about language as a *national* argument" (24).[16]

A few years before the War of 1812, the Federalist Fisher Ames writes (with a mix of defensiveness and transatlantic deference):

> Nobody will pretend that the Americans are a stupid race; nobody will deny that we justly boast of many able men, and exceedingly useful publications. But has our country produced one great original work of genius? If we tread the sides of Parnassus, we do not climb its heights; we even creep in our path, by the light that European genius has thrown upon it.[17]

Out of this concern about the adequacy of the English language emerge questions of inadequacy and degeneration. The English language, for instance, clearly does not have its roots in the new country, and (influenced by naturalists) the language can be at risk, therefore, of what Willard calls a "rank growth of what is gaudy and disgusting, [which] may be forced to a pernicious maturity."[18] The War of 1812 helps to set the stage for this surge in the politics of language and especially literary nationalism. As John C. McCloskey argues, "American triumphs on the sea in the War of 1812 tempered the American mind into a belief in its power to express itself in a literature independent of any foreign influence." He adds that, "with America's victory in this second war with the mother country, a new-found note of confidence came into literature."[19]

McCloskey's account of self-confidence drawn from such "triumphs" is a good example of a climate for self-assertion running ahead of itself. Amid considerable internal political opposition, America fights to a draw, yet acts as if it has won a victory. "Far from bringing the enemy to terms," writes historian Donald R. Hickey, "the nation was lucky to escape without making extensive concessions itself."[20] Notwithstanding many mismanaged campaigns (as shown by Walter R. Borneman[21]), declarations to the contrary proliferate. The country's weak *casus belli*, grievances about British interference with American shipping and British impressment of American citizens, rebound in bellicose statements made by James Madison, Henry Clay, and others, functioning as classic speech acts, attempting to enact the very thing they are talking about. Before war is declared, Madison writes, "We behold . . . on the side of Great Britain a state of war against the United States."[22] Going to war hinges on the British response to an ultimatum by Congress, and unbeknownst to Congress, the British have caved in, suspending the Orders in Council that had interfered with American shipping. Without the delay in communications across the Atlantic, many historians believe that the war might never have taken place; the declaration of war may have been "a bluff, designed to shock the British into concessions" (17). In the end, victory is declared, much as war has been initiated, in the seam of a language calling for a severance from its origins.

The following is a good example of the deployment of "unsupported" assertion. The "Battle of New Orleans was of no military significance to the war," Borneman has shown, "but politically it came to fill a huge void in the American psyche—not only propelling Andrew Jackson to the presidency, but also affirming a strong, new sense of national identity" (2–3). On the heels of a negotiated political victory, the issue again after the war is linguistic and cultural severance. "Somehow, with British armies arrayed along its borders and a British blockade locking up its ports, the United States managed to sign a peace treaty on Christmas Eve, 1814, that preserved its preexisting boundaries, even if it made no reference to one of the war's most egregious causes" (2). On the eve of war, language becomes part of a trilogy of inseparables in the House of Representatives—"we are identified with the British in religion, in blood, in language"[23]—that marks the experience of civil separation, and the basis for framing oneself anew. On December 11, 1811, Richard M. Johnson picks up on this trilogy: "The ties of religion, of language, of blood, as it regards Great Britain, are dangerous ties to this country, with her present hostile disposition—instead of pledges of friendship they are used to paralyze the strength of the United States in relation to her aggressions" (460). Exacerbated by the war is the pointed concern with language because, as Benjamin T. Spencer has noticed, "it was in the patriotic exultation after the War of 1812 that there arose, especially in certain periodicals, a sustained movement for the creation of a literature the relation of which to British letters should be as worthy as that of our military and naval forces to those of England."[24] Among the first generation after the War of Independence, the war could be seen as a watershed in self-aggrandizing identity, an object lesson not just in self-assertiveness but in staying power.

The war, to overstate the case, is won by saying it was won: Hickey sums up a wide consensus of historians: "although most Americans pretended they had won the war—even calling it a 'second war of independence'—they could point to few concrete gains to sustain this claim."[25] The saying-so betokens a formal assertiveness. In turn it would beckon a future to "back up" the present. For the literary elite, especially for a group of writers who would shortly help to found the *North American Review*,[26] a trumped-up dependency on the English language paradoxically stands for a sense of entitlement that they felt was being left behind. Writing of perceived inadequacies, Francis C. Gray distorts facts, as he unifies language with nation:

> Our language presents another obstacle to the celebrity of our writers. The excellence of modern authors is estimated by comparing their productions with other works written in the same language, most of their readers being masters of one language only. This comparison is just in Europe, where those who write in the same language generally reside in the same country, and possess the same advantages. But our language, our literature, our taste are English, and we determine the merit of our literary productions by comparing them with those of men, who enjoy better means and stronger motives for the cultivation of letters than America affords.[27]

In the years following 1812, there arises a discourse that concerns framing for the "same language" and for the inexpressible. Alliances and divisions are not straightforward. While opinions "radical in the realm of language"[28] promote the confidence for a national literature in journals such as *The Portico,* the *North American Review,* or the *Port Folio,* many conservatives have less certainty, if indirectly relishing the idea. Clearly lamenting the break with the classical, clergyman Henry N. Day draws from American know-how:

> [W]e shall not look for proof of the widely diffused prevalence of an aesthetic awakening and growth in society at the present time, in the number of our professional artists, or in the perfection of their products, as compared with those of other ages. We must seek it in the useful, rather than in the fine arts. We must not reject it because it shows an immature, rude, or even a gross and perverted taste.[29]

From several directions, periodicals and essays promote an "awakening," and Webster begins his massive project of separation, *The Dictionary of the American Language,* for a society in which "the circulation of information and opinion through print was held to be of the greatest importance."[30] The linking of language, especially written, to the creation of nationhood, of course, has long roots. Tracing the formation of how language becomes a "language-of-power," Benedict Anderson singles out the printer-journalist (he uses the example of Benjamin Franklin) as creating an imagined community based on written language.[31] For Philip Spencer and Howard Wollman, "the spread of a written vernacular" is central to a conceit of nationhood: "When an ethnic group's language develops a wide literature of its own it can go on to develop into a nation; where it does not, it is likely to fail in such a development."[32] The rhetoric that joins writing to an idea of nation is central to what Homi Bhabha calls "discourse," here an "attempt . . . persistently to produce the idea of the nation as a continuous narrative of national progress" (1). Further, he states pointedly that this ideology focuses on the nation "*as it is written*" (with its display of "temporality of culture and social consciousness").[33]

Looking at writing after the War of 1812, Joyce Appleby stresses the importance of readers in the early nation: a mature generation born right after Independence "took on the self-conscious task of elaborating the meaning of the American Revolution" and wrote for a nation composed increasingly of "participating readers."[34] Edmund S. Morgan notes that George Washington's reputation is premised on his performance in reading and writing. He shows how Washington continually transforms "what looked in the historical record like shortcomings" into triumphs through formal and written acts of "conscious creation" of character.[35]

It is difficult to understand roots and conceits of nationalism. Historians, thus, have come to see national identity more in terms of an effect than a cause. Even when ethnicity is a mainspring of collective identity, Richard Jenkins argues, in an allusion to Max Weber, that "the belief in common ancestry is likely to be a consequence of collective political action rather than its cause; people come to see themselves as belonging together—coming from a common background—as a consequence of acting together."[36] Weber suggests that speech acts or acts of assertion enable a nation to perceive itself. Many New England settlers, for example, often did not feel themselves described by their geographical designation. They saw themselves, as noted by Spencer and Wollman (31), as more faithful to the written code of the Bible and its vision of Protestant England than the English themselves. In this sense, as Stephen Fender argues, their Protestantism was portable, requiring neither churches nor clerics to be moved to a new locale: an "essential precondition of emigration, the thesis of portability." There was "no need of confession, absolution or extreme unction, or even of admonitions and moral support from the local vicar."[37] Thus, what many, such as Stuart Hall, Ernest Gellner, and Tom Nairn, explore in terms of production or narration of nation premised in a long past[38] can translate for these settlers into a premise of acting together, even coercion. Cressy notes that "The Massachusetts government attempted to control the flow of opinion" (22) and to dispel English perception of New England as a "distant backwater" (32), shorn of continuity.[39] Even on the eve of the twenty-first century, the poet and cultural critic Robert Pinsky echoes this recurring question of acting together, in his example without a priority of a perceived past: "Reason is dismayed or humbled . . . by an implied quandary: How can memory do its cultural work in the absence of continuity?"[40] "Acting together" can take on dramatic and literal urgency. What Pinsky regards as acts of cultural memory plays out in early self-conscious demands: George Washington, as Morgan explains, "wanted honor" and famously "carried himself as though he merited it."[41] Discourse that begins with such self-translation ends by restoring that which was never conceived or realized as always conceived or desired. In this construction, disadvantages are recast as advantages, and inadequacy is limited. In other words, "acting together" can defensively blur what one is not and, on the offensive, claim what one wants to be without naming conditions or costs. In this emphasis of claiming without naming, Washington literally acts out what he is not (yet) but is (framed to be).

The discourse of the inexpressible proves to be invaluable in this rhetoric of claiming what cannot be named or achieved. Its inadequacy and loss are recast instead upon a slowly widening definition of adequacy. Let us look at, for instance, how Charles Brockden Brown in 1801 props up a perceived inadequacy by his dangling of the word "enlightened": "We are united by language, manners, and taste, by the bonds of peace and commercial intercourse, with an enlightened nation. . . . In relation to the British capital, as the centre of English literature, arts, and science, the situation of *New* and *Old-York* may be regarded the same."[42] But, he asserts, America "will, at length, generate and continue a race of artists and authors, purely indigenous, and who may vie with those of Europe" (iv; emphasis added). Impatiently shortening that length, he points not to the absence of this pure production, but to its lack of public recognition or, more to the point, to its own self-acceptance: "This period is, *probably, at no great distance;* and no means seem better calculated to hasten so desirable an event, than those literary repositories, in which every original contribution is received, and the hits and discoveries of observation and ingenuity are preserved; and which contain a critical examination of the books which our country happens to produce" (iv; emphasis added). The temporal dare of "probably" will reappear fiercely in Walt Whitman's pivotal Preface of 1855, as we will see, notably without a definitive change in status or behavior, but in perspective. Brown then undermines the critic who might derail the journey from absence to presence. He sets up the foil of the inability of writers to withstand scrutiny: "It was thought that American writers would not *bear* criticism: that, as this was a *young* country, its authors must be treated with peculiar indulgence, and be encouraged by praise, rather than intimidated by censure." But this position, he says, is "applicable rather to the supposed incapacity of the critic, than to the business of criticism itself. If the critic have formed to himself an ideal standard of excellence of the most elevated kind, or is enslaved by the authority of any individual example, there is danger" (iv–v). Brown tilts the seesaw toward the future author, but only in relation to a warning, a dare of immanence, as well as imminence. Critics have second-class status, as he says, because their ideal standard of excellence may be too elevated or be "enslaved by the authority of any individual example" (v).

In April 1799 the Friendly Club founds *The Monthly Magazine and American Review,* edited by Charles Brockden Brown. Its first issue offers a self-referential letter to the editor that begins, "You have undertaken, it seems, to amuse the world with a monthly publication. I hope you have well considered the difficulties that lie in your way, and have not forgotten the old fable of the farmer and his ass. . . . I am far from thinking that your publication will deserve the fate of the ass; but I am much afraid that such a fate will befall it." In a conservative double bind, the letter promises "to extract the quintessence of European wisdom; . . . to speculate on manners and morals in the style of Addison and Johnson" and, then, warns (and again, dares): "You have promised all this; but you will excuse me if I question your power to perform it."[43] This appears at first a surprising discourse. Brown and Fisher Ames, for example, are among a redoubt of conservative members who, like those of their less conservative counterparts, impatiently imply an achievement of "genius" (nearly) as good as done. Writing about Ames in "Federalist Criticism and the Fate of Genius," Edward Cahill perceptively notices that Ames "struck a rather odd pose for such a thoroughgoing advocate of conservative Federalism."[44] Cahill explicates that posture in Ames. Instead of pointing to deficiencies in letters and suggesting the appropriate patience fitted to an inferior, Ames sees genius as "an omnipresent and timeless force, and that the circumstances of American society have only rendered it *inactive and invisible*" (687; emphasis added). Ames's Federalist politics allows him to embrace, as ever-present if as yet inexpressible, a future Milton or Shakespeare, who in effect remains openly buried (and potentially animated) by the public who desires to bury their great writer in something akin to a Poets' Corner.

Walt Whitman famously assumes the mantle of reanimating inactivity and invisibility. Many others transform disadvantage to advantage, absence to presence, defensiveness to victory, but Whitman's 1855 Preface especially draws on the vitality of the topos of the inexpressible, exploiting the vitality of frames, personae, metaphor, voices, joke structure, parody, and mimicry. Well known for an inventory of progressive signs, his Preface especially ranges over the youthfulness of Americans, leisure, and patience. Each of these, though, has already been regularly scapegoated in journals and articles. In Whitman's well-known phrase, the discourse almost instantaneously "overturns" or recasts these perceived deficiencies; in his phrase, "the signs are effectual" (26). The adjective is unerringly and contextually precise for same-language inexpressibility, and, as part of the topos of inexpressibility, the line is itself a notable frame. To say the signs are effectual is to make the sign into an action, as frames can do. "[E]ffectual" conveys not just a sense of adequacy but what might be vulgarly called a direct hit (and a set-up as in "being framed") for the English language. Under compression of a frame, an end is fully adequate to its unarticulated means. The framed voice of the Preface has thus concluded: "[The English language] is the chosen tongue to express growth faith self-esteem freedom justice equality friendliness amplitude prudence decision and courage. It is the medium that shall well nigh express the inexpressible" (25). Ames takes similar steps to convert the inexpressible into action: "Genius," he writes, is "to the intellectual world what the electric fluid is to nature, diffused everywhere, yet almost everywhere hidden, capable by *its own mysterious laws of action* and by the very breath of applause" (emphasis added). Ames continues that such action is capable "of producing effects that appear to transcend all power, except that of some supernatural agent riding in the whirlwind. In an hour of calm we suddenly hear its voice, and are moved with the general agitation. It smites, astonishes, and confounds, and seems to kindle half the firmament."[45]

Although critics have always noticed the historic importance of Whitman's Preface of 1855, its relations to the history of inexpressibility and to the actions of what is "yet *almost* everywhere hidden" (emphasis added), have not yet been looked at carefully. In the Preface resides the full spectrum of claims for imagining literary and national communities, ranging from "the genius of the United States is not best or most in its executives or legislatures . . . but always most in the common people" to more sweeping assertions, such as "The Americans of all nations at any time upon the earth have probably the fullest poetical nature" (5–6).[46] Perhaps most overlooked is that the Preface harbors the topos of the inexpressible, of which even the Preface's profuse expression is but the tip of the iceberg. The impasse of inexpressibility building after independence—a doubt of failure or silence in the English language—is embedded in the Preface. How the Preface goes about adapting a poetics of the inexpressible is both immediate and longstanding, entwined in rhetoric, strategy, and politics: literary anxiety, tensions with the past, and perceived cultural loss, amid national and imperial expansion, are conjoined with the topos of the inexpressible and poetic framing.

Inside the body of the Preface of 1855 is an articulation of the inexpressible that turns perceived cultural disadvantage to advantage. The rhetoric of turning disadvantage to advantage dates back to settlement and, earlier, to discovery. "So urgent was their [the emigrants'] need to turn their cultural loss to advantage that they fell upon, as if inventing it anew, a whole, traditional rhetorical complex," writes Fender.[47] An early example of this kind of turn in promotional writing can also be seen in a move away in early reports of voyage from "the stony reality" (2) of potential problems of settlement toward persuasion:

> Influenced by the promotional writings of the Richard Hakluyts (uncle and nephew), and building on the experience of the Roanoke settlement of the 1580s, a sequence of sea captains explored the coastline between Virginia and Newfoundland looking for a place to establish a colony. The reports of their voyages, often written to gain funding for future expeditions, presented America as a land of plenty and immeasurable promise.[48]

Rhetoric of promise and praise, joined with a state of being "unequal to the subject,"[49] has a history not only in promotional writings of settlement but also in the topos of the inexpressible. "The English language befriends the grand American expression," the Preface again suggests; "[i]t is the medium that shall well nigh express the inexpressible."[50] "Well nigh" suggests almost, but not quite. "Well nigh" undercuts "the grand American expression" because "American expression" appears already to be undermined by the same-language problem of the English language itself, not always perceived as its "friend." "National literature seems to be the product, the legitimate product, of a national language," Walter Channing has written in his now famous summary of 1815.[51]

This impasse, the articulation of a language condemned by its same-language history to a curtailed or truncated future, is stamped throughout. It is forged under the longstanding topos of the inexpressible, and recognizable conceits of expansionism and temporality attributed to the Preface are thrown into a different light. Its discursive strategies of literary potential and projected independence, established primarily in the Preface of 1855, are not unique. Yet this discourse needs to be heard in the context of its time, and an understanding of how important the history of poetics, in particular the inexpressible, is to a discussion of the English language as a medium for what it may not *yet* express. The Preface offers characteristic textual strategies that pose a series of questions about a moment of language, discourse, and history. How do local contexts and historical genres inform its language of inexpressibility, this discourse, this *framing* of English to distance itself from itself? What does it mean exactly for desired language in the Preface to lie ahead of ("shall well nigh"), but already lie inside, its own and current body of expression, namely English—and suggest itself at the same moment as a "medium" for what it is not yet expressing? What impasse occurs here that perpetuates such circular arguments?

It is important to step back momentarily and acknowledge that most concerns with Whitman's language have been identified not with his prose, but with his poems, including a longstanding look at Whitman's style. Harold Bloom's controversial claim in 1994 for "Walt Whitman as Center of the American Canon"[52] rests primarily with an analysis of style in the poems, and a steady and diverse following continues to discover in Whitman's style justifications for Philip Fisher's description of Whitman as "a grounding fact for all later American culture, as Homer was for Greek culture, or as Shakespeare became for England."[53] Such identifications of style in Whitman's poems include continuing discussions of Whitman's groundbreaking free verse, but also more recently the injection of "intellectual and aesthetic activity"; as Helen Vendler corrects in *Poets Thinking,* for instance, "Whitman has never been granted much intellectual capacity."[54] Yet, even at the outset, a reviewer in July of 1855 from *Life Illustrated,* focusing on style, practically gives up even trying to name it, landing on his own inexpressibility: "[L]ines of rhythmical prose, or a series of *utterances* (we know not what else to call them)."[55] Later that year, in September, another reviewer in the *United States Review* tautologically decides to let Whitman's style speak for itself, saying, "The style of these poems, therefore, is simply their own style. . . ."[56] A conundrum in style can sometimes yield to a compensatory and exaggerated focus on statement. "If Poetry has passed him by," Oscar Wilde quips in 1889, "Philosophy will take note of him."[57] William Carlos Williams in 1955 pursues a similar drumbeat, finding a message where he expects "light," alluding to poetry: "He had seen a great light but forgot almost at once after the first revelation everything but his 'message.' . . . "[58]

In brief, Whitman's "message"—what Charles A. Dana names in 1855 "bold, stirring *thoughts*"[59]—continues to pick up the long thread of a particular focus on an inordinate style. At present such discussions, often located on the spectrum between unity and lawlessness, appear in larger contextual references, best described by Betsy Erkkila in an excellent collection *Breaking Bounds:* "rethinking the very meaning we bring to such terms as American, literature, history, culture, and Walt Whitman himself."[60] Earlier, addressing Whitman's style directly, Erkkila writes,

> These clusters [in *Autumn Rivulets, Whispers of Heavenly Death,* and *From Noon to Starry Night*] radiate in ever-widening concentric circles from a focus on self, life, body, light, day, and the social world toward a focus on the cosmos, death, soul, darkness, night, and the spiritual world. At the same time, the clusters and the poems they include continually fold back on one another chronologically and thematically, temporally and spatially, in a manner that suggests the image of ensemble—of "form and union and plan"—that is the final design and desire of *Leaves of Grass.*[61]

As difficult a register as style creates for his poems, the poems have consistently been granted release for their innovation, formal experimentation, and social responses. In Harold Bloom's essay on Whitman, for example, a search for style and design yields ground to an analysis of another of the founding tropes commonly cited for Whitman—originality.[62] Whitman's prose has not always fared as well. It has been denigrated as "not very good" as or having the "unfortunate result of distracting critical attention from Whitman's finer achievements. . . . "[63] Even the Preface of 1855 is often ignored by those searching for style, reconfigured as "meaning," adjudicated through "thoughts" or discourse. For the most part, it is often cited as an adjunct or notation to the poems, not as the independently substantial document that it is.[64] Yet the Preface proposes certain histories and futures not found in the poems themselves. It provides, therefore, new insights into the period, the culture, and poetics. In terms of rhetoric it reveals framing, overwriting, and a humor that all but empties itself of meaning. To hear all this, however, it is necessary to know a background in poetics as well as the contemporary documents. Detailing strategies of control in still earlier literature of the settlers and founders, Robert Ferguson interestingly articulates something, difficult to name, that is important about the rhetoric and a struggle pertaining to style of foundational papers in this way: "... it is the combination that counts. Thematic simplicity and rhetorical complexity seem a peculiar blend, but they always connect in a language of political statement."[65] This combination of "thematic simplicity and rhetorical complexity," still difficult to parse, usefully helps to put a finger on why so much attention is paid to "meaning" (or crises of meanings). Yet, in terms of poetics, we can begin to hear once more Whitman's historically mediated "thoughts," what Ferguson, again, aptly names a problematic "language of many levels" (25).

To see the complex exploitation of "levels" allows us to overhear, at first, Whitman's overdetermined voices that have not been heard in relation to the topos of the inexpressible. We will hold off on the formal inquiry into the inexpressible and begin simply by touching upon the elements encircling it, such as questions of a received language and its inheritance. The English preacher Jonathan Boucher is noted for framing such self-consciousness of American language: in 1807, he writes: "Thus, the United States of America, too proud, as it would seem, to acknowledge themselves indebted to this country, for their existence, their power, or their language, denying and revolting against the two first, and also making all the haste they conveniently can, to rid themselves of the last."[66] Such frames of inadequacy spread in America to rings of self-doubts and self-defensiveness regarding not just language but literature and culture. Evaluating America's "moral and intellectual power" in 1830, William Ellery Channing for example asks, "The great question is, how far is it [the country] prolific of moral and intellectual power."[67] He adds, "These are the products by which a country is to be tried." He perorates, "Do we possess, indeed, what may be called a national literature? Have we produced eminent writers in the various departments of intellectual effort? Are our chief resources of instruction and literary enjoyment furnished from ourselves? We regret that the reply to these questions is so obvious" (275). Whitman's Preface of 1855 does not address this proliferating attitude that we have seen in kind.[68] It draws from the history of the topos of the inexpressible, a topos of human inadequacy; and it draws from framing inadequacy (of a language, a literature, a "genius") that is inextricably linked with it. Because these frames, surrounding a received language, grow out of the soil of contemporary criticism, I pause and listen to the self-debate among these earlier critics. In 1822 George Tucker, for example, all but concedes a fate of exclusion from "genius": "It will scarcely be denied, that if we examine the individuals of the two continents, with a view to compare their senses and their bodily powers, no difference can be observed." George Tucker concludes that "genius is not the exclusive gift of any country."[69] In an 1856 letter to Emerson, Whitman's stance calls up Tucker's self-protective claims that no poet presently is up to the mark: "Of course, we shall have a national character, an identity" (1336). In a shade of difference, it reappears in terms of producing character, nonetheless to blindside mimicry: "The genius of all foreign literature is clipped and cut small, compared to *our genius*" (1330; emphasis added).

Faithfully representing naysayers, the temporal frame in the Preface first accurately recapitulates and mirrors the perception of the missing "genius," who is still only yet to come, a replacement for the "priests": "There *will soon be* no more priests" (24; emphasis added). Such an utterance, held for a moment as truth, at first seems initially and routinely expanded in a bare shift to unreliable narration. After we hear that the "superior breed" (24) has yet to "arise in America and be responded to from the remainder of the earth" (25), the shift begins: "The English language befriends the grand American expression" (25). The temporal frame, that is, shifts, exaggeratedly rescinding mimicry and the apparent acquiescence, making it a matter of choice: "[i]t is the *chosen tongue* to express growth faith self-esteem freedom justice equality friendliness amplitude prudence decision and courage" (25; emphasis added). According to Washington Irving, it has been anything but; in 1838, he writes, "Perhaps, with the same language, a lingering allegiance to their models, good or bad, and the similarity of our manners and tone of mind, arising from a common origin and maintained by the tremendous influence which their literature, disseminated cheaper than our own, exerts upon us, this [the absence of a national poetry] is unavoidable."[70] The blatant unreliable narration of the initial voicing in the Preface makes this seemingly nonfictional account fictitious, this stance, a fiction.[71] Through such frames around the inexpressible "chosen tongue," point of view is repositioned.

This readjustment of point of view has a long social history in the discourse of choosing to come to America. David Cressy calls " the climate of hyperbole and expectation," as he notes in tracts such as William Morrell's *New England, or a Briefe Enarration of the Ayre, Earth, Water, Fish and Fowles of that Country . . . in Latine and English Verse* (1625), and premised on the literary convention of an idyllic setting, *locus amoenus*,[72] a "poetic encomium."[73] A practice of adapting literary conventions is established, and the topos of the inexpressible, already the epitome of adjusting point of view, becomes central in this history. Framing around what can never be expressed in a received language refits and recategorizes what is made to appear stable. One part of the the Preface's temporal frame—oversimplifying I will, for the moment, designate it simply as a "first" voice—echoes the arguments of those who profess inadequacy, such as Orestes A. Brownson: "Feeling ourselves inferior, we could have not confidence in our own taste or judgment, and therefore could not think and speak freely. We could not be ourselves. We could not trust the workings of our own minds. We were safe only when we thought as the English thought, wrote as the English wrote, or sang as the English sang." He continues:

> We Americans in literary matters have had no self-confidence. There is no repose in our literature. . . . This proceeds in a great measure from the fact that we have found our model of excellence, not in our own minds and hearts, nor in human nature generally, but in the literature of that land from which our forefathers came. Instead of studying man, we have studied English literature. . . . "[74]

In the Preface, this voice is picked up in an action of contemporary mimicry, colluding as a record of the voices which speak of a country's lagging achievement in language and literature: "but the genius of the United States is not best or most in its executives or legislators" (5). He adds, "[i]t *awaits* the gigantic and generous treatment worthy of it" (6; emphasis added). A "second" voice of the temporal frame, as we will see, takes the offensive, refits expectations of achievement to state the achieved but, given the absence just established, does so self-consciously.[75] This voice depicts not only the unreliable narration of the first voice (as a lie), but its very genre (fiction). This slippery temporal move renders the initial "facts" more unreliable than they first appear. The framing of generic and fictional unreliable narration, within the nonfictional mimicry, sets up competing discourses of disbelief. There is first a genre switch from nonfiction to fiction. The nonfiction is the first voice's recapitulation of the state of letters, the underachievement. Making the first voice's account a fiction, the second voice frames a different fiction: the achievement is immanent, actually here. The pivot is a time difference between one sense of "fiction" as untrue if framed by another "fiction" in a narrative. When the first recapitulation of underachievement is refitted from nonfiction to simply a narrative in the second's presentation (of achievements as immanent), its mimicry is pinned to narration, rather than to documentation: here, mimicry is translated into fiction, as is a perceived inadequacy of desired language and character.[76] Thus when the formerly "reliable" mimicry of the first voice (heard as nonfiction since it is recounting the palpably obvious) is made into a fiction and a lie by the second voice's decision of narrative, a once reliable speaker, speaking of underachievement, is *framed* for a moment as a fictional inner speaker: the narrator, thus, who refits the first voice's mimicry into a fiction, creates an "unreliable" character out of what appeared to be a solid speaker of certain standing perceptions of literature. As this local unreliable character is created (through the second voice), so too the larger inadequate character is recast for a moment from its freight of failure, its being tied to the binding and instantaneous "fact" and documentation. When the first voice with its mimicry and recapitulation comes back (as it does), it has been tinged with unreliability, even though the second voice framing it has told "lies" too in the process. In this set of choices between unreliabilities and what constitutes "fact," the opinions that denigrate literary strength are dared from competing fictions of narration, creating joke structures (which I will go into further in chapter 4) and new nonfictions. Facts, framed as fiction, are replaced by claimed self-evident truths, such as the one that the nation's champions have arrived and are available.[77] *Time* has been injected into the frame of the inexpressible; what at first appears a factual dead-end is transformed into a future as a dare. The Preface, thus, depicts competing defeats of defensive mimicry and, in the collision, an offensive unreliability (represented by the second voice). They all are framed in mock declarations of simplicity by the statement: "What I tell I tell precisely for what it is" (14) and "How beautiful is candor!" (19).

Within the Preface the verbs often carry the temporal frame of inexpressibility. "The American poets *are to enclose* old and new for America is the race of races," the first voice says in future tense: "Of them a bard *is to be* commensurate with a people" (7; emphasis added). Then the unreliable narration slips out: "To him the other continents *arrive* as contributions . . . he gives them reception for their sake and his own sake" (7; emphasis added). The mimic's future construction ("is to be") gives way grammatically to the unreliable narrator's plain present tense ("arrive," "gives"). Though they look as if they are present-tense verbs, "are to enclose" and "is to be" have divested themselves of their residual present-tense quality of lacking (what would have been suggested by "encloses" or "is") and "are to enclose" and "is to be" acquire instead a resonance of possibility. Between two denotations of possibility—"chance" and "realization"—lies the changeover from the mimicry, who speaks but of the future, to the unreliable narrator, who stays in the present (and marks it with present-tense verbs). Therefore two presences that have not yet been shaped except as constructions in a frame are presumed: the step into the future, as present momentarily creates the real present as past (that is, finished, done, over—and one that does not exist as it has existed, that is, as in the manifest "contributions"). In this exchange the reader is presented with a frame of disbelief: a slip from the future (initiated by mimicry) into the present (framed by an unreliable narrator). Future achievements pass for the past. They are realized. The complexities of time shifts and genre are thereby elastic, assimilated and condensed into a seemingly simple presence.[78]

Therefore these verb tenses are functional. In the Preface, for example, the first voice, initially designed to represent "fact," historically refers to the "endless gestation of new states" as a source for poetry that has *yet* to come: again, "Of them [the American poets] a bard is to be commensurate with a people" (7). Contradicting in present tense the second voice speaks, designating poetry as immanent, *not* predicated on the future:

> To him [the American bard] enter the essences of the real things and past and present events—of the enormous diversity of temperature and agriculture and mines—the tribes of red aborigines—the weather-beaten vessels entering new ports or making landings on rocky coasts—the first settlements north or south—the rapid stature and muscle—the haughty defiance of '76, and the war and peace and formation of the constitution.... (7–8)

The first voice's free fall sets up the second narrator's dead-serious stand.

The verb tenses of the speakers, thus, are integral to the tension. The first voice, preferring the future tense, appears to echo contemporary critics who fan out impatience, acknowledging the absence of what it wants (which covers both desires and lacks): a national bard. The non sequitur of a second voice, who at first is cast as more unreliable than the first, recasts the first, pulling a straight present tense from a future command. Thus mimicry carries anxiety in contemporary voices, but is undermined by the unreliable narrator. This narrator formally renames the first voice, turning it, redundantly, into foolish nonfiction. Fisher Ames has expressed constrictions of imitation: "Is there one luminary in our firmament," asks Ames, "that shines with unborrowed rays?"[79] Ames's rhetorical question proclaims that there is no "luminary," and the first voice acknowledges the same in the Preface by using the future tense. In contrast the second narrator, reconstructing that report, refutes contemporary verdicts and edicts. The mimic who returns reasserts a current lack: "The largeness of nature or the nation were monstrous without a corresponding largeness and generosity of the spirit of the citizen" (6). By being forced to separate and put back together what at first appeared to be one voice, the listener, in effect, is dared to keep the facts straight (precisely what the second voice has been suggesting in his claim for a "national" poet).

Celia Britton describes a related strategy: "[r]ather than seeking a solution to the problem as defined by the dominant culture, it changes the terms of that definition—twisting the parameters of the subject's situation in such a way as to turn lack, negativity, and otherness themselves into a means of resistance and self-representation."[80] Though the formerly dominant culture of England in this case is but a beat from a newly dominating culture in the U.S., she has caught some of the dilemma of the mid-nineteenth century of settlers recently revolting against an imperial power. Rhetoric twists what the local critics call "lack" into advantage. For example, the 1807 *Port Folio,* surveying American literature, sees a decline: "with no people, whose history is recorded, have letters flourished" in a time "[p]rior to this auspicious period" of "ample leisure."[81] Leisure, far from a flaw, is actually positive by the time the second voice appears again: "His [the American poet's] love above all love has leisure and expanse ... he leaves room ahead of himself" (12).[82]

Within the Preface the projected language (or its perceived absence) becomes a prop. "Embouchure," for example, appears: "His [the bard's] spirit responds to his country's spirit ... he incarnates its geography and natural life and rivers and lakes. Mississippi with annual freshets and changing chutes, Missouri and Columbia and Ohio and Saint Lawrence with the falls and beautiful masculine Hudson, do not *embouchure* where they spend themselves more than they embouchure into him" (7; emphasis added). "Embouchure" is not just found fit for use but is made fit by relegating its humor to the framed first voice, thereby offensively removing the language's potential to be mocked. By adding a French word and frame, the first voice can remake English, which has been at the center of potential postcolonial debate, just one of the many sources for American English.[83] Here, framing helps to explain, therefore, the preponderance of borrowed language in his Prefaces. From the Preface of 1872, "n'importe" (1000), "surplusage" (1000), "*eclaircissement*" (1001), "*sine qua non*" (1002), "literatuses" (1002) rain down on us.

There is another layer of metaphoric resonance. The first voice has echoed earlier critics, and much of Whitman's rhetoric and cast reappears;

George Tucker, for example, has examined and compared the "individuals of the two *continents*" in an attempt to find Americans *not* wanting, and Royall Tyler has cited "manners, customs, and habits of a *strange country*" imported in the "English Novel" that "renders the homespun habits of her own country disgusting."[84] For the second voice in the Preface neither the potentially superior continent nor, from the other side, its looming "looms" of influence signal anything other than a contribution ("the other continents arrive as contributions," 7). And the second voice's apparent throwaway, "he gives them reception for their sake ... " (7), demonstrates that there is *already* something to offer; he is putting it to the first voice as he has put it to Tucker and Tyler. Perhaps no exploitation by the frame, however, is richer than metaphors, and Whitman's Preface plays with resonances of youth, "embarrassments of infancy," common in the articles and newspapers at mid-century for the country's lack of age.[85] Identifying "the causes that have retarded the progress of literature in The United States," *The Port Folio* sees that its "cause which will primarily suggest itself is, *the youth of the country*."[86] The Preface makes these descriptions part of its grist. Youth becomes a heroic person, who, again, "leaves room ahead of himself" (12). The Preface, moreover, recasts youth and leisure: "Nothing is better than simplicity ... nothing can make up for excess or for the lack of definiteness" (13). Richard Shryock calls such embedded narratives "actions"[87]; rather than attempting to say something with pointless humor that but prepares the frame, the Preface attempts to do something.

Within the frames there is also doubling on important words. "Inexpressible," for example, dramatizes a rhetorical play with point of view. The unreliable narrator suggests the English language (befriending the "grand American expression") will "express the inexpressible" (25). The word "inexpressible," a point of contact between the two voices, is also its moment of self-division. It comes from the first voice, which wishes to designate the future-bound and literal connotation of "yet-to-be expressed" poetry. Crucially—and this is rhetorically complex—the first voice's literal connotation initiates a different, more liberal, connotation in the second voice. Neither voice uses it figuratively, and so the double play on literalness reveals the gap between the two. A desired national poetry is thus literally—and concomitantly—coined "inexpressible." These fictions, incompatible, are generically crossed. In the Preface of 1876, for example, the second voice says, "Poetic style, when address'd to the soul, is less definite form, outline, sculpture, and becomes vista, music, half-tints, and even less than half-tints" (1013). The first voice reappears, responding silently to critics: "True, it may be architecture" (1013). Then it cedes its place again gradually to the second voice: "but again it may be the forest wildwood, or the best effect thereof, at twilight, the waving oaks and cedars in the wind, and the *impalpable odor*" (1013; emphasis added). Trying to describe poetic style, both fictions end up with impalpability: for the second voice, the literal meaning, "inexpressible"; for the first voice, the literal inability to say, defined in exposed adjustments, the "may be," the "or," its tools for echoing "an utterance adjusted to, perhaps born of, Democracy and the Modern—in its very nature regardless of the old conventions, and, under the great laws, following only its own impulses" (1011). In Whitman's frame small equivalences, such as "perhaps" in "adjusted to, perhaps born of," indicate a transition from fact to fiction and back again, recast. The uncertainty of the first voice is a reflection of corroborating defensiveness and an integral part of the frame: "perhaps" echoes the critics' conundrum of what comes first, poet or language? Thus the problem and frame, first voice and second one, are turned inside out, making the uncertainty ("perhaps") small, syntactically negligible not negligent, but crucial. If frame texts can be said to be about "what they cannot name," the condition makes this literal and exactly acute.[88]

Since there are no easy signals for these switches in voices, it can be difficult to recognize just "who" is speaking. Look at the he-is-not-here-yet first voice in this mimicry: "Of all nations the United States with veins full of poetical stuff *most need* poets and *will* doubtless have the greatest and use them the greatest" (8; emphasis added). The second he-has-already-arrived voice bowls it over: "Of all mankind the great poet *is* the equable man" (8; emphasis added). Correction is all but impossible *because* it has already been granted; the second voice claims that the correction has been achieved and, thus, cannot come in the future ("he has passed . . . "). Giving the first voice credence, even for a moment, is to be gulled. But neither is the second voice certain. Point of view remains continuously less-than-certain: "The poems distilled from other poems will probably pass away" (26). And in March of 1891, Whitman's piece on "American National Literature: Is there any such thing—or can there ever be?" (1258) ends on an ambiguous question itself: "The whole matter has gone on, and exists to-day, probably as it should have been, and should be; as, for the present, it must be. To all which we conclude, and repeat the terrible query: American National Literature—is there distinctively any such thing, or can there ever be?" (1264).

Unsurprisingly, defensive posturing in the Preface exploits a form of the shaggy dog tale (which I will discuss later).[89] Because this is important for Whitman's Preface, I will map the area here in outline. Jan Brunvand explains that in no-point shaggy dogs, "a wholly unrelated and pointless punch line is told to a group containing some dupes who believe that they are hearing a genuine joke. When those in-the-know laugh, the suckers wonder what's wrong with their sense of humor."[90] Afraid to be outsiders, listeners laugh. But they do not, cannot, understand a humorous punch line as fiction that in fact is not humorous. Either they are suckers, or they redirect their attention from what they (do not) know to how they go about knowing.

In the Preface what is being put up is not primarily whether there is or is not a poet, but what is inherently central in every shaggy dog story—again, *point of view*. What is often uttered, thus, is invalid, to be overturned. The American poet, according to the first voice, is inexpressible, not here yet, yet to come. But according to the second voice he is already present, he is in existence; again, "he has passed" (10). Mimicry makes frames of perceived facts. The mimic's words curl back, making fiction out of perceived "real" declarations. To say this another way: mimicry seems to frame what is there—no poet—and that point of view is necessary for this frame. There are voices—"Past and present and future are not disjoined but joined" (13)—that humorously point to a lurking shaggy dog that demands "a wittily unexpected and sudden ending, all the more unexpected in that the 'lead-in' and the 'lead-up' have to be deceptively leisurely and almost diffuse."[91]

This joking demands listeners who, like the audiences of the shaggy dog stories, refuse meaning but share materials and a point of view that enable them to transform defensive stances into hurtling offense. They can accept, to use Ted Cohen's phrase, a "special invitation."[92] This "intimate community" begins from settlement (" . . . the movement of English-speaking emigrants to the New World," argues Fender, is motivated in part by drawing from Virgil, "millennial prophecies of a Golden Age restored," 63); onward past Puritan ideology of "a special people, an only people—none like thee in all the earth" [93]; to the contested cognitive work of metaphor itself: "For this [cognitive] disclosure to occur effectively, metaphor must be articulated in a mode wherein we are invited to attend to *how* it achieves its effects." He adds that "we are invited—by the tensional gap . . . —to traverse it in imaginative terms."[94]

Elastic, the frames are everywhere in the Prefaces. Here is a description of the verse form in the 1876 Preface: "Thus my form has strictly grown from my *purports and facts,* and is the analogy of them" (1013; emphasis added). The methods of writing, not only the writing, are an analogy of "purports and facts." In Whitman's frame the most important two words in their implication for both the shaggy dog story (and its variants) and, here, the local context from which the strategy emerges are the words "I say" (1011). This seemingly innocent pair has a simple singular pronoun (which gains its charge from representing two voices) and a verb (which is more than verbal due to the dramatic frames). Neither of these two words, then, should be taken merely at face value. They are an extension of the jokes-that-are-not-jokes. The frequently uttered disclaimers in the Preface, "in my opinion" or "True, . . . ," similarly, are anything but transparent; they are of course part of what makes uncertainty small, syntactically and literally negligible, and therefore crucial to making of *non*fiction. Present tense verbs, such as "is" ("Here [in America] the theme *is* creative and has vista" [8; emphasis added]) collide with future ones, such as "shall" ("Their [Americans'] Presidents *shall* not be their common referee so much as their poets shall" [8, emphasis added]).

The frames heard in the Prefaces register those voices in the early republic that are demanding an original language, refuting degeneration theories of language adapted, for example, from the work by Comte de Buffon's *Histoire Naturelle*,[95] and embracing what Christopher Looby calls the "sense of nation fabrication as an intentional act of linguistic creation."[96] It was a demand for a so far inexpressible language in writing.[97] "This country has a literature notwithstanding all that has been said in this paper to the contrary," Walter Channing says, setting up his rejoinder: "But it is not the least indebted for it to the labour of its colonies. I now refer to the oral literature of its aborigines."[98] His statement argues for the oral: "Their words of description are either derived from incidents, and of which they are famed to convey most exact ideas, or are so formed as to convey their signification in their sounds . . . and are in themselves the very language for poetry, for they are made only for expression, and their objects are the very element for poetry" (313). He hyperbolically attributes that the Indian "reposed" in the oral origins of his language and, thereby, "in the knowledge of that which was peculiarly his own" (314). By contrast he equally exposes the magnitude and length to which he has gone in writing to reveal this oral language of the Indian "now as rich as the soil on which he was nurtured" (313). Needless to say for Channing's view of Indians and their language, the Indians' oral and more perfect or pure confluence of nature and art, unlike its less "peculiar" and perfect written counterpart of English in America, has, as he says, "never been submitted by its authors to the test of comparison" (314). Thus while the Indians are "most perfectly contented with their language," they are resigned to contentment, according to Walter Channing, only by, "if it may be so called, their literary condition."[99] This "literary condition," rather than "literature," cannot by his patronizing definition compete in writing with (his own act of inadequate) writing that is as yet unspeakable (in an English language), but therefore also ever more important in growing hegemony.[100] Edward Channing also wants to proceed with writing, where potential reputation lies. The act of writing in the following quotation is yoked to oral "uttering" in its conception: "[L]et him [the writer]," he says,

> turn to the rougher and more intrepid ages of his country, before men troubled themselves about elegance or plan, and wrote right on as they felt, even though they were uttering a thought for the first time . . . whether they were to be ranked among the classicks, or barbarians in poetry, whether theirs was to be called an Augustan era, or merely the plain old English days of Elizabeth.[101]

This discourse of inadequacy combined with declared impatience, deriving from an imported topos of the inexpressible, creates an unusual slowness and complexity of delivery. I have opened with a reading of Whitman's 1855 Preface to unravel not only the weave of the text, but also the warp it is woven on; the lines consisting of framing, the inexpressible, and oral humor must be reconstructed. Some threads are easier to follow than others. A dependence on early-nineteenth-century debates about language is clear enough even though its rhetorical modifications are often exceedingly complex. The rhetoric of the Prefaces can be traced, but their poetics—their formal dependence on certain literary forms derived from poetry—will require a wide-angle lens. This is just the beginning of thinking about what happens when a self-conscious and written search for a language, distancing itself in place so to speak, emerges from roots in the inexpressible, framing, and overwriting in expanded slow motion.

CHAPTER 2

HE INEXPRESSIBLE

"It [the English language] is the medium that shall well nigh express the inexpressible" (25). Whitman's statement could point to something almost inexpressible, but not quite. Or it could point to something possibly inexpressible, but not impossibly. The statement falls somewhere between a positive assertion ("the English language is inexpressible") and a double negative ("the English language is not inexpressible"). It is hard to get a footing here. The rhetoric is hyperbolic and defensive. It harbors a perceived impediment of expression, English over English, that I looked at in the first chapter. The conversation over the doubled language in the nineteenth century eluded easy answers: is the English language so close to being inexpressible that it *is* basically inexpressible, or is the desired expression only *nearly* inexpressible in the English language, making room for hope in the expression of the nation after all in distancing English from English?

We are on shifting rhetorical terrain. Whitman's statement begs the question of whether the inexpressible can be expressed. Literary tradition, though, is quite clear on this: the inexpressible cannot be expressed. If the concern is God, or highest love, language often may not cross the gap between what can be expressed and what cannot. Chaucer's Parson can never succeed in expressing God, and Cordelia says, "What shall Cordelia speak? Love, and be silent."[1] Even within the heritage of inexpressibility, Whitman's claim is revealing. It leaves open the possibility (positioned in "well-nigh") that what is inexpressible can and will be expressed in time. More than this, the statement actually carries with it the implication that, perhaps, the inexpressible has *already* been expressed because the Preface is an utterance in which the poet is offering up his own poems as an example of a perhaps achieved expression.

The Preface of 1855, as I have shown, realizes (to put it too simply) a "double" voicing in its contemporaries. Two paired voices in the Preface characterize this. On the one hand, the inexpressibility of English, as we have seen, can be bookended by anxieties of cultural inferiority and, on the other, by a (long history of) self-promotional rhetoric or praise that it takes to frame such fears as needless. To review quickly: the first voice in the Preface echoes that a literature cannot be expressed, while the second voice jumps ahead to say that it already has been expressed and in fact may already have passed the reader by. The inexpressibility of the first voice echoes the despairing discourse of Walter Channing, Fisher Ames, and others. The dare of the second voice to express what cannot be expressed has been hinted at in the very same texts. "True, we labour under disadvantages," Channing first writes. Then he changes directions. "But if our liberty deserve the praise which it receives, it is more than a balance for these. We believe that it is. We believe that it does open to us an indefinite intellectual progress."[2]

The Preface performs a number of adjustments to a longstanding literary convention, the topos of the inexpressible. To hear more clearly the expectations in the early part of the nineteenth century of (possibly) expressing the inexpressible language and literature, therefore, it is important to know the lineage of the topos. What happens in that period rests on earlier fundamental foundations and alterations of the topos. An ever increasing responsibility by the speaker to meet the expectations of the inexpressible—at the limit, *to distrust* its unreachable perfection altogether, or *to trust* the human responsibility to inhabit the challenge of words themselves—stubbornly finds a home historically in this topos of the inexpressible, a rhetoric traditionally bound with perceptions of perfection and inadequacy. In tracing the topos's development from the Middle Ages to an impasse of English in the nineteenth century, it may appear as if I am oversimplifying it or the topos; in the appearance of each, there are differences in makeup, appearance, timber, and gravity. Because my focus is on the intersection of this topos with a perceived inexpressibility of language in the nineteenth century, I have not lingered over these differences (though I know they are important). This chapter helps to illuminate this complex and important topos that will enable writers to traverse a perceived impasse of language, an acutely perceived inexpressibility.

Whitman's Preface fully utilizes the inexpressible topos's dealing with what can and cannot be expressed, and so we must, first, see how the Preface came to squeeze time and opportunity from a topos that conventionally looks to timelessness and human inadequacy. This brief history of the topos will enable us to see the basis for this particular adaptation. In this short survey we will especially take note of how a topos traditionally concerned with having *too little,* or insufficient, language for expression comes to find itself potentially with way *too much* language—not knowing how to select and choose just the right expression for itself. It takes a little time to cross this distance. But it was abetted by a predominantly political turn toward discovering an overlap (or excess) of language; an expression in English already had a footing in a topos that had been heading in the very same direction: the remote possibility of expressing the inexpressible, given time and the proper selection of words.

Although much about the topos has been studied, for many in English and American literature the terrain is unfamiliar. It is not easy going since the topos of the ineffable and the topos of the inexpressible are so intertwined in practice that they are often used interchangeably. When the classical topos of the inexpressible intersects Christianity, the "ineffable" emerges, and its prevalence crests in the Middle Ages. The difficulty hovers in this Christian context not over the struggle of language sufficiently to praise leaders or rulers, as in the *Iliad,* for example, but to fitly praise God and represent divine love. This difficulty is articulated by St. Augustine: "not supposing we have found what we seek, but having found (as seekers do) the place in which to look. We have found, not the thing itself, but where it is to be sought."[3] The topos is later taken up by early Christian writers, because the sacred frequently manifested itself in the Bible, the Lives of the Saints, and devotional treatises. The topos of the ineffable expands *occupatio,* the rhetoric where a speaker says, "Words fail me" and goes on anyway.[4] In Chaucer's parody, for example, the Squire claims to give up on describing the epitome of beauty in a king's daughter, saying, "It lyth nat in my tonge, n'yn my konnyng; I dar nat undertake so heigh a thyng." Tacking defeat finally not to human insufficiency but his own insufficient position, he confesses: "Myn Englissh eek is insufficient.

/ It moste been a rethor excellent, / . . . I am noon swich, I moot speke as I kan."[5]

In *European Literature and the Latin Middle Ages,* Ernst Robert Curtius properly collects the roots of such utterances under the inexpressibility topoi.[6] *Topos* is Greek for place, and in classical rhetoric it is a conventionalized topic to which texts, and originally orations, continually refer. Topoi originate in what Curtius calls "helps toward composing orations" (70); in conventions "set forth in separate treatises," they "penetrated into all literary genres" (70). Curtius locates beginnings of the inexpressibility topos in panegryic, in which "the orator 'finds no words' which can fitly praise the person celebrated," as well as more generally in what he names the "'emphasis upon inability to cope with the subject'" (159).

Like many conventions, topoi have long existed as part of what Curtius sees as a vast literary toolbox, taking on different meanings at different moments in history. What might be called the high road and the low road in Bunyan's *Pilgrim's Progress* can, for example, reappear as the highland-lowland literary device seen in much of Hemingway's fiction.[7] Like a Romanesque church rebuilt by Gothic craftsmen, any rebuilt topos necessarily carries with it a foundation that can have different inflections in different times and places.

Topoi, as it is becoming apparent, are something more than just topics, such as Jacob's ladder or the tree of knowledge. Each topos carries with it a technical mélange of styles and modes of representation peculiarly suited to it. In literature, two of the most common are the eulogy and the humility formulae, spilling over into literary genres and techniques. Eulogies came to be characterized by the overuse of poetic devices,[8] and Curtius shows "how close the contact between poetry and the rhetoric of eulogy could be" (155). The second topos, humility, exploits authorship itself, particularly the rhetoric of self-abasement. Like the other topoi mentioned above, the ineffability comes with a heritage of stylistic and narrative associations. Just as the eulogy relies on poetry and the humility topos relies on devotional formulas,[9] so did the ineffability topos have a literary mode for its representation—framing. This strategy deals with the gap between what is expressed and what cannot be represented. Framing, that is, goes hand in hand with the topos of the ineffable. Framing is especially useful, then, as we will see in chapter 3, for concerns with perceived and self-opposing constraints of inexpressibility, those of inadequacy and perfection. Frequently a concomitant of the inexpressible, a high style can often seem artifical and remote. "Rhetoric," C. S. Lewis once observed when writing about the European tradition, "is the greatest barrier between us and our ancestors."[10]

The topos of the ineffable can seem historically remote, or even arcane. It has a great link, for example, to mathematics. Joining religion and mathematics, André Kukla claims that we are able to "know certain truths which it is beyond the power of language to express." He continues, "Mathematical and many religious ineffabilists also agree" that an "attempt to express the ineffable must systematically embroil us in contradictory assertions."[11] The ineffable topos can fundamentally assert "unrepresentability," which Kukla says is "undoubtedly the prototype of ineffability" (135). Some of the more common nodes of intersection of the ineffable with religion and its characteristic self-contradiction include 1) the well-known writings of St. Augustine, named by Peter S. Hawkins as the "most influential interpreter of this rapture," that is, of unmediated and unrepresentable contact with God, in which God's language is paradoxically referred to as silence[12]; 2) the work of fifth-century philosopher and grammarian Bhartrihari, for whom the idea of a supreme reality Brahman and word (*shabda*) transcended spoken and written language[13]; and 3) Buddhist philosophy in which, as Ben-Ami Scharfstein explains, the "ability of words to capture (to 'name') the Tao in the sense of reality in itself" is attacked (*Ineffability,* 86). Each of these approaches names a major point of contact between religion and the ineffable. St. Augustine, for example, writes, "... God should not be said to be ineffable, for when this is said something is said. And a contradiction in terms is created, since if that is ineffable which cannot be spoken, then that is not ineffable which can be called ineffable."[14]

The ineffable in the Christian era originates in a warning which delimits the precincts of the sacred. The action of admonishing is indicative of this religious branch of the topos in which language, as Anne Howland Schotter points out, can "warn against its own inadequacy—if the signs would warn against being taken for the thing they signified." This strategy of warning, common to the topos itself, conversely represents, as we have seen, a strategy of praise. If St. Augustine cannot use language to express God, he can nevertheless employ it to praise Him.[15] Scharfstein puts it succinctly, "*Ineffable* is often the most effective superlative we can use."[16] Though in keeping with a "sermo humilis" with regard to perceived higher states of being, the topos nonetheless is among the most elaborate and formalized figures in writing. It requires a "verbal ingenuity and confidence,"[17] a recognition both of limits and an "intimation of a transcendent" (9). Occasionally split by a reference to its secular past, the topos travels through Italy, France, and Spain (most famously perhaps in the writings of St. John of the Cross).

In different ways, medieval writers lean heavily on the topos. Dante Alighieri generates in *Paradiso* a large-scale drama of the ineffable in relation to God's Word; as does the famous *Pearl*-poet who, as Schotter argues, "makes the inadequacy of *language* in conveying the Divine an implicit theme as well." She writes, "[a]t the same time that he [the poet] exploits the most splendid resources of his medium, he includes some of its pedestrian characteristics as a warning against excessive trust in language," whether on a rhetorical or theological level.[18] The theological implications and Augustinian model for "what cannot be said" continue to dominate the poem, as Schotter points out: "By using language which warns against itself, the poet is able . . . to suggest the Divine Word through the limited medium of his own words" while warning listeners against the inside dreamer's lack of humility.[19] The topos also appears as a conventional trope of humility in Chaucer's *Troilus and Criseyde:* "And ek for me preieth to God so dere / That I have myght to shewe, *in som manere,* / Swich peyne and wo as Loves folk endure, / In Troilus unsely aventure."[20]

Yet, the drive in this failure for the poet to use, as Schotter suggests, his "most splendid resources" leans into human capacities to express wonder. The ineffable filters, therefore, through many genres, including love stories and quest romances. The expression of an inability to speak appears throughout the Middle Ages in secular descriptions of language's inadequacy for any *marvellous* subject to which "'words could not do justice.' . . . It even has a form specific to alliterative poetry in the formula '*it is to tor* [too difficult] *to telle,*' which the *Pearl*-poet himself uses in *Sir Gawain* to describe indescribable luxury" (28).

Thus, the topos's strategic quest for praise of the divine *and* for a listener's approval revives the idea of wonder in the Renaissance, notably in Shakespeare's plays. As Marjorie Garber points out, an already thin line between praise and wonder in the topos is exploited, by which near-transgression toward the unspeakable opens out, she argues, from praise (ineffability) into wonder (unspeakability or inexpressibility): "And it is here, in the realm of 'wonder,' that the inexpressibility topos in Shakespeare has its most powerful effect. Instead of eloquent silences at moments of great emotion, the audience is confronted by characters who try to express the inexpressible by acknowledging that they cannot do so." She emphasizes the adaptation of the topos to new ends, saying that the "fundamental use of this topos . . . is for aggrandizement of the subject, whether it be a person, a feeling, or an event."[21] In Garber's view, such an emphasis calls attention to a "created artifact" and more specifically "a mode of expression." Turning to focus on the frame and the "aggrandizement of the subject" rather than on the actual inadequacy is a large turn toward what Garber says "we [in the audience] can only imagine" (41).

In both Spenser's and Milton's use of the ineffable, there can also be seen a concern for the audience's role. An important change of focus occurs from the unapproachable subject (such as God) to the speaker (what might be called the participant with the topos). It occurs side by side with an emerging shift in language from the ineffable (and its focus on the unreachable divine) to the inexpressible (and its still larger emphasis on the speaker). Maureen Quilligan describes the founding and primary problem of *Paradise Lost* in these terms: it is how to create a bridge in the tradition of the ineffable "between the sinful limits of the audience's understanding and the unspeakable bliss of prelapsarian union."[22] She discovers Milton's rejections of Spenser's own use of the topos, a rejection, that is, of "self-conscious mediateness of Spenser's sort of allegory," in favor, she writes, of crafting a more direct and literal language (67). In Milton's rendering of the ineffable, according to Quilligan, there are "signals to the reader" that can awaken the "option that Christ literally works within its [Milton's] fiction" (78). It dovetails with Garber's displacement of the ineffable's characteristic demand for praise toward deference in the Shakespearean audience for wonder.

Both Quilligan and Garber note the diminishment in the religious emphasis on *warning* (due to human transgression) and the rise of *inadequacy* (and a discourse of reception by the speaker). This shift is also present in what Stanley Fish's well-known interpretations of the ineffable amplify and make monumental: they appear in his introduction to what he calls "self-consuming artifacts." He writes, "What is required is a mode of action that is simultaneously assertive and self-effacing, a difficult balance which Augustine achieves . . . by continually calling attention to the ultimate insufficiency of the very procedures he is discussing (and therefore to the insufficiency of his present effort)."[23] He adds that "Augustine, in effect, has made language defeat itself by making it point away from the temporal-spatial vision it naturally reflects" (42). Fish moves directly to discourse, or what he often calls a "mode of action" (40).

> Of language such as this one cannot ask the question "what does it mean?" for in everyday terms it doesn't mean anything (as a statement it is self-consuming); in fact in its refusal to "mean" in those terms lies its value. A more fruitful question would be "what does it do?"; and what it does is alert the reader to its inability (which is also his inability) to contain, deal with, capture, say anything about, its putative subject, Christ. The sentence is thus a ploy in the strategy of conversion, impressing upon the reader, or

hearer, the insufficiency of one way of seeing in the hope that he will come to replace it with something better. (42)

Fish is describing of a new stage of the inexpressible.[24] The prevailing pattern or strategy of a sermon, according to Fish's perceptive analyses of Donne's sermons (especially), is *didactic:* "to educate is to change, and in a sense, to convert; the end of education is not so much the orderly disposition of things, but the illumination and regeneration of minds" (20) by which "the reader is first invited to consider a problem in terms with which he is likely to be familiar (and therefore comfortable) and then forced by some unexpected turn in the argument to *re*consider not the problem, but the terms" (32). All in all, the "sermon, preacher, and parishioner dissolve together into a self-effacing and saving union with the source of their several motions" (70).

In Fish's redirection, language itself becomes more central. Fish's apprehension of the inexpressible actually is in accord with its religious traditions of warning in the ineffable: the language "becomes a vehicle of humility, for its most spectacular effects are subversive of its largest claims" (70). But, centrally, the discourse also identifies a version of Nancy K. Miller's idea of recasting, or *"truth effect"* which creates a familiar pact that "stages a meeting with symmetrical desire in the other constituted by the readers."[25] The conventional act of warning in the Anglican sermon, thus, is fused with a discourse of participation and conversion. The sermon, as Fish concludes, "thrusts the forms of language before us so that we may better know their insufficiency, and our own."[26] A summary would sound like this: the substitution of something higher or better is indicated by the increasing irrelevance or disappearance of language, preacher, and parishioner into a *self-consuming artifact* (seen from the traditional side of warning in the ineffable topos), or, it may be said (in terms of Miller's "pact" or "affective event," 12) into *self-aggrandizing discourse.* A simpler summary would run this way: in the move from the ineffable to the inexpressible, there was a shift from authorial warning to the audience's (tremendous) capacity to react.

Unlike the Anglicans, therefore, who, as Fish writes, *"display* language"[27] to better map language's own insufficiency, Fish notes that the Puritans prided themselves on their capacity for *truth* through language. Their sermons make "linguistic forms serviceable by making them unobtrusive" in an actual attempt to "claim everything"; they do not disavow language's claims (75).

Inadequacy is being recast in new terms. Each attempt or instance of utterance becomes an impediment, therefore keeping inadequacy of expression in the foreground. Each word in this emerging inexpressible is not hard won, that is to say, not won at all, as traditionally determined. Instead, it is hard *lost*—a near-hit, obtruding with each utterance as just missing, if still missing. To say this in another way: inadequacy is being fundamentally measured not in terms of the more traditional forbidden territory of the Word, but through an excess of expression in the wrong directions.

This line of argument, which may seem like nitpicking, is not. We are heading toward the terrain of Whitman's Preface from an emerging seriousness about the possibility of carrying what is perceived as inexpressible in language. That is not the case with the ineffable in medieval and early Renaissance texts. There it is couched in language that organizes humility around its inadequacy. Seeking assistance from the Muse, Spenser in *The Faerie Queene* invokes the inexpressible's humility; with the conventional show of deference, grounded in the shortcoming of his language, he implores Queen Elizabeth: "O goddesse heavenly bright, / Mirrour of grace and majestie divine, / . . . Shed thy faire beames into my *feeble eyne,* / And raise my thoughts, *too humble and too vile,* / To thinke of that true glorious type of thine, / The argument of mine *afflicted stile.*"[28] The insufficiency of words appears again in Una's "great grief," which "will not be tould, / And can more easily be thought" (7.41). George Herbert puts it succinctly in "The Flower": "We say amisse / This or that is: / Thy word is all, *if we could spell*" (1.19–21; emphasis added). In the traditional ineffable, self-defeat, which anchors itself to language, ultimately mocks the extraordinary and elaborate efforts of the human tongue to reach what forever exceeds its grasp, even if by the Renaissance, the ground is tilting toward questions of reception. Inadequacy is a measured failure, a direct contrast to the highest human verbal performance and its attempt at achievement. St. Augustine and Dante draw upon this map for their preparation of a truth that is outside human time and space. (To help point out the gap between human experience and a truth inaccessible to human reach, poets such as Dante, Chaucer, or Spenser conventionally used allegory and analogy.[29])

But most interestingly, in the theology of English Puritan sermons of the Renaissance, there exists, as Fish suggests, a remote possibility of actually carrying the truth in language: "the faculties are put in good working order and made answerable to the task of comprehending truth."[30] By the time the Puritans reached America, this remote possibility fell in line with the notion of "*un*fulfillment": "The future, though divinely assured, was never quite there," Sacvan Bercovitch explains of the American Puritans' trust in a divine plan of progress made manifest not just in New England, but in the New World at large.[31]

This understanding of the inexpressible, it has to be emphasized, is canted differently from the absolute human inadequacy and depravity of the ineffable of Catholic and Anglican forebears. Bercovitch writes that "threats of doom, derived from Christian tradition, imply a distinction between the *two realms* [human truth and God's permanent and universal Truth]; their [the Puritans'] language itself, expressing their special sense of mission, incorporates the threats within the broader framework of the absolute" (29; emphasis added).[32] The "rhetorical synthesis of man's time and God's was first outlined by John Cotton and John Winthrop," Bercovitch adds. "It was developed by their colleagues and heirs into a comprehensive definition of New England's errand into the wilderness, a dream of a society in which '*the fact could be made one with the ideal.*'"[33] Thus, the "New Englanders," he adds later, "acted as if they were damned while presuming they were saved" (51). Though the Puritan aspect of inadequacy is connected to damnation and related, therefore, both to Augustinian humility and to the topos of ineffability, it itself shades into (always) pending fulfillment, restoration, and potential success that were guaranteed not by the Puritans themselves but by their God (16).

Perry Miller explains that in this practical revision of the ineffable is a need to reach truth *through* language, "by deductions from the content of their conception of Him, whereas most of their predecessors, they believed, had arrogantly pretended to extract deductions from His inscrutable essence"[34] and inevitable human failure. Miller adds: "If the Puritans, for all their admonitions to impartial perceptions of the divine Being, nevertheless emphasized certain conceptions of Him at the expense of others, and even came close to identifying these conceptions with His essence, it was because they were impelled by the spirit which informed their articulated creed" (14).

The Puritans' articulated creed participates in the colonies' history and circulation of promotional writings of discovery, catalogues of unspeakable excellence (commercial) and abundance (raw materials), and, at the same time, a lost Golden Age.[35] The language retains a hope of merging the ineffable ideal with the factual world. It presents a perpetually remote possibility of expressing the inexpressible in language, to have, in Miller's words, "discoverable truth as already discovered, set down in black and white" (20). I do not want to overstate. God, of course, theoretically remains an unknowable essence for the Puritans, as Miller puts it, "in common with Augustinians of every complexion, medieval or Protestant." At the same time, however, "they believed that for centuries philosophizing divines had *mistaken the limitations* of the mind for the limits of reality" (13; emphasis added). From the point of view of orthodox apologetics, Miller concludes that "the space between revelation and the inconceivable absolute" is "the one fissure in the impregnable walls of systematic theology" (21). In other words, they make implicit (not explicit) room for the absolute ineffable, in practice, to be less absolutely inexpressible. Inadequacy is measured, importantly, by too many "wrong" words, each and every one just barely out of place, time and time again: under different conditions or circumstances, the inexpressible might be otherwise.

As we have just seen, the history of the topos has evolved a branch which has made room for the possibility of time and expression: again, a *"space* between revelation and the inconceivable absolute" (italics added) is what Miller calls a fundamental fissure in the ineffability topos. This making of room for expression in the topos is a key development for a perceived impasse of language in the New World. In chapter 1 we have seen that impasse slowly evolving side by side with a rhetoric of high expectations and national hyperbole. We have heard these high expectations for a language emerging from an overlapping one, and the inadequacy therefore to find a literature or author. In 1819 Richard Henry Dana, Sr. writes with impatience both of missing authors and false starts toward them: " . . . we at once become exceeding angry—begin to talk in large and general terms of American genius and enterprise, forgetting that first-rate authors are not as easily made, as prime sailors and soldiers."[36]

Yet, with the historical *fissure* of the ineffable—the shift of the ineffable to a remote, that is, a *remotely possible,* inexpressibility—come high expectations to express what is perceived to be out of reach. In this emerging emphasis of the topos, therefore, human inadequacy, traditionally absolute, can be reattached in the topos to moment-to-moment potentially "avoidable" failures. We can now clearly identify a few of these strategies, appearing in the impasses that we have heard in chapter 1. These strategies, crucially, find *too much* of the ("wrong") language, rather than, more traditionally, *too little* of the "perfect" one. For a perceived overlapping English, these strategies are central.

The philosopher André Kukla helps us to identify such strategies. Each strategy pertains to the emerging possibility of moment-to-moment inexpressibility, even if it still remains impossible. One of the purposes of his research is to identify a "new taxonomy" for the ineffable. As he explains, he applies a *"new taxonomy* of ineffabilities to the phenomenon of religious mysticism" and then looks at the consequences "generated by the new taxonomy."[37] This taxonomy introduces the temporal to the traditionally timeless ineffability topos. He puts it this way: "we could introduce a *temporally* indexed notion of any of the varieties of ineffability" (153; emphasis added).

Two of Kukla's new categories or strategies should be looked at closely: they pertain to the (remote) possibility of introducing time, and an elimination of inappropriate or "excess" language, for expressing what cannot be expressed.[38] One category is called the "unselectable." He explains that "despite the fact that a suitable sentence ... comes to mind, the speaker always evaluates it as an inappropriate thing to say" (xii). In this case, there is an excess of the inappropriate language. He explains further: "We may, under certain circumstances, come to entertain the possibility of saying an *unselectable sentence;* but *we always decide against it in the end.* It always seems to be too contentious, or too troublesome, or too trivial a thing to say" (146; italics added). Here are two short examples of this strategy, as we can now hear them, in the context of an English language that has been perceived as carrying its excess of England's English language and literature. Whitman classically formulates inexpressibility in what he calls "imaginative literature" ("A Backward Glance," 662). First he claims inevitability: "The Nineteenth Century, now well towards its close ... never can future years witness more excitement and din of action—never completer change of army front along the whole line, the whole civilized world. For all these new and evolutionary facts, meanings, purposes, new poetic messages, new forms, and expressions are inevitable" ("A Backward Glance," 659–60). Yet Whitman does not "dare" to *select* from among these the "expressions" long sought in the nineteenth century. "Let me not dare, here or anywhere, for my own purposes, or any purposes, to attempt the definition of Poetry, nor answer the question what it is."[39] Though, as he says, this decision is a general statement for "any purposes," it is also in context of the calls for an original literature rhetorically suited to his "own purposes" and those who have been demanding the inevitably of such expressions. The gist, it turns out, is not a warning based on the timeless impossibility of naming "Poetry," generally—but a calling to answer *in time* the very same question for themselves with other words, in what appears in an "illustration" still to be found selectable: the time now "had come," he writes " ... to illustrate all through the genesis and ensemble of to-day; and that such illustration and ensemble are the chief demands of America's prospective imaginative literature" (661–62). The shift from a perfect expression of "Poetry" to a practice, declaration, and self-illustration of the same points to the "prospective" but yet to be found selected "imaginative literature," whose *time* is now here. Here we see the temporal, as Kukla suggests, injected into the traditional topos of the ineffable.

A second category is what Kukla calls the *unabducible*. In this case, no *suitable* expression for the desired inexpressible "ever comes to mind for consideration as a possible speech act" (xii). In this case, too many unsuitable expressions (of the English English overlap) crowd out the desired American expression. For example, in J. Hector St. John de Crèvecoeur's own Pine Hill in Orange County, the soil itself becomes a metaphor for potential inadequacy in language. Soil appears a conventional metaphor in Crèvecoeur's letters, published in 1782: "Men are like plants; the goodness and flavour of the fruit proceeds from the peculiar soil and exposition in which they grow."[40] But in an already self-conscious context of a nonnative soil for the English language, the metaphor, takes another direction. In the tradition of the ineffable, it arrives as a stamp of inadequacy in terms of (failing) attempts to speak through a nonnative language, forever foreign to the soil. Yet, from the angle of the *unabducible,* no suitable language has been available *so far.*

Words uttered in the name of God or country—for example, Crèvecoeur's "What then is the American, this new man"?—have been *from the start* drawn from a residual attachment to the "knowledge of the [former] language" (alongside an equally paltry and former attachment to "love of a few kindred as poor as himself," 49). Making room for a language still out of reach, the question "What then is the American, this new man?" is framed as unabducible. The "new" and suitable language may spring moment to moment from the (same) inadequate soil of the "former language." What must be spoken by the farmer that cannot be (easily) spoken is buried in the metaphor of ineffability: once the proper fruit is cultivated, there is a remote hope, now drawn from time as much as from stubborn soil, of expressibility: for words to portray the new nation, its laws, as Crèvecoeur says, "the new government he [the American] obeys, and the new rank he holds" (49).[41]

The dense language makes recapitulation useful: the ineffable with its emphasis on subservience to God or an extraordinary event both praises the unreachable object and recognizes the failure to achieve it. But this adapted inexpressible is (perpetually) in the making, continuously displacing its own potential with itself, daring itself into existence ahead of itself, then retroactively representing it as potentially already there in the overlap of words, just *not yet* perceived as fully suitable or selectable. The inexpressible is put into an overwritten form of improper selection, since writing out the problem of English over English leads to a hyper-self-conscious defensiveness and an on-the-offensive obtrusiveness. It also insists on a temporal emphasis of the (yet-to-be-expressed) utterance. Crèvecoeur writes in the voice of the American farmer, "I wish I *were able* to trace all my ideas; if my ignorance prevents me from describing them properly, I hope I *shall be able* to delineate a few of the outlines, which *are* all I propose" (51; emphasis added) The ineffable has here been transformed: time ("were able," "shall be able," "are") has replaced eternity, and impatience in time ("I wish I were able . . . .") has become a substitute for inadequacy. The result in the inexpressible is a frame outlining what is as good as done in a rhetoric of what is to come. Crèvecoeur's plain, nearly unobtrusive self-contradiction dramatizes this: "The American is a new man" (56). Something of futurity has already passed, combined in a present tense linking verb of indescribable perfection.

In other quarters, we can hear more literally a promotion for finding England's English words unsuitable as a way to champion American ones. Noah Webster writes in 1828, "but, in the United States, many . . . terms are no part of our present language,—and they cannot be, for the things which they express do not exist in this country. They can be known to us only as obsolete or as foreign words. . . . The necessity therefore of a Dictionary suited to the people of the United States is obvious."[42] In this instance, Noah Webster urges Americans to begin all the more to hear England's English as precisely "unsuitable." Rather than making the case defensively, Webster attacks the perceived inexpressibility, underscoring good reasons for the unsuitability of England's English in the very same "overlapping" American English—and providing good reasons of course for his dictionary.

In the discourse of same-language inexpressibility, the inexpressibility of unsuitable sentences ("unabducibility") or inappropriate ones ("unselectability") resonates most strongly. The new taxonomy of Kukla helps to identify a shift toward what cannot be spoken (and its potential for correction), rather than what cannot be represented originally associated with the ineffable and its inevitable utter human inadequacy. For example, to frame what is still out of reach due to improper selection of one's *own* perfectibility, in a larger frame of the same-language question, Benjamin Franklin in 1732 invokes the standard and religious ineffable and its concern with the unobtainable "perfection." Changing the register of the topos to the inexpressible, he humorously compares man's perfectible state to that of a chicken: capable within itself to find its own perfection perfectly suitable:

> If they mean a Man is not capable of being so perfect here as he is capable of being in Heaven, that may be true likewise. But that a Man is not capable of being so perfect here, as he is capable of being here; is not Sense; it is as

> if I should say, a Chicken in the State of a Chicken is not capable of being so perfect as a Chicken is capable of being in that state. In the above Sense if there may be a perfect Oyster, a perfect Horse, a perfect Ship, why not a perfect Man?[43]

For Franklin, perfection of oneself should be considered at least *possible* in relation to oneself, and in particular one's own language and laws. Pamphleteer Matthew Wheelock's statement that "to expect perfection in human institutions is absurd" once provoked in Franklin a passionate defense of de facto perfectability in America: "Why did you yourselves not leave our Constitutions as you found them?"[44]

This shift from what cannot be "represented" ever to what cannot be found "expressed" (or suitable or selectable *yet*) is a companion to the increasing visibility of the term "inexpressible." In the founding period, the newer view of the ineffable is plain in Joseph Addison's comment from 1711: "I gazed with inexpressible Pleasure on these happy Islands."[45] This emphasis, of course, has appeared even earlier, for example, in Milton's desire to transfer the burden of unspeakability from the object of attention, such as the Word, to its embodiment in the listener. It also marks a gradual turn away from the mystical or religious states of being associated with the topos, and it anticipates the ultimate secularization of the topos that will include, as well as emotive intensity, punning. Notice the play with plurality in Catherine Gore's *Sketches of English Character* (1852): "A pair of standard footmen seems to be the real pair of inexpressibles." Alluding to the emerging colloquial use of the plural for "breeches" or "trousers" documented earlier in 1790, the following stanza joins plurality to the inexpressible: "I've heard, that breeches, petticoats, and smock, / Give to thy modest mind a grievous shock, / And that thy brain (so lucky its device) / Christ'neth them inexpressibles, so nice."[46] The euphemism of "unmentionable" mixes with the rarified air of the Romantic "inexpressible" and the sublime.

The sublime anticipates both the pleasure, and later grief—the aesthetics and ethics of perhaps inarguable silence—that will inhabit the term.[47] Writing of the German and French philosophical despair, George Steiner notes that the "instrument"[48] of language leaves an inarguable silence where outrage or futility lies. He muses that the "first articulate word spoken will bring down the curtain" (52). New modes of international expression for the unspeakable horror, grief, and despair of the First and Second World Wars have been outlined in Steiner's "Silence and the Poet." Beginning with his repetition of Adorno's famous adage, "'No poetry after Auschwitz'" (53), he goes on to consider the inexpressible, namely here silence, as the possible proper alternative to speech: "Precisely because it is the signature of his humanity, because it is that which makes of man a being of striving unrest, the word should have no natural life, no neutral sanctuary, in the places and season of bestiality. Silence *is* an alternative" (54). The inexpressible, in a direct attack on earlier presumptions of the ineffable, is then shot through postmodernist expressions of "nothingness," whether in black humor, tragicomedy, or absurdism. Even in this common snapshot, M. H. Abrams's encapsulated history reminds us of the inexpressible's wide, modern spread into the absurd:

> The current movement, however, emerged in France after the horrors of World War II (1939–45), as a rebellion against essential beliefs and values in traditional culture and literature.... After the 1940s, however, there was a widespread tendency, especially prominent in the *existential philosophy* of men of letters such as Jean-Paul Sartre and Albert Camus, to view a human being as an isolated existent who is cast into an *alien universe;* to conceive the human world as possessing no inherent truth, value, or meaning; and to represent human life ... as it moves from the nothingness whence it came toward the nothingness where it must end—as *an existence which is both anguished and absurd.*[49]

This links essential human meaninglessness with unspeakability, rather than with dreams of ineffability. It strangely echoes a felt inexpressibility of self-distancing English. Both this and the modern perspective have in common an inexpressibility framed by an unreachable "center," a missing representation in *language itself* of anything but the same language itself. We must not risk confusing discourse with content; ideologies sitting on different sides of the fence have been organized by a discourse of meaninglessness and inexpressibility. Richard Poirier peripherally, however, notices the connection to the inexpressible. He puzzles how an "age-old skepticism about language should have become so pronounced"[50] in the nineteenth century, and, further, how language in that period is already, as he names it, postmodernist, standing "in the way of transparency" (135).

The topos of inexpressibility has always been ideal for engaging and challenging the very *terms* of what Poirier calls "transparency" (135), the moment in which language reaches its end, its object, its idealized state. Frost's "The Oven Bird," for instance, famously takes up the challenge in this song: "what to make of a diminished thing."[51] Frost's oven bird is not a British nightingale but a common North American ground bird. Like Keats's bird in "Ode to a Nightingale," Frost's has a question of immortality, but unlike the nightingale, this bird demands duration, time, from the ineffable: "The bird would cease . . . / But that he knows in singing not to *sing*" (emphasis added). Without articulating the inexpressible, he frames "the question" literally, at the limit of unobtrusiveness, attempting to eliminate excess, "in all but words." Thus, a bird does not "sing" in birdsong; in all but words, his song is framed as speech (this bird "says") and it is furthered to a question that itself is framed—one that never is (or never needs to be) directly asked (120). Moreover, throughout it all, he is a "loud" bird. This comic and dead-serious frame of excess of the "wrong" words in inexpressibility is also modernly nothing but words.

In the end the topos never entirely loses the self-conscious rhetoric of *occupatio,* where a speaker says, "Words fail me" and goes on anyway. The topos has moved away from the unavailability of human language to meet divine and timeless perfection. Instead the inexpressible is refitted to an imminent realization of "an excess" of language itself, hard to adduce, select, and pinpoint, that needs precisely time. Beginning with the inadequacy of the human condition, Crèvecoeur's framing, as we have seen, refits its inaccessible perfection of statement to a temporal and temporary impediment of language itself. His statements turn disadvantage to advantage and refit the topos of the inexpressible, exploiting words themselves. More precisely he crosses out the estrangement with another's (own) language. At any moment (if not yet realized, moment to moment), the words may be reified. Henry Adams in 1918 catches the temporal refitting through the metaphor of a pencil or pen, striking out with this instrument word by word what is *not suitable* in an effort to leave in what may be:

> Satisfied that the sequence of men led to nothing and that the sequence of their society could lead no further, while the mere sequence of time was artificial, and the sequence of thought was chaos, [Adams] turned at last to the sequence of force. . . . The form is never arbitrary, but is a sort of growth like crystallization . . . for often the pencil or pen runs into sidepaths and shapelessness, loses its relations, stops or is bogged. Then it has to return on its trail, and recover, if it can, its line of force. The result of a year's work depends more on what is struck out than on what is left in.[52]

Resorting to a new construction of the inexpressible by seeing *too much language* rather than *too little* or inadequate words certainly seems a roundabout way to achieve *saying.* Yet, it signals, as we will see, an even larger and more important understanding of framing, self-distancing, and refitting in relation to time. The topos of the inexpressible becomes a practical matter of words inextricably tied to human expression in a framework of time.

CHAPTER 3

RAMING

"It [the English language] is the medium that shall well nigh express the inexpressible" (25): here, as we have seen in chapter 2, Whitman is drawing on the topos of the inexpressible, a convention of rhetoric that begs to say what cannot be said. The rhetoric of the inexpressible, again, traditionally depends upon an unbridgeable gap between inadequate human speech and its object of praise (one thinks immediately of God or beauty or a visionary state). To the tail end of other encomiums—perfection, wonder, promotion—Whitman, as we saw, adapts the topos of the inexpressible.

The adaptation in the Preface of 1855, drawn from contemporaries' discourse, is particular and startling: the inexpressible does not center on *a human being* (who cannot express perfection) but with a *language,* English, perceived not to be able to attain its perfected American expression. By focusing the topos of the inexpressible on a perceived inadequacy of a language, rather than on the limitations of being human, Whitman's Preface adds complexity to a sophisticated rhetoric.

His adaptation especially puts pressure on the frame of inexpressibility.[1] This chapter first looks at the history of frames of inexpressibility because the roots of this rhetoric are crucial to the adapted and temporal frames in Whitman's Preface. A frame constitutes how the topos of the inexpressible is normally delivered: in other words, the topos of the inexpressible historically constitutes a frame. That frame is defined by two parts: first, an object of perfection, and, second, the inadequate human speech that inevitably misses the mark. Traditionally the binary frame is the means by which the division between the (human) expressible and the (out-of-reach) inexpressible is delivered. The structure of the topos is essentially binary; its literary infrastructure, the two-part frame.

The first part of the frame of the topos of the inexpressible is usually taken to be precisely that which cannot be expressed, something larger than life, again whether God, beauty, or the sublime. The second part of the frame is drawn from the humility of being human; by definition, their language is unable to express unspeakable greatness or praise. The binary topos can be drawn out into narrative. This classic and narrative embodiment of the topos, rooted in dramatic tragedy, focuses typically on two characters (such as John Marcher and May Bartram in Henry James's "The Beast in the Jungle"; Victor Frankenstein and Robert Walton in Mary Shelley's *Frankenstein;* or the Ancient Mariner and the Wedding Guest in Samuel Taylor Coleridge's "The Rime of the Ancient Mariner"). When the topos lends its infrastructure to fiction, the first part of the frame can be realized in a heroic character, the one who embodies a larger-than-life realm, such as Heathcliff in *Wuthering Heights.* The second part of the frame, the inadequacy of human speech, is revealed in its choral characters, such as the servant Nelly Dean, who laments what she cannot bear to witness or express: "something," dreaded, as she says, from which she can "foresee a fearful catastrophe."[2] Together these characters establish what lies outside the range of human limitations and expressibility, what Stephen Booth goes as far as to call the human experience of "indefinition."[3]

Far and away the most fundamental code of this inexpressible frame is this two-part structure. Whether tale or narrative, dream or love vision, this frame is essentially binary. In very early periods, the two parts take place in a poem. The frame poem, such as the medieval "Alisoun," may be organized as poem of "warning" and survival, related to the proverbial wheel of fortune poems. In such a frame, the wheel of fortune takes the "heroic" role of the unspeakable (sometimes seemingly arbitrary) power, situated in an inscrutable divine plan of God. In the second part of "Alisoun," the speaker offers his utterance of humility as a warning of the transitory nature of human existence and utterance. Davidoff notes a less well-known instance of the frame by the poet Henry Bradshaw: "With the grace of god / the tyme for to vse // Some small treatyse / to wryte breuely //

To the comyn vulgares / theyr mynde to satysfy."⁴ The divine part emerges in "the grace of god"; the humility, in "Some small treatyse." The writing by those human beings who are humble signifies a "vulgar" inadequacy to speak the larger and spiritual truths, as it also signals a moment of survival and penance. The Old English "Seafarer," for example, is a frame of self-warning on earth: "I can narrate a true story about myself, / speak of the journey...," it begins, and later concludes, "Glory is brought low. / The earth's nobility grows old and withers."⁵ Some medieval frame poems, acknowledging especially the inexpressible, have in common a choral attitude that allows the survival of those who recognize limitations and inadequacy, while acknowledging anonymity, suffering, or grief as the cost of such limitations and human generations. This is represented especially in the medieval spectrum, as in Boethius' *Consolation of Philosophy,* the *Pearl,* or the fourteenth-century poem "The Quatrefoil of Love."

Many of Chaucer's poetic framers, such as the narrator of *Troilus and Criseyde,* are choral figures of self-declared inadequacy and loss, characters who cannot bear to tell the tale but who go on to tell it. Representing the nameless crowd, they remain alive in anonymity and lament (inadequately) the death of the great and singled-out hero. In such divisions of the inexpressible frame, the binary is rooted to the early Greek chorus. David Lenson explains the choral root of that division:

> Tragedy from its origins possesses a language divided against itself, a fusion of choric, collective utterance and the more uniform, individual meters of the epic tradition. The first actor, a development from choric verse said to have taken place in the sixth century in the plays of Thespis, apparently did not use the same language as did the chorus from which he arose.⁶

From this break with the chorus, Lenson suggests, comes the division and idea of heroic progress marked by the individual: "Should one live briefly as a completely defined individual? Or should one only endure in the timeless anonymity in which life, love, and death are passed as burdens from generation to generation—but in which even such burdens are a cause for exhilaration?" (8). In Chaucer's *Troilus and Criseyde* the choral narrator sings of the singled-out Troilus, "As he that was withouten any peere / Save Ector, in his tyme, as I kan heere."⁷ But of course the attempt to sing of unutterable greatness shows his own tongue but human and choral. The human vanity of expression appears here, as the narrator prays to God for greater adequacy: "And for ther is so gret diversite / In Englissh and in writyng of oure tonge, / So prey I God that non myswrite the, / Ne the mysmetre for defaute of tonge" (lines 1793–96). The convention of human inexpressibility and human vanity, inclusive of all forms of human expression (including in Chaucer's period a "diversite in Englissh"), is coined in Chaucer's concluding lines: "Repeyreth hom fro worldly vanyte, / And of youre herte up casteth the visage / To thilke God that after his ymage / Yow made, and thynketh al nys but a faire / This world, that passeth soone as floures faire" (lines 1837–41).

In the Middle Ages, the exemplum is a related form of this binary frame that participates in its own self-regard and education of values. Scanlon observes that even "the exemplum was not static, but active and dynamic."[8] He offers the exemplum as "a narrative enactment of cultural authority" (34) in which ideology and history connect. In the sermon exemplum especially, in which the education of values is at a peak, frames can divide into two: choral and heroic, the surviving and the dead or canonized, the anonymous and the named, the common and the enigmatic, the framing and the framed—all models of "before" and "after." For example in *Liber exemplorum ad usum praedicantium,* a thirteenth-century Franciscan collection, the bishop (as the focus of what Scanlon calls "communal desire") specifically "remains nameless" (63), while the institution of the Church, emblematic in Mary, offers divine intervention and resurrection. Thus, for didactic purposes of vision and warning, the choral part is defined primarily by what it is *not:* miraculous, dead, silent, singular. The choral framer represents a communal world that can be represented; its antithesis, a world of perfection and singularity beyond the adequacy of human language. In *Pilgrim's Progress* the earthly world of Christian continues to be set against a heavenly world of eternity. A before-and-after structure continues to typify these binary frames.

Hovering over these early frames, then, is what cannot be represented in language.[9] In *On Christian Doctrine,* for example, St. Augustine refers to the fallen word and the ineffable: "Have we spoken or announced anything worthy of God? Rather I feel that I have done nothing but wish to speak: if I have spoken, I have not said what I wished to say. Whence do I know this, except because God is ineffable?"[10] It becomes commonplace in such instances of the inexpressibility topos that language falls short. Possibilities for what constitutes inadequacy in language, however, continue to find paths. The topos of the inexpressible in which divine (and hence impossible) language cannot be matched by human effort lives on, for example, in the inadequacy of language to express isolation. With increasing modernity, the inadequacy of words often emphasizes the indescribability and isolation of physical pain. Elaine Scarry puts a finger on this unnameable when she explains in "The Inexpressibility of Physical Pain" that "pain comes unsharably into our midst as at once that which cannot be denied and that which cannot be confirmed."[11] This isolation and entrapment of the choral figure is central to frames that put in counterpoint an imagined and unreachable perfected state, epitomized in Randall Jarrell's "The Woman at the Washington Zoo": "The world goes by my cage and never sees me ... You see what I am: change me, change me!"[12] Margaret Atwood's "Siren Song," for example, also experiences choral entrapment of inexpressibility. Her female narrator complains, "I don't enjoy singing / this trio, fatal and valuable."[13] She balks especially at its human, choral, and in this case male-dominated repetition: " ... Alas / it is a boring song / but it works every time." Moment to moment, the song is isolating, fully inadequate to her own self-representation across the line of narration: " ... will you get me / out of this bird suit?"

Such pain, irony, and indescribability are famously apparent in the work of World War I poets, for instance, Wilfred Owen, Siegfried Sassoon, Isaac Rosenberg, and Edmund Blunden. For them, silence is not eloquent[14]; it is silence and suffering. Blunden, for example, writes of his forefathers who are dead, "There is silence, there survives / Not a moment of your lives."[15] Human and choral fallibility around the inexpressible, as a pattern of survival and silence, also live on in work like *Waiting for Godot*. A sense of humor laced with the persistent choral pattern stakes out what is communal and human in the tradition of the inexpressible: "the passing beyond humanity may not be set forth in words."[16] Words in the following passage exist as a physical and human condition of existence, themselves the second part of the inexpressibility frame. They constitute an act of waiting, while the first part of frame has been laid out, what always lies just around the corner, in this case Godot. The words' continuous patter stakes out what literally never can be witnessed, Godot, since here Godot does not exist but as the words themselves that express the wait for him.

ESTRAGON: Charming spot. (He turns, advances to front, halts facing auditorium.) Inspiring prospects. (He turns to Vladimir.) Let's go.
VLADIMIR: We can't.
ESTRAGON: Why not?
VLADIMIR: We're waiting for Godot.
ESTRAGON: (Despairingly.) Ah! (Pause.) You're sure it was here?
VLADIMIR: What?
ESTRAGON: That we were to wait.
...
VLADIMIR: He didn't say for sure he'd come.
ESTRAGON: And if he doesn't come?
VLADIMIR: We'll come back to-morrow.

ESTRAGON: And then the day after to-morrow.
VLADIMIR: Possibly.
ESTRAGON: And so on.[17]

A continuum exists, then, between medieval and modern frames of the inexpxressible.[18] An unbridgeable gap between words and the representation of something that is not possible to represent adequately in words persists especially in poetry and in the topos of the inexpressible; and it does so generally in crises of isolation, physical pain, or acts of mass cruelty. The modern or secular forms of the inexpressible have rhetorical foundations in the religious emphasis on the inadequacy of language to speak a perfection that only God knows, itself a line that runs, for instance, from Thomas Hoccleve to Edmund Spenser to Henry Vaughan. In all of these frames coming from the topos of the inexpressible, to reiterate, there remains a division between the urge to speak and what cannot be sufficiently met with words.

These frames relentlessly resist, or they enclose without ever naming, certain experiences of words. In poems or prose, such frames can begin with a perception of perfection or achievement, and they focus on human loss or inadequacy. They find roots in paradox, contradiction, and uncertainty of order, often refusing to draw a clear line between editing and authoring;[19] whether imaged through a development in the English language (Chaucer's increasingly complex tales of warning and authority in his dream visions); or seen through Renaissance and early modern practices of gathering and framing (Tottle's *Miscellany* and *The Boke of Margery Kempe*); or traced through their formal modernist development (Frost's "Oven Bird" and Eliot's "Prufrock"). Unabating of self-division, they are based on a core of perceived human limitation to represent a perceived perfection. They highlight the line that delimits language to express adequately or at all.

So, once more, the frame is defined by two different parts: first, an object of perfection, and, second, the inadequate human speech that inevitably misses the mark. The object of perfection defines a heroic character; the inadequate human speech, a choral character. The topos of inexpressibility is particularly suitable, therefore, to the mediation of an anxiety regarding the practical status of a language's own efficacy, as we have seen debated at length regarding the English language in America. Richard Shryock explains that an essential role of a frame therefore "is to mediate."[20] He continues that this is "an unusual tool in that it can bring about change not only to the receiver but also to the sender" (13). Therefore, the English language may be considered in the nineteenth-century frames that we have seen as *both* a state of inadequacy to reach the inexpressible (outside the reach of any individual speaking an already English English language, giving credence to choral affirmations of failure) and—to use recent jargon—"agency" for achieving the very same perceived inexpressibility in itself, American English.

Consider, then, in this precise situation, the possibility of an overlap, in which the choral character and the heroic character are put together as one. Theoretically, then, the character expressing what cannot be expressed is *one and the same* character embodying what cannot be expressed: this hypothetical character, an amalgam of both hinges of the inexpressible, is, I think, difficult to picture. But in the context of Whitman's contemporaries, this overlapping character is not a *human* character. It is a *figure*—a literal figure of speech. This figure, made of two figures of rhetoric (inadequate English and desired American English), is held together in the English language itself. In other words, for Whitman and his contemporaries who hear a problem with an overlapping language, the English language may be said to characterize *both* parts of the frame of the inexpressible topos at once: the inadequate expression of the past *and* the desired expression of the future.

To put it bluntly, the same words are local and foreign at the same time. They are both inadequate and (almost) adequate. Here, attempting to say-what-cannot-be-said is no longer based on a *division* between the human and the larger-than-life. Instead it is based on a language's *overlap* with itself, in which inadequacy and perfection are held in one and the same grip of the English language. Perfection is perceived in this compressed frame as lying not across an impenetrable line of eternity but *inside* its own expression of inadequacy. Impatience therefore comes to the surface.[21] Here, Washington Irving reveals such restlessness, inside his claimed patience, by attempting to push back a demand to express what is in effect already latent in the same English language:

> We wait with hope, but we wait with patience. Of all writers a great poet is the rarest. Britain, with all her patronage of literature, with her standing army of authors, has, through a series of ages, produced but a very, very few who deserve the name. Can it, then, be a matter of surprise, or should it be of humiliation, that, in our country, where the literary ranks are so scanty, the incitements so small, and the advantages so inconsiderable, we should not yet have produced a master in the art? Let us rest satisfied—as far as the intellect of the nation has been exercised, we have furnished our full proportion of ordinary poets, and some that have even risen above mediocrity, but *a really great poet is the production of a century.*[22]

Such literary discourse framing the unreachable "perfect" poet is at heart not a literary matter, but a political one. Writers want (both in terms of lack and desire) an economical (fast and efficient) way to get a culture that they fear does not meet their rising economic success. This quest for rapid perfection unwittingly generates frames of unreachability. The classics can define an unreachable literature, yet another form of expression both perfected and out of reach: "The Greek and Roman languages," Theophilus Parsons writes, "are far more perfect, better contrived vehicles for thought and feeling than any modern tongue. No writer can, therefore, now equal the classic authors in mere style...." "On the other hand," he continues, "an excessive and indiscriminate admiration of these last [the old English writers] might make him careless, diffuse, and declamatory."[23] Finally, he says, "the fact is, that while some of our countrymen are vain enough, they scarce know of what ... they are not apt to be proud in the right place" (33). After hitting this note of "unselectability" (to use André Kukla's term again[24]), he adds *time* in his demand for literature, a literature that is inextricably linked to a "spirit of freedom" that has *already* happened: "Much yet remains to be said upon the subject, for which this is not the place or occasion. We would however remark, that if there be any truth, which reason and experience concur to teach, it is, that genius and liberty go hand and hand; and it is equally true, that we live under institutions whose very essence is freedom, and which must cease to exist when they are no longer animated by the *spirit of freedom* which *called them into being*" (33; emphasis added).

Here, a same-language postcolonial condition has led to a complex impasse. How can this overlapping condition of the inexpressible in the English language find a way out? The answer has to do with a collapse into the English language itself: once the heroic and choral parts are in *one* place, one language, English, they belong to *time frames* in which the (heroic) inexpressible American English and the (choral) expressible English English exist in time and can be recast exactly one from the other. Compressed together, the two Englishes are no longer divided by a line that separates the human from the eternal and unreachable. In Whitman's Preface, as we have seen, the desired American English, in an echo of the statement above, is *already found* within the inadequate English one. Yet it must first be distanced from itself—separated into two—but just as quickly reintroduced as one all over again: only it appears a new English, already achieved. Each part of the frame in this adapted topos of the inexpressible is characterized, as we have been seeing, not by *human characters* of inadequacy and perfection but by *time frames* (that comprise the English English that is not yet and the American English that is yet to be). Finally, these time frames, carved from the topos of the inexpressible, must be put back together as *already one*. They must be seen as one, in particular the American English, in a (newly perceived) advantageous way, rather than *already one* in a (perceived) disadvantageous way, already English English.

This, then, is why Whitman explicitly inserts time into a timeless topos. Whitman's Preface not only adapts the topos but transforms it. He makes the story of an overlapping English a story of the inexpressible, yes, but then again the inexpressibility topos always comes with frames in its rhetoric. So Whitman's Preface also makes a story of *time frames* from the inexpressible, rather than a frame story of characters. Further, by including time in a topos that normally deems it irrelevant to effort, Whitman's Preface revisits inevitable failure in the traditional topos as potentially inevitable achievement of the English language at *every moment* in human time.

Participating in a suspended discourse of a dare of self-same language, Whitman's rhetoric, as I have shown in chapter 1, distances itself from itself to recast it. The conversion of disadvantage to advantage by featuring time frames in which to let it happen (in a topos that normally lies beyond the reach of time) gives new dimension to the self-limiting English language, one to be recast, self-translated, back into an English that had already taken shape: "The English language," Whitman asserts, "befriends the grand American expression . . . it is brawny *enough* and limber and full *enough*" (25; emphasis added). Drawing on a rhetoric from a literary form for dealing with the problem of hard-to-express subjects, the convention of the topos finds a different footing in the Preface. It translates a traditionally timeless otherworldly topos into a practical world of possibilities in language. In a same-language context, this inadequacy suggests a failure of words from (translations of the same) words, rather than a totality of human failing in relation to the eternal. Whitman's Preface tersely attempts to reverse the tide and perceptions of inexpressibility in English words: "The English language befriends the grand American expression."[25]

In this way, the inexpressible veers from its characteristic division of death and life, or "then" and "now." Its division is obfuscated, again, by the usual division between what can and cannot be expressed being rooted in *one* simultaneous instrument of expression, English. This adaptation of the inexpressible causes temporal somersaults: it situates the inexpressible in a past achievement turned backwards from a future that exists in the present. In 1820 Theophilus Parsons voices the now familiar call for a literature, "In this country, it should be the business and the object of literary men, not to reform and purify, but to create a national literature. We have *never yet had one,* and it is *time* the *want* should be supplied."[26] Whitman's

Preface will respond to such impatience, supplying both time and need. In a long and literal act of pretense, verbs fuse the impatience of a missing literature with a future as good as achieved:

> America does not repel the past or what it has produced under its forms or amid other politics or the idea of castes or the old religions... accepts the lesson with calmness... is not so impatient *as has been supposed* that the slough still sticks to opinions and manners and literature while the life which served its requirements *has passed* into the new life of the new forms... perceives that the corpse is slowly borne from the eating and sleeping rooms of the house... perceives that it waits a little while in the door... that it was fittest for its days... that its action has descended to the stalwart and wellshaped heir who *approaches*... and that he *shall be* fittest for his days.[27]

This package of redirected time frames will be repeated countless times. It forges a promise for the heir that cannot be named, but has already passed, and predates its own existence. Lodged in the "corpse," the past-up-to-present just short of a desired "literature" is itself descendant of the future, born to the heir of a national idiom yet to come. This sequence of verbs presumes a past that has not yet been. Equivalently that same past presumes a future that has already come. Simultaneous is the realization (both in time and imagination) of it in the present as having already been forged. There is only the framing, and a residual present. The middle ground of becoming, and with it the possibility of never becoming or never being expressed just right—is gone.[28]

The immediate cultural anxiety about language is not addressed, but redressed. It is not overcome but bypassed casually and unhurriedly by a bystander: "Now that he [the greatest poet] has passed that way see after him!" (10). The frame around the already achieved inexpressible, referred to in a past tense that forges the future, refits the more traditional frame of the topos originally bound to human inadequacy; it suggests inadequacy of any single individual who by chance may have missed the boat *in time* to participate in the expression. Whitman's frames attempt to revisit disadvantage as already advantageous, and advantage as already disadvantageous. The frame presents a before as if it were an after, or an after as if it were a before, or both. Manfred Jahn makes this point, pointing to the simultaneous revisitation of both data and frame: "Frames and textual data enter a mutual dependence relationship corresponding to what is traditionally known as the hermeneutic circle; more recently, it has also been termed the 'interactive model' of the reading process (Harker 1989,

471). The adequacy of a frame is continuously put to the test by incoming data, and the analysis of the data depends to a considerable extent on the current frame. The frame tells us what the data is, and the data tells us whether we can continue using the frame."[29] This same simultaneity occurs in Whitman's concluding statement in his first Preface, "The signs are effectual. There is no fear of mistake. If the one is true the other is true. The proof of a poet is that his country absorbs him as affectionately as he has absorbed it" (26).

These frames are both simultaneous and intensely tendentious.[30] The simultaneous elision of what can be expressed with what this language cannot express takes place in the same literal and written space that is occupied by itself, the English brought over from England. While writers are self-consciously overwriting in professed statements of English over English, something else is happening. They are, in effect, overdetermining an outcome: they are pointing to an alternative to failure. This brings up a problem: how can the two perceived Englishes wrapped up in one (the one choral and inadequate, and the other perfect and complete) ever appear to succeed? The traditional topos, consisting of one part praise and one part inadequacy, inevitably leans toward failure or human limitation. In Whitman's Preface, this topos steals time back from the heroic and eternal branch of its history: joined with the choral branch of its frame, as one, inside the same English language, the heroic branch joins its human counterpart in time. Time replaces the eternal. And then the human potential for expressibility forces itself back into time, rather than being stuck as forever inexpressible outside eternal time. In the traditional topos perfect expression is out of time. It can never be achieved because inside human time there can be no success. But the moment the topos is placed in time by compressing the frame, perfectibility becomes possible because time is on its side. It is at least now possible on the scale of time, whenever it happens. Whitman and his contemporaries never make any exact predictions about when an American literature will emerge: they simply play out the assumption that in the fullness of time it will come, or has happened.

In both the Preface and the discourse preceding it, one of the values most identified with the coming or perhaps yet-to-be-realized literary perfection is originality. This arises straight from the question of an overlapping language. An overlapping English in particular puts pressure on the lack of an "original" English or an identifiably original language and literature from within its own expression. A writer for *The Democratic Review* in 1847 remarks that "when the colonies finally asserted their independence, it was only against the political power of the mother-country. They retained her language, her letters, and the fame of her great writers, as their birth-right as Englishmen, or the descendants of Englishmen."[31] He claims, "We are to make the metals, torn from the virgin soil of a new country, flow into these old moulds, and harden into these antique forms. We must take these shapes, or not be at all" (267). Painfully articulate, the essayist in *The New American Review* of 1812 focuses on perceived deficiencies of originality:

> We repeat, then, that we wish our native poets would give a more national character to their writings. In order to effect this, they have only to write more naturally, to write from their own feelings and impressions, from the influence of what they see around them, and not from any pre-conceived notions of what poetry ought to be, caught by reading many books, and imitating many models. This is peculiarly true in descriptions of natural scenery. In these, let us have no more sky-larks and nightingales.[32]

Channing has covered many of these perceived ventriloquisms in his influential "Essay on American Language and Literature," first published in 1815. "There is something peculiarly opposed to literary originality," Channing writes, "in the colonial existence which was unfortunately so long the condition of America." He says, "The language in which we speak and write is the vernacular tongue of a nation which thinks it corrupted on every other lip but its own."[33] To Channing, America lacks a stage in "the development of the mind itself."[34] And what he finds missing has to do with the lack of an original language. Denying Algonquin or Iroquois, he points imperially to the language of the settlers—unique to their "new" land, (especially) their future.[35] "It is hardly to be hoped," he writes pessimistically, "that we shall ever make our language conform to our situation, our intellectual vigour and originality."[36] In contrast to the vast American landscape, the English language can appear cramped: "An original literature implies a race either not derivative from another since its refinement had reached the point of literary cultivation; or one which, if secondary, has, in new seats, under a new body of influences, formed for itself a fresh and complete identity of its own," writes E. W. Johnson from *The American Review: A Whig Journal of Politics, Literature, Art, and Science*. He continues:

> Now, we are not the first of these; nor, though tending to it, have we yet become the second. Until our language—which has, we suspect, passed through all the structural changes of which it is capable—shall have taken a new genius and other forms, growing into quite a different dialect, our

future Letters must be the same, at least in their vehicle, the instrument of speech they are to use.[37]

Writers hear the history of England vibrating inside their language and resist it, feeling, as Ernest Hemingway observes a century later, "like exiled English colonials."[38]

Despite claiming in his *Dissertations on the English Language* (1789) that the American language would someday become a language in its own right, Noah Webster expresses the inevitable contamination, a perceived originality lying in wait amid the impediments[39]: "As an independent nation, our honor requires us to have a system of our own, in language as well as government. Great Britain, whose children we are, and whose language we speak, should no longer be *our* standard; for the taste of her writers is already corrupted, and her language on the decline."[40] The insufficiency of originality is often ascribed to the inheriting of a literature already formed. "They began with too much civilization," complains one reviewer in 1850.[41] In *The Knickerbocker Magazine,* the argument is put in this way: "we speak the language of a literature already formed."[42] In 1847, N. Porter, Jr. has made clear, "We might as well talk or dream of the American language. England and America must continue to employ the same speech."[43] Sometimes the insufficiency of originality is seen in an inability to recognize it in the first place. Walter Channing has put this question directly: "The candidates for literary distinction among us, or those that may be, are therefore destined to a high distinction," and asks, "But let us inquire, who are to award it?" (35). Still searching, he concludes with another inquiry: "whether our prospects are more promising, than our retrospections are melancholy" (35). Nor can we hear the rhetoric of insufficiency of Channing or George Tucker or Samuel Miller short of its hyper-self-consciousness.[44] In 1822, Tucker asks if the inadequacy is "owing to the *inferiority of our natural genius,* as some have alleged, or to causes that are temporary and accidental?"[45] His impatient oversimplification already suggests that what is being said is not what is being said. His emphasis on the temporal ("causes that are temporary") suggests a confidence, moreover, in an expression of originality, or what he calls here "genius." But like the out-of-reachness in the inexpressible topos, nothing so far being expressed is felt to match this originality.

Poetry is pivotal to these discussions of originality because it is taken to be the epitome of original expression. Whether circling language or literature, the self-same English language is witnessed as impeding poetic development. This concern is persistent. It leans self-consciously into the "high" art of poetry for a self-battering: "You can hear in Scott, the rattle of her armor, and see in Ramsay, the gentle waving of her plaids," Washington Irving observes, "But *we* have none of these. We are not rocked unconsciously into poets."[46] In Henry Wadsworth Longfellow's view, the connection between a missing perfectibility, language, and poetry is made explicit: "It is from this intimate connexion of poetry with the manners, customs, and characters of nations, that one of its highest uses is drawn. The impressions produced by poetry upon national character at any period, are again re-produced, and give a more pronounced and individual character to the poetry of a subsequent period.... In this view, poetry assumes new importance with all who search for historic truth."[47] Even questions of economic dependence[48] often are foreshortened in one breath with concerns of language, epitomized in the idea of poetry: "we shall never be national in poetry, till we break the spell; and we shall probably never break the spell [of colonialism], till our national character is more distinct from theirs" (386).

The word "originality" oscillates tellingly within this debate over literary achievement and poetry. The perceived hand-me-down language puts pressure on the very word, and it shows up in different shapes. The adjective "original" initially appears in documents of self-diagnosis, relating one country of origin to another. It is synonymous with other adjectives, such as "distinctive," as in this sentence by Walter Channing: "Our descriptions, of course, which must, if we ever have a poetry, be made in the language of another country, can never be distinctive." More frequently it becomes a noun—abstract, self-evident, equivalent to "natural genius." "The importance of a national language to the rise and progress of the literature of a country," according to Channing, "can be argued from all we know of every nation which has pretended to originality."[49] Channing's use of the word "originality" has a particular inflection; it is an invention or, as Channing's declaration clearly implies, a pretense. Here it can be heard in the light of speech acts analyzed by Shoshana Felman in her work on J. L. Austin. Channing's statement does not in practice attempt to trace or describe the origins of an American character; language tries to "accomplish an *act* through the very process of... enunciation."[50] Originality is (more than) half act, half reception. Derrida notes this in his often quoted analysis about the declaration of the Declaration of Independence: "[o]ne cannot decide... whether independence is stated or produced by this utterance."[51] Furthermore, he continues, "Is it that the good people have already freed themselves in fact and are only stating the fact of this emancipation in [*par*] the Declaration? Or is it rather that they free themselves at the instant of and by [*par*] the signature of this Declaration?...

This obscurity, this undecidability between, let's say, a performative structure and a constative structure, is *required* in order to produce the sought-after effect.⁵² Declarations such as Channing's reinvent "originality"—the word is never the same each time it is uttered. Ferguson also picks up this performative note: early important public texts of the Revolution, he says, "are composed to be seen and believed in without necessarily being read or mastered . . . they seek substantiating form at every turn" (9). He adds, "These abstractions have very practical implications for both the literal word on the page and the space around it" (13). He explains, "One reduces the public text into an article of faith or icon."⁵³

"Originality" has often been tied to something like a place, an idea, or a characteristic (as in Pascal's definition of intellect as originality from *Pensées* ("[t]he greater intellect one has, the more originality one finds in men"⁵⁴). But when "originality" concerns the perception of an absence in the context of a coinciding language there is a paradox: a demand that writing make itself out of itself. In *An Examination,* 1807, Joseph Dennie sets the apologetic tone: "There is no light, in which our country can be contemplated with less satisfaction to genuine patriotism than in her literary relations."⁵⁵ In the worlds of trade and practical science, successes are profusely noted by many. Samuel Miller, for instance, writes, "In the Mechanic Arts, so far as respects the ingenuity of individuals, and the important service rendered by numerous inventions and improvements, America yields to no nation under heaven."⁵⁶ Charles Brockden Brown's defensiveness on this subject stands out:

> No one is so absurd as to suppose that the natives of America are unfitted, by any radical defect of understanding, for vieing [*sic*] with the artizans of Europe, in all those useful and elegant fabrics which are daily purchased by us. Similar and suitable circumstances would show Americans equally qualified to excel in arts and literature, as the natives of the other continent. But a people much engaged in the labours of agriculture, in a country rude and untouched by the hand of refinement, cannot, with any tolerable facility or success, carry on, at the same time, the operations of imagination, and indulge in the speculations of Raphael, Newton, or Pope.⁵⁷

By 1845 resounding counterobjections have built up, but frequently based on instantaneous spottings of the desired unreachable originality, here called "genius": "We are no friends of precise prophecy," says the writer in the *The American Review*: "We cannot say of genius, it will be here or there, but the spirit of God breathes it, and lo! a Homer, a Shakespeare."⁵⁸ Melville goes so far as to see the future animating the present itself. "The Future is endowed with such a life," he writes, "that it lives to us even in anticipation."[59]

These attempts to ascertain the future are new directions in the history of the inexpressible. The focus here becomes temporal, a bid for language (just) in time, rather than the more common verbal array of paradox by which the inexpressible allows for speech only in an initial attempt. (I will follow this in chapter 5.) The problem of inexpressibility is exacerbated in certain ways, that is, when a resolution is specifically sought *not* in silence. To Fisher Ames, for example, those fetters, predominantly based in language, unfold a declared strategy of achievement, producing a rhetoric of "genius" straight out from the tags of "stupidity": "Nobody will pretend that Americans are a stupid race; nobody will deny that we justly boast of many able men and exceedingly useful publications. But has our country produced one great work of original genius?"[60]

Indeed a variety of strange schemes were proposed to establish the elusive originality, the promise of which is built even into Ames's rhetoric of deficiency. One is considering alternatives to England's bequeathed English. In 1828 a motion submitted in the Pennsylvania State Legislature to make German coequal with English fails by one vote.[61] There are curricular plans to quash all English influences of language ("If the borrowers and imitators are only encouraged," notes Edward Channing metaphorically, "the swarm will go on thickening"[62]). English influences to be suppressed include classroom education, forms of speech and grammar, and manners.[63] Schools begin to remove Latin and Greek from the curriculum[64] and abolish copying English texts in handwriting exercises. "The best authors," Theophilus Parsons claims,

> they whose effect upon the mind would be to give it strength and elevation, may be and should be *studied,* with assiduity; but no writer, however excellent, however perfect in his own style, or however good that style may be, should be *imitated;* for imitation always tends to destroy originality and independence of mind, and cannot substitute in their place any thing half so valuable.[65]

Some schemes were explicitly political and economic. Reducing imported British books and altered taxation laws are the practical suggestions for encouraging people to read American work: "... our opinions and feelings are controlled by foreigners, ignorant of our condition and necessities, and hostile to our government and institutions. And it will continue to be the case until, by an honest and judicious system of RECIPROCAL COPYRIGHT, such protection is given to the native author as will enable our best writers to devote more attention to letters, which, not less than wealth, add to a nation's happiness and greatness; and should receive as much of the fostering care of government as is extended to the agriculturist or manufacturer."[66] Herman Melville notably complains of imported influence, "You must believe in Shakspeare's unapproachability or quit the country"; then, he expounds, "But what sort of a belief is this for an American, a man who is bound to carry republican progressiveness into Literature as well as into Life?"[67] And in the same period a "climate" already ripe for literature, compared to that of the English landscape, frequently takes on literal and figurative casts around a difficult-to-define but certain end:

> Every foot of soil has its proper quality; the grape on two sides of the same fence has new flavors; and so every acre on the globe, every family of men, every point of climate, has its distinguishing virtues. Certainly, then, this country does not lie here in the sun causeless; and though it may be not be easy to define its influence, men already feel its emancipating quality. . . . "[68]

The preoccupation with originality can often become quite extreme. Coming out of the work of the eighteenth-century taxonomists, some barely resist comparing English to American bodies as a way to see if the shape of hands or brain can promote or impede cultural success. As George Tucker writes:

> Now, if we suppose, with some philosophers, that the operations of the mind are but the workings of matter in its most subtle form, it would not be irrational to infer, that where, on a comparison of different subjects, the grosser parts of the material man appeared to be the same; or if different, superior, there would be the same relative equality or superiority, in those finer parts which constitute the mind. Judging by this rule, we must believe that our intellects are at least as flexible, as alert, and as susceptible of vigourous and continued action, as those of Europeans.[69]

He then self-servingly asks "our haughty adversaries for some further proof that nature, who has been so bountiful to us in the formation of our bodies should have acted a niggardly part in the structure of our minds."[70] Proposed solutions to the problem are perceived as inordinately difficult. In 1809 Ames, borrowing from an old trope, says America will never succeed at it: "—giants are rare; and it is forbidden by her [nature's] laws that there should be races of them."[71] Paradoxically just out of reach, but inside its own settler language, is a desired "original" language. To use a metaphor, it is a ventriloquism that hopes to distance the puppeteer from its "dummy" language, but recast the dummy as its own original.[72]

It would be useful, I think, to briefly sum up our journey in this chapter. The topos of the inexpressible rests on a binary frame, in line with the conventional contrast between the heroic and the choral. With the introduction of time into the topos it adapts in dealing with the perceived problem of English inside English. The binary shape transmogrifies: distancing a more original inexpressible English from inside the same inadequate English depends on spinning a conceit of adequacy, even superiority, from within inferiority.[73] In the remainder of this chapter I want to outline how this spin, as aggressive as it is apprehensive, works. The strategy of recasting, which dares itself to be disproved, takes many shapes in the nineteenth century. A few important ones are doing end-runs around inadequacy, renaming what is inadequate as adequate, and inviting in the reader to "co-author" a text.[74]

In his end-run around inadequacy, Henry Wadsworth Longfellow captures how the perceived dead end of originality can be recast. First it is recognized:

> To an American there is something endearing in the very sounds—Our Native Writers. Like the music of our native tongue when heard in a foreign land, they have power to kindle up within him the tender memory of his home and fireside;—and more than this, they foretell that whatever is noble and attractive in our national character will one day be associated with the sweet magic of Poetry. Is then our land to be indeed *the land of song?* . . . Yes!—and palms are to be won by our native writers![75]

It turns out that "the land of song" is already there, as the missing "song" is turned back into its own writing of its presence. Longfellow continues, "Already has a voice been lifted up in this land." Then he explicitly raises the disadvantage: "[w]e cannot yet throw off"[76] America's allegiance to Britain; then he evades, as the native "tongue" (116) is translated in the turn from disadvantage to advantage. He ends with what we have seen as the present tense typical of the second voice in Whitman's Preface, the voice of the already-achieved American literature: "[w]e *are* thus *thrown* upon *ourselves*" (117; emphasis added).

Rather than being merely stuck in the present conditions, the recast, desired author, like the inexpressible itself, remains alive. The possible appearance of an original becomes, at any moment, a matter of saying so. What has been a perceived inertia in American language and authorship is turned by the frame of the inexpressible into a flicker of movement by which promise is packed into a past achievement and then "recalled," if not named. Samuel Miller, for example, sees a want of leisure as "by no means friendly to great acquisitions in literature...."[77] Whitman's Preface alights on it and recasts leisure to advantage. Attacking the inability to produce books based on the absence of leisure (or a leisure class), his Preface famously assaults its implicit denigration: the Preface will magnify a feared absence and recast it as imminent (conducive to the production of literature), and therefore all but immanent.

In this end-run, the acute awareness of the overlap in English pushes recasting to extreme self-consciousness concerning language itself. This inexpressible for this self-same language is not other-than-language, but words themselves. Let us take a step backwards. Usually, as George Steiner points out, origins of the topos traditionally look to God, or statements of light, music, or silence, not words themselves, for fruition. "It is just because we can go no further, because speech so marvelously fails us, that we experience the certitude of a divine meaning surpassing and enfolding ours. What lies beyond man's word is eloquent of God. That is the joyously defeated recognition expressed in the poems of St. John of the Cross and of the mystic tradition."[78] Yet, unfolding the topos in which language *itself* is the desired object of expression shifts inadequacy from the human being to inadequate time or reception or selection. A desired and failed representation of God or the divine, therefore, is replaced by super self-consciousness. Words cannot express—and yet are the only eligible means to express—what lies precisely with the same (English) words.

Frequently not just recasting, but tongue-in-cheek recasting (a subset of recasting), therefore, appears and falls just short of irony. It produces self-reflexive written layers of "conversation" of English with English, and sometimes a conversation of a character with the notion of character.[79] Tongue-in-cheek, Brown ruminates, for example with a character of his own creation of character, named "The Rhapsodist": "though he [The Rhapsodist] not unfrequently derives half the materials of his thoughts from an intimate acquaintance with the world," the Rhapsodist nonetheless "is an enemy to conversation." Conversation, however, can be successful, though he speaks to himself; Brown continues, "He loves to converse with beings of his own creation...."[80] The Rhapsodist will rhapsodize, in effect, about the reader as such too.[81] The Rhapsodist claims to the ineffable "[t]ruth," but relinquishes his authorial position to its oral counterpart, conversation: "Truth demands this sacrifice from me."[82] The stated aversion to written authorship is an aversion to authorial statement (possibly inadequate) in the inexpressible topos. Any aversion to an authorial position is recast from the Rhapsodist's (potentially inadequate) words to those same words' reception—that is, if received favorably. Not modernly ironic, this aversion to authorial and perfect "truth" is fastened to structures that resist attack, and invite revision, and especially approbation. Here both the risk of putting out an authorial "truth" and, of course, much more pointedly, the risk of missing it are recast, tongue-in-check, but seriously, in terms of successful invitation and reception, as the Rhapsodist makes clear, rather than in terms of successful delivery. We can hear this tongue-in-cheek recasting again in the narrator of Nathaniel Hawthorne's "Wakefield," which suggests the following: "there will be a pervading spirit and a moral, even should we fail to find them. . . ."[83]

A second strategy in recasting involves renaming the inadequate as adequate. I have offered many examples between defensive anxieties of expression and offensive desires of perfection. Perhaps, though, it is useful to have two brief additional ones. In 1836, Edgar Allan Poe articulates, first, inferiority and, next, a patient confidence. What he calls an "excess of *our subserviency was* blameable," but he also designates a conservative impatience toward "misapplied *patriotism*": "We *are becoming* boisterous and arrogant in the pride of a too speedily assumed literary freedom . . . and thus often find ourselves involved in the gross paradox of liking a stupid book the better, because, sure enough, its stupidity is American."[84] By focusing on deference to oneself (which is merely stupid) rather than subservience to others (which is "blameable"), Poe shifts total inadequacy to a (more nearly) adequate state, one potentially capable of correction. He does so by changing tenses, leaning from past tense into a present that with correction predicates a self-correcting and more favorable future. Charles Brockden Brown also turns to verb tenses to re-present an impasse in the present time frame and recast an option of advantage for a favorable future time frame. In doing so, he will rename as "heavenly" what is already named a "deficiency." The redefinition forges at least two *time frames* (of failure and success), mutually impossible for coexistence, from a single overlap of inexpressible authorship in the English language at present. Brown writes, "Satisfied that the present circumstances of the writer if disclosed, would render his most glaring deficiencies excusable, I am content to recommend myself as a candidate for *future approbation* only."[85] This self-effacing "I" transforms instantly into an authorial "we" in this invitation to recast "glaring deficiencies" as "heavenly" in the future: "Whenever this heavenly spark is discovered, tho' surrounded by the wettest rubbish, and smothered in the depth of rudeness, and obscurity, it is our duty to recall it into being, to place it in a more favourable situation . . ." (466). The inexpressible future is recalled, the present placed, and the "heavenly spark" put back into a perpetual "favourable situation."

A third strategy of recasting entails an explicit invitation to the reader.[86] This direct address can be explicit and jarring. Brown's Rhapsodist comes right out and invites the American reader to join this "conversation," that is, to join the literature in English of his "own creation." "I have unwarily admitted in my bosom, a belief that literary fame is a prize *not altogether* unattainable, and that I am, even now, entitled to share *with you* the honour of publication."[87] With such invitations, listeners in this economical frame not only "share" the "honour of publication," but are invited to co-create a pose of authorship. The risk of inexpressibility, exacerbated by an English language overlap, then can easily slide into the practical "resolution" of an advantangeous overlap of the author and reader. The responsibility of inexpressibility for the author shifts to success of reception by the reader.

Such a strategy has long been seen as common. In this period, which expresses what Stephen Railton calls a "rhetorical stance and strategy" (*Authorship and Audience,* 20), language is preoccupied with itself and audience. He instances *The Scarlet Letter* as a "rhetorical project" that blurs the line between readers and authors, leaving them with a determination of origin, a "project of their own."[88] The Rhapsodist engages this strategy of displacement. Engaging the inexpressible "truth" of the topos, the Rhapsodist at first relinquishes perfection of solitary authorship for the more fluid ongoing conversation in speech with the reader: "In short," he says, "he will write as he speaks, and converse with his reader not as an author, but as a man."[89] Here the reader is put on an equal and privileged footing with the writer, suggesting that there must be what Ted Cohen calls a "shared awareness" among a "close community."[90] The problem of a dual language thus is suspended. Membership in this de facto community between author and audience puts them on equal footing. The risk, in other words, is recast in terms of successful invitation and reception (by author to audience) rather than in terms of successful delivery (in what may be perceived as a compromised language).

Each of these three strategies casts the delivery of the (inexpressible) English itself, already imbibed in the same language, English, as nearly beside the point. Responsibility is shifted from proper humility (in deference to an other-than-human-language realm) to evasive action, renaming, and inviting the reader in. Whitman's Preface illustrates how all three strategies can be used at once with devastating effectiveness. In his 1855 Preface, an echo first agrees with Channing and others, announcing that there is not yet any native American poet ("the United States with veins full of poetical stuff *most need poets,*" 8; emphasis added). However, he goes around them with sweeping claims that those poems are as good as achieved

("The United States themselves are essentially the greatest poem").[91] The anxiety of Channing and other writers, even in this small but indicative example, is not so much addressed as reconditioned through defensiveness being turned into an offensive: Whitman's prose then places the poet's arrival within a frame of self-congratulatory and already achieved recovery, renaming what was inadequate as adequate, here the "psalm of the republic": "Let the age and wars of other nations be chanted and their eras and characters be illustrated and that finish the verse. Not so the great psalm of the republic. Here the theme is creative and has vista" (8). The emphasis then shifts from the source to an enactment of the problem by the audience,[92] projecting an assumed unanimity where none had been before, yielding, to borrow a term from Stanley Fish, a "self-identifying community"[93]: "the kind of community that is open only to those who are already members of it," those who can recognize one of their own members coming through: "Here comes one among the well beloved stonecutters and plans with decision and science"—(where "decision and science" and practicality are often construed as an impediment to the American "psalm")—"and sees the solid and beautiful forms of the future where there are now no solid forms" (8). As Fish explains, "That community can no more be described or 'caught' than can the minds of those who populate it" (37); or, as he says, an act of writing that "can never, be specified" can "generate the community; generate it not by creating its members (who are already what they are), but by providing a relay or network by means of which they can make contact with and identify one another" (40). Fish artfully identifies a discourse that is committed to "not being about anything" and instead, precisely, "puts pressure on those who read it to demonstrate, in the very act of reading, that they are *already in*" (40; emphasis added).

By attaching itself to time—that is, something so far not achieved in time frames, rather than impossible to achieve in human time—the longed-for inexpressibility of an "original" language, seized from inside itself, anticipates more modern discussions. The text becomes inexpressible in a literal way: the text is the very site of forces resulting from the point at which the object of the inexpressible is language itself and not something "beyond" language. In this way, the performance of the problem overtakes the problem itself. There is of course no real answer to an imagined problem of an "original American" language, and the problem in the first instance is a coordinate pinned down by the topos of the inexpressible. The strategy of recasting, or renaming, or invitation is a set of options opened, not closed, by self-distancing and self-observation. Thus, the discursive focus on what Benedict Anderson names the imagined community, specifically "an idea of steady, solid simultaneity through time" (63)[94] engages inexpressibility (a topos known, again, for its concern with perfectibility). This kind of engagement with the topos of the ineffable, encouraged by a self-identifying community of settlers, a demand for perfectibility, and a perceived self-same language, produces framing that contributes to anticipating and predating patterns of discourse also associated even more self-consciously and more modernly with "not being about anything," anything, that is, teleological. Not surprisingly poets are among those most interested in this topos explicitly, and specifically in the inexpressible "thing itself" (a good example is Wallace Stevens's "Not Ideas About the Thing but the Thing Itself"). The form of engagement, however, bears tell-tale signs of early lineage with the discourse of framing derived from a perceived inexpressible and same-language frame. As we have also seen, they are constructed around time as they adapt a topos of inexpressibility that is grounded in a conceit of what can never be expressed. They exploit rhetorical confusion, indeterminacy, and vagueness suggested by concerns with a path of built-in inexpressibility of a received language.

W. B. Yeats famously makes the distinction: "We make out of the quarrel with others, rhetoric, but of the quarrel with ourselves, poetry."[95] In a same-language English, these frames from the inexpressible make the quarrel with "others" as "ourselves," a self-conscious matter of rhetoric and poetry as one, if at all. My concern here is not simply to suggest the existence of a pattern in relation to a revived topos, but to examine its links to a politics and poetics of inclusion and exclusion. In this chapter, I have tried to delineate these frames. In the next chapter I will link them to patterns of dead serious humor associated with dead-ends and exclusions, transmogrified by the inexpressible.

CHAPTER 4

Translating English into English and "Damned Serious *Humour*"

The postcolonial defensiveness of self-imitation, as chapters 2 and 3 have shown, developed through the discourse of the inexpressible. It points away from the ineffable and the eternal toward temporal inexpressibility (even if not explicitly articulated) for those settlers and descendants who sought refuge from a language or literature that was "inherited" from England. An inexpressibility that demands words to be recast from the (same) words sets up new footing for identifying the dead and alive in character and language. The uncomfortable stance of the misfit who is an insider rather than an outsider is clear in the following complaint from *The American Review* in 1845: "To quote from Holy Writ, '*We,* measuring *ourselves* by *ourselves,* and comparing *ourselves* among *ourselves,* are not wise.'"[1]

In the search for an "original" language and literature from inside one and the same language, English, an adapted topos of the inexpressible comes on the back of the promotional writings (outlined in chapter 1), the traditional topos of the inexpressible (followed in chapter 2), and framing practices (covered in chapter 3). In each instance a language is measured. Uncertainly "waiting for our literature,"[2] conservatively patient James

Russell Lowell recognizes—and attacks—a literal call for a new language: "It was even seriously proposed to have a new language. Why not, since we could afford it? Beside, the existing ones were all too small to contain our literature whenever we should get it. One enthusiast suggests the ancient Hebrew, another a firenew [sic] tongue of his own invention" (203). Calls for the language frequently cite inappropriateness. One of the most common complaints against its accuracy of fit, unsurprisingly, is American mannerlessness or "rudeness." As *The Port Folio* reviewer writes in 1807:

> [W]hen we come critically to analyze it [public speaking in the United States], and to try it, by a standard severe and accurate, we shall see its diction turgid and redundant, without the delicate embellishment of a correct taste, or the polish of an exquisite finish. With as much force, these strictures apply to our written compositions. Though bearing sometimes proofs of genius, rich and luxuriant, they are clothed, for the most part, with a drapery of uncouth deformity and wild licentiousness.[3]

"No matter for rudeness," Edward Channing nine years later weighs in: "It is enough that all is our own, and just such as we were made to have and relish. A country then must be the former and finisher of its own genius. It has, or should have, nothing to do with strangers."[4] One of the many impediments in the path of expressibility and literature, a longstanding perception of rudeness, is here acknowledged ("No matter . . ."), refitted as sufficient and "our own," and then achieved ("to have and relish"). The declaration shakes off a designation of rudeness from a detrimental past (death) to recast it for the future (and life). That temporal pivot turns on the phrase "just such," an inexpressibility that is at once both absent and present. Putting a stake in a nonexistent presence of the new consensus that denigrates rudeness, it conversely embraces it.

These speakers, though among the most privileged, effectively characterize themselves as "outsiders"; that is, they feel that their qualities (such as rudeness) and their language (not native to the country) are not essentially matched to expectations of themselves. They defensively see or create themselves into misfits. Offensively—on the offensive, and embracing traits such as rudeness—they transform the pejoratives back into positives. In this self-changeover, by which the "hick" outsider is first shaped from an insider's position of power and fear, that same self-created outsider becomes a proud purveyor, a self-translated insider. "A country," as Edward Channing observes, "has formed and finished its 'own genius'" (207). This framing acknowledges certain English views on American rudeness, corroborating William Cobbett's observations, for instance, of "Trenton, which I should have liked better, if I had not seen so many young fellows lounging about the streets, and leaning against door-posts, with quids of tobacco in their mouths, or segars stuck between their lips, and with dirty hands and faces," or Americans heading west, "'born with an axe in one hand, and a gun in the other.'"[5] Rudeness, in Cobbett's portrait, is inappropriate for expressibility. Yet it is the tag imposed by those who are not "our own," the English, and at the very same time feared by those who are "our own." What transpires—the translation of a self-disparaging insider *back into* an affirmative insider with a reinscription of the same word—is important. The new insider will create or, better, hear new enjambments in outdated critiques.

Although the first wave of self-confidence after the war of 1812, as Benjamin T. Spencer points out, has "to an appreciable degree spent itself" (125), continuing *"structures of expectations,"* as the linguist Deborah Tannen might call them,[6] still echo throughout the period: "In selecting the most prominent of the literary and political magazines of England as our professed model," observes a writer in the 1829 *American Monthly Magazine,* "we trust we shall not be understood as expecting to equal it. In the present state of American literature, we do not think this is possible."[7] In the next issue, the same conservative vision of entitlement, fingered by putative artistic inadequacy (offered by analogy with the Goddess of Crafts and Wisdom), is self-consciously dramatized through analogies, including one with the Goddess: "The consequence is, we have taken leave of our political parent, as is the case of most wilful children, better educated than endowed. Our British inheritance is that of an English younger brother—proud, but poor—well taught, but ill treated—blood enough, with none of the heraldry—pretensions in abundance, but little of the patrimony."[8] In the creative self-translations, the movement begins with the defensive insider ("poor") pushing himself out ("an English younger brother"); then pushing offensively back onto an (improved footing on the same poor) insider, "proud": in these dramas, youthfulness translates into pride, and pretensions are shorn of pretentiousness (translated back into "blood"). All these translations, here beginning literally with dashes, are early and visible frames growing large. This exaggerated written discourse translates one's own story, itself "inexpressible" since it retains the wrong selection of language and perspective, back onto itself. But this time, it acts anew and, in particular, orally and spontaneously.

Delineating written frames that intersect oral patterns of discourse, Robin Tolmach Lakoff sees the division of "planned, nonspontaneous written discourse on the one hand, and spontaneous, direct oral communication on the other."⁹ "[W]e must understand," she explains, however, "... that some of the characteristics we have ascribed to 'oral' discourse, for example, are not necessarily characteristic of the oral medium per se, but rather their choice has more to do with ... the usefulness of an appearance of spontaneity, rather than to the use of the vocal channel itself" (241).

Examples of attempts to hearken to *actual* oral, and especially poetic, roots are not uncommon. For nationalist rhetoric W. B. Yeats draws on Celtic folklore. A call from *The Knickerbocker Magazine* in 1838 wistfully links nationalism, literature, and poetry to intimations of the oral:

> We have the sublimities of nature, and by seizing on these, our poets might be immortal. We have noble rivers; eternal forests; the most stupendous mountains; and seasons full of glorious associations. The fall of the leaf, the dreary winter forests, the ocean prairies, and the picturesque Indian landscapes of the west, furnish materials totally unknown to England, capable of founding a distinct school, and yet how rarely are they sung!¹⁰

But from the start, efforts are perceived as compromised. As the writer above bemoans, "We repeat it, therefore, that there is a dearth of bold, natural genius in our poetry. We have no lord of the epic or the drama" (387), both of which are oral in origin. And *The North American* Review in 1832 offers an explanation for the compromised beginnings: "The origin of poetry loses itself in the shades of a remote and fabulous age, of which we have only vague and uncertain traditions."¹¹ Some point to a recovery of oral history of the Indians, especially their emblematic landscape. The Indians provide in G. M. Wharton's patronizing words, "one grand theme peculiar to the country," in effect, a solution comprised of the Indians' "mystery": "There is a mystery around these unfortunate sons of the forest, which adds not a little of the sublime to our thoughts about them."¹² So the writer from the *The Knickerbocker Magazine* a few years earlier has said, "Perhaps our only materials are in the dreamy traditions of the red men." He adds, "but they can never win our sympathies, as our own fathers might have done."¹³ In an act of appropriation, Spencer notes, it is the "possibility of an American epic based on the deeds of the white conquerors" that just happens to be "urged with equal zeal."¹⁴ The desire for heroic epics reflects a demand for song and, quite literally, voice to meet the "lofty" expectations. Ralph Waldo Emerson rhetorically echoes the territorial climate of lament (to establish disagreement with such readings): "There is no speech heard but that of auctioneers, newsboys, and the caucus. Where is the great breath of the New World, the voice of aboriginal nations opening new eras with hymns of lofty cheer? . . . We hearken in vain for any profound voice speaking to the American heart."[15]

For spontaneous discourse, complex written statements of the inexpressible turn instead to the received English language, including dead metaphors, for spontaneous discourse. Tannen helps explain oral spontaneity's links with the written form: "In speaking, what's said is said and can't be unsaid. In view of this, speakers often make use of the device of taking back something said, knowing full well that its effect has occurred; the message has been heard."[16] Through framing, written discourse accommodates this give and take. Here again is Channing's passage on rudeness: "No matter for rudeness. . . . It is enough that all is *our own* and *just such as we were made to have and relish.* A country then must be the former and finisher of its own genius. It *has, or should have,* nothing to do with strangers" (207; emphasis added). The butt of an attack, "rudeness" is revised into an asset of character: "should have" has qualified "has." Framed by a complex written discourse, the explicit addition of the inexpressible *just such* (rudeness/perfection) insists on a future tense of completion, rather than the past tense of anticipation ("just such as we were made to have"). In effect, the addition of the hurried "has" to "should have" is a signal of oral discourse that retains what is crossed out (rudeness). And recasting itself in accordance to an anticipated constraint of reception, the discourse fulfills the listeners' consensus and "requirement" (here the demand to repitch "rudeness" from the inside out)—these are all moves typical of oral discourse. Consider, "It [a nation] has, or should have, nothing to do with strangers." By the time rudeness is finally relished—transported from a dead description of American manners to a place holder for speaking the American inexpressible "just such"—rudeness returns as "just such," literally itself (and specifically *not* what "strangers" translate it into). The sentence exhibits what John Berryman will much later call in his own work "damned serious *humour.*"[17]

Berryman's crucial phrase, not often underscored, nods in important historical ways to a history of self-translation, and the linking of the literal with the inexpressible in precisely a "damned serious *humour.*" Translation studies often separate the word uttered from the same word received. This history of a shuddering between the original and the "translation" is long. Giving highest honors to "imitation," compared with "metaphrase" and "paraphrase," John Dryden famously writes in 1680, "The third way is that of imitation, where the translator (if now he has not lost that name) assumes the liberty, not only to vary from the words and sense, but to forsake them both as he sees occasion; and taking only some general hints from the *original,* to run division on the groundwork, as he pleases."[18] Dryden implicitly acknowledges the potential for a "new" text coming from any "imitation" of an original—"if now [the translator] has not lost that name." Later, Walter Benjamin extends that idea into what he called an "afterlife": "For in its afterlife—which could not be called that if it were not a transformation and a renewal of something living—the original undergoes a change."[19] For Donald Carne-Ross, however, the notion of an original text takes one step back: it is *already* a translation from the preverbal to the verbal. This brief sketch of translation begins with an original's unique existence, advances to a more modern understanding of kinship with the "original" (inside the living totality of a "pure language"), and then proceeds to a lateral "transposition" of the original from the nonverbal to the verbal, in Carne-Ross's words, "essentially an instrument of criticism."[20]

The notion of "imitation" used by Edward Channing and others to denote perpetual "borrowing"[21] is fearfully too close for comfort as kin to England's "originals" since they are uttered in one and the same breath. Imitation is also in no way (yet) a transposition, as in Carne-Ross's interpretation, from a nonverbal inexpressible original (if much desired). Instead in the self-translation of English into English, the word "imitation" cited by Channing and others is founded in fears of mimicry, directly juxtaposed with the perception of nothing but a stubbornly perceived unoriginality. The idea of translation too often turns into a literal enterprise in relation to an utterance that imitates *itself;* that is, it makes dead metaphors of itself immediately upon utterance. Literal meaning, as Gábor Bezeczky explains, can make a word a matter of both "fact" and rebirth: "It is impossible to tell a lie in this language because words cannot be used outside their proper fields of application. . . . This also prevents speakers from mistakes and 'planned mistakes' or 'calculated errors' as metaphors are sometimes considered."[22] The idea that literal language does not pertain outside its "proper fields of application" is essentially what happens: it rectifies English "errors" of metaphor in the American landscape. America, Edward Channing writes, "will have but feeble claims to excellence and distinction, when it stoops to put on foreign ornament and manner, and to adopt from other nations, images, allusions, and a metaphorical language, which are perfectly unmeaning and sickly, out of their own birth-place."[23]

This preoccupation with birthplace and the first subject has often led writers to Anne Bradstreet, often named "America's first poet." John Berryman directly addresses her in "Homage to Mistress Bradstreet." A deep engagement with this premise of an "original" is played out in language that frets over originality. Written one hundred and forty years after Channing's above comment, "Homage to Mistress Bradstreet" reinstates the literal through radical translations of dead metaphors and syntax. Such translations attempt to forge a lineage of firsts: first poets; first utterances (language newly literal); first insiders of an American English. Recognizing a colonial and conservative impulse, Berryman astutely says, "[a]n American historian somewhere observes that all colonial settlements are intensely conservative, *except* in the initial break-off point."[24] His own grammar resets grammar, here grounding himself in a "patient woman,"[25] alive three hundred years earlier, ready for rebirth. In his address to this first poet, the smallest "it," for example, also patiently undergoes translation toward its own first—from a body buried in a relative clause to a body of sound as first uttered or, at least, heard anew, literal and therefore strange: "Out of maize & air / your body's made, and moves. I summon, see, / from the centuries it" (133). In enunciation, the word "it" changes its tune from a displaced pronoun to one made alive and new. Its separation from the routine and relative clause traces it back, and forwards, to its own body of sound: toward its own self-protection as a potential expressible and independent word. As a syntactically and disproportionately loud pronoun, "it" traditionally stands for something else, a noun, another "body." Translated physically from its position in the sentence, "it," however, is first indeterminate, literally no more or less than a place holder, withdrawn from its figurative function. At first perception, "it" seems to serve the noun "body," but that precisely suggests an absurd attachment, a tie to time and place that the word "body" defines, and specifically what its dislocation here rejects. It is *it,* a sound initially made funny by keeping back its function: it rejects its body, here literally so, its noun "body." In this overlap, it is serious in not warning against speech, but in protecting speech itself.[26]

This is, as Berryman said, "damned serious *humour.*" It is also dead serious humor. It playfully revives "it" as a body of sound, remade literal, after having been left for dead, now ripe for writing as recovery under the umbrella of new discovery of firsts. It reveals a written discourse that acts oral by leaving in full effect what has been orally crossed out ("it" attached to a dead body literally). It leaves, instead, a living past of anxiety about writing in relation to self-translation. Pascal Covici, Jr. notes that "[a]lthough most significant American authors do not generally receive the title of humorist—more and more of them, however, write humor—a great many of their works force readers into the same sudden shifts of perspective that humor brings about." The "revelations brought about by much American literature occur in large part because that literature functions in many of the ways that humor does," he adds, "even when it is essentially very unfunny indeed."[27] Berryman's displaced "it" deliberately discomforts the supposed insiders of the language, those who frame themselves in terms of mimicry. Self-consciously extracting language from misguided reception or imperfect, simplistic ventriloquism, it signals the change in audience from defensive listeners to parodic interpreters.

"Much of their [British] personality and wit is lost upon us in this country," notes a writer from the *American Monthly Magazine* in 1830, "and even that which we understand, is too exaggerated for our simplicity to enjoy fully."[28] But on an offensive tack, that "simplicity," unable to accommodate British "wit" (or even the desired American tongue), shades into the literal. Thus through the literal the supposed inadequate expression of insiders of their own language becomes a rail by which words themselves, rather than silences in the traditional topos of the ineffable, are regenerated. For example, Berryman writes, "Versing, I shroud among the dynasties; / quaternion on quaternion, tireless I phrase / anything past, dead, far, / sacred, for a barbarous place."[29] The "I" here is buried, shrouded, inhabiting two bodies at once. Both outsider and insider, "I" produces acts of simultaneous translation and conversion—and acts of speech itself ("Versing," "phrase")—around a dead body, the historical "I." Earlier, Berryman's use of "most" qualifies written narration with oral interjection: "we were, most, used up" (134). Caught between modifying "we" and "used," "most" lies neither way; it is buried alive between its conventionally "heard" functions, reviving now simply as utterance, from a *character* created inside out from another and earlier (Bradstreet's) narration. Dying as a teller of tales, the narrator lives instead through speech. Instead of achieving what is often referred to as a spontaneous participation of listeners in oral performance, the written text draws out humorously and to no end, a written frame of erroneous perspectives, a parody of storytelling.

In his prefatory "Note" to *The Dream Songs,* Berryman initiates such displacement of the errors in expressibility, which lead nowhere but back to the beginning: "Many opinions and errors in the Songs are to be referred not to the character Henry, still less to the author, but to the title of the work."[30] This self-conscious and ultimately aggressive regression playfully defrays and dares authorship and its responsibility. This sense of humor joins more seriously in a national dare entered by Herman Melville in 1850:

> Let us boldly contemn all imitation, though it comes to us graceful and fragrant as the morning; and foster all originality, though at first it be crabbed and ugly as our own pine knots. And if any of our authors fail, or seem to fail, then, in the words of my Carolina cousin, let us clap him on

the shoulder, and back him against all Europe for his second round. The truth is, that in one point of view, this matter of a national literature has come to such a pass with us, that in some sense we must turn *bullies,* else the day is lost, or superiority so far beyond us, that we can hardly say it will ever be ours.[31]

Berryman's poem "Homage to Mistress Bradstreet" directly addresses this inheritance of anxiety and action of bullying. His strategies in the poem defamiliarize by making insiders' conventions of English both strange— and then again—literal. The narrator in "Homage to Mistress Bradstreet" addresses his own ancestor: "When the mouth dies, who misses you?"[32] By mouthing and defamiliarizing, Berryman's narrator reinitiates himself as an outsider—like storytellers, speakers, narrators who exhort to themselves *as* narrators to "Talk to me" (140)—in a master plan of ultimate insiderness (with Bradstreet, the "original" author) and inevitable relation.

Look, for instance, at the odd, unfunny humor in Berryman's "Can be hope a cloak?" (142). The very subject—"hope"—does not immediately present itself, making space for an inaudible pronoun. The beginning of a sentence is replaced with a middle. The ear attempts initially to revive and replenish "can be" with an appropriate pronoun or noun. Stripped at first of its subject, the verb "can be" acts positively, by sounding like an active verb, with "hope" as the object of its action: "[c]an be [might have] hope." "Can be" declares ultimately, by grammatical deformation, what the syntactical question attempts to remove: "hope" as literal. For a passing moment the phrase "[c]an be hope" replaces the rhetorical question that figuratively turns hope into a cloak: "Can hope be a cloak?" The question mark signals figurative language, a metaphor ("cloak"). As figurative, "hope" is laughed at, but the word "hope" is made unfamiliar and is not laughed at—not at all. The action of deformed grammar and colliding syntax, therefore, joins "hope" and "cloak" more closely into one sound, latched by a long "o." The utterance mocks metaphor-making at the same time that it reinvents the sound of the word, "hope" (and also "cloak"). By placing "hope" self-consciously near the act of making (in "hope a cloak," a transformative "is" heard before "a"), the metaphor "hope is a cloak" is turned into self-conscious action. It shows the maker making literal and funny what should be a metaphor, revealing what it is meant to conceal.

As local performance within itself, this action is funny. But in terms of the longer view of the poem, it is also not funny. In truth, there is no pronoun or person speaking the subject's part. "Hope" is formally the subject. Yet in the long view of the poem's frame, the speaker created by the utterance is actually dead. "Can be hope a cloak" is attributable to a dead speaker, the female poet Bradstreet. The line declares itself self-consciously, thus, as a moment *of* narration, an instance *of* voice (regardless of initial statement). In the longer view, it frankly declares itself against the odds of the insiders' common grammar and syntax. The line is alive, but to or for whom? Once the pronoun or noun has been initially "stripped" to loosen the speaker's identity, laughing at the utterance is laughing only at the character who has been made to say it. In particular such a stripping allows the character potentially to include the listener. The sentence, therefore, refuses to represent anyone in particular; but it articulates *everyone.*

Similarly opening a common case for everyone, James Russell Lowell, again, in 1849, allows no one, so to speak, into the possibility of exclusion (in part countering specious arguments of America's being left out of renowned literary recognition):

> After the United States had achieved their independence, it was forthwith decided that they could not properly be a nation without a literature of their own. As if we had been without one! As if Shakespeare, sprung from the race and the class which colonized New England, had not also been ours! . . . But this ownership in common was not enough for us, and, as partition was out of the question, we must have a drama and epos of our own. It must be national, too.[33]

He continues, "Mere nationality is no more nor less than so much provincialism, and will be found but a treacherous antiseptic for any poem. It is because they are men and women, that we are interested in the characters of Homer. . . . Literature survives, not because of its nationality, but in spite of it" (202). Whether or not it is its "destiny to produce a *great* literature, as, indeed, our genius seems to find its kindliest development in practicalizing simpler and more perfect forms of social organization" (209; emphasis added: "great," not "national"), Lowell positions America's "social organization" at the top of the ladder, however, precisely in favor of its potential for a "national" literature; any expression of nationality is as automatically universal as any other nation's, if not perhaps more so, because of its politics: "our literature . . . should be national to the extent of being as free from outworn conventionalities, and as thoroughly impregnated with humane and manly sentiment, as is the idea on which our political fabric rests" (209). The least representative may be the most representative: "Here we arrive at the truth which is wrapped up and concealed in the demand for nationality in literature. It is neither more nor less than this, that authors should use their own eyes and ears, and not those of other people" (210). It is a bid against imitation and, in particular, "costume": "the consequence," Lowell writes," is a painful vagueness and unreality" (210). So in Berryman's demand for "Can be hope a cloak?," the least representative "it" is also the most eligible after all for the "most" syntax, if the listeners are using their own eyes and ears; that is, invited by an insider awareness of grammar, all are just as quickly rebuffed by alien syntax—a wake-up, worse, to slipping grotesquely into consent to an alien costume (or language) of *convention,* fitted to the wrong ears and eyes: in Lowell's vivid simile, "It is like putting Roman drapery upon a statue of Washington, the absurdity of which does not strike us so forcibly because we are accustomed to it, but which we *should recognize at once* were the same treatment applied to Franklin" (210; emphasis added). That recognition "at once" (in Berryman's alien syntax) makes "hope" bounce back and survive *literally* as the subject.

Funny from the point of view of form, this survival of "it" is both trivial and serious. It is structurally amusing, dead-serious in its literalness of refounding the word through sound. "Hope," a word refitted by a narrator, makes a rebel of the reader who orates with one's own mouth. Many lines in "Homage to Mistress Bradstreet" read as these examples do. Prepositions or transitive objects often move into subject locations ("But whisper / I am not utterly," 40.3–4), making adverbs function as substantives. Verbs are frequently replaced or displaced by understudies of verbs, adverbs, and adverbial phrases ("Silky my breasts not his, mine, mine, to withhold / or tender, tender," 38.2–3). Thus, named verbs have less action than the other parts of speech enacting the verbs' roles. Missing subjects are doubled to make pronouns appear, underscoring their proportionate absence. Run-on sentences are often resolved on an indeterminacy ("—I cannot feel myself God waits," 35.1), just as mid-sentence beginnings draw attention to the artifice of origins ("Bone of moaning: sung Where he has gone / a thousand summers by truth-hallowed souls; be still. Agh, he is gone!" 44.1–3). As Joseph Mancini, Jr. argues, Berryman's reader "accurately and simultaneously hears and speaks the poem"[34] or, to put it another way, Berryman, after orally impregnating a written text, talks about hearing poems "with your eyes."[35] By separating the prepositional phrases from their adverbial functions, by compressing time sequences into one, and by putting adjectives after nouns, the narrative breaks apart speaking from receiving, context from text, utterance from origins. The pattern isolates single words, "it," "me," "you," "unchained," making them peculiar, funny, literal, non-meaningful, unword-like, moments of spontaneous action and sound. To hear such words is to *say* them again to oneself—to keep the inexpressible alive as *merely* literal.

Such designed utterance that exploits the insider/outsider rhetoric that is a staple in the oral tradition makes grammar careen in new paths. When insider-outsiders momentarily stop being self-conscious about their own language, they become dislocated insiders, attuned to figurative language that is previously unnoticed. In each case, a separation of pronoun from action (whether by interruption, dislocation, or mixed grammar parts) removes the verb function, distributing its attributes among the surviving parts of speech, compelling them to be alive or, at least, to center momentarily. The passing privilege of verb action is forced, invented by translating inadequate pronouns to empowered "I's," and, finally, to inexpressibility as past, not present, tense. Doing this impels a need for a continuous stream of presumed outsiders, or misfit-insiders. These outsiders include, again, narrators of the inexpressible, who, one by one, openly re-presented inert language as alive, strange, alien to the ear, if not to the mouth. Look at these seven far-from-simple words in one sentence from Berryman's second stanza: "I summon, see, / From the centuries it" (133). In this direct address, "you," the subject of "see," is for a moment hidden. "I," therefore, is not the subject, as it appears, but part of the object. Thus narrating "I"—outsider "I"—is created from the inside out when "I summon" is framed by the narrating "[You] see . . . ." The whole sentence is framed by a narrator who openly covers "see" in parallel next to "it" so that the buried "you" is reinvigorated as an insider to its own sentence. The narrator also subverts both narration (the fact of the frame) and "you" for a moment to make the words "see" and "it" disproportionately literal, odd, full of life, foreign to the ear, unmediated. "I" seems to be doing everything, summoning and seeing, but "I," as it turns out, is not the subject. Buried "you" literally is. Thus, as points of the sentence's momentum, "see" and "it" have exaggerated literalness and undue importance, each hanging upon the other in translation. In "see / From the centuries it," "you" does the seeing. "You" is made an outsider to be refashioned as never anything but an eye, *the* "I"—a "new" insider.

That temporal shift of presumed inadequacy to retrospective success, framing the inexpressible and always beyond past tense, is key to identifying the juncture between oral discourse and written frames that allow the appearance of acting oral. To say this differently: if a written text such as this is heard acting in the oral tradition, it does just what it continuously *proposes* to do, continuously adjusting itself to constraints. It performs itself or, as Henry B. Wonham heavy-handedly regards one form of exaggerated and oral discourse, "The meaning of a tall tale, in this oral scenario, is indistinguishable from the event of performance; significance is the product of a transactive process that occurs in the rhetorical space between narrative presentation and response."[36] Teller and listener are either indistinguishable or, put the other way, at any moment eligible as both, accomplished at both, never inhabiting the moment of the "rhetorical space" of what cannot be expressed. When that "rhetorical space" takes place in writing, it frames the future as the retroactive past: the past is itself a descendant of the future, born of the "heir" yet to come. In 1840, Evert Duyckinck makes this backwards case, and desire, clear, pointing to written authorship (a calling "sacred and apart"[37]) as the epitome of such reasoning: "While other occupations are laid aside and forgotten when they have attained their immediate purpose, the Author's employment is fresh and constant; it unites both means and end in itself; it is the race and the prize. . . . It is something to anticipate . . . the backward glances of the next generation" (20). In the tall tale, as Wonham again notes, language makes that glance itself its prize: it "feign[s] agreement" from readers "where none exists"[38] until the reader stops laughing *at* and begins to laugh *with* the same idiosyncrasies.

Like expression demanded in a dare from the inexpressibility topos, the tall tale is fundamentally a dare structure built on initial lament, framing feared inadequacy, skipping over any actual change in favor of conversion, or recasting something vague and large but agreed upon. What Wonham calls an "invitation for collusive agreement" (23) in the tall tale is a transformed rebirth, like the inexpressible topos, of the earlier modes of religious conversion. Designed to recast self-confidence from physical dangers of disappearance, or potential nonexistence, tall tales especially forge a coming together of tellers and listeners. An agreement to agree supersedes *either* multiple meanings *or* any expressible, single rendering of experience. Typical shaggy dog stories resemble these folk narratives that "invite interpretive commitment from listeners who lack either cultural experience or experience of the genre, or both."[39] But there is a large difference between the tall tales and shaggy dogs. A shaggy dog story is, as Roger L. Welsch points out, "a parody of a joke."[40] It is not as funny as the tall tale. The idea is to draw it out as long as one can, adding as many irrelevant details as possible before coming to the punch line that fizzles. Part of the joke of a shaggy dog story, thus, is that actually there is no joke, that is, no funny punch line. At the same time the whole experience of the shaggy dog story itself is not laughter at the absence of a joke, but something more than its encapsulated important fizzle. Its story is often barely a story at all and—like its core "meaning"—proves difficult to corner. The "insider" and "outsider" positions, therefore, are structurally blurred. Here is a prime example reported by Jan Harold Brunvand: "Two characters, animals or humans, are in a dangerous situation. Often they are floating on a piece of ice which threatens to split up; sometimes in a canoe or on a high perch. One looks at the other and says 'Typewriter.' (Or, 'Radio,' 'Trees,' or other meaningless comment.)"[41] This story ends with the teller laughing; yet the seemingly confident laughing (at very little) creates a crisis of understanding in the story's audience. Did the listeners get it or didn't they? Did they miss something obvious? Does the teller know more, or perhaps less, than they do?

Yet, one kind of shaggy dog, the no-point shaggy dog, takes this further. It seriously and actively invites listeners to constitute speakers, and offers everyone the potential to be an insider on a fizzle line. Here is a classic, again noted by Brunvand: "A man asks in a drug store for a pint of chocolate ice cream. 'We have no chocolate, but I can give you an aspirin.' 'How did you know I had a wooden leg.' 'I could tell by the rubber band around your head'" (68). And here is another that, as Brunvand observes, would be delivered "in a long drawn-out style with minute details, repetitions and elaborations" (44) between each of the following sentences: "A man keeps a barracuda (or sharks) in his swimming pool and no one knows why. Finally he agrees to tell his reason, but in going out to the pool to explain, he falls in and the barracuda eats him" (67). Since the dividing line between insiders and outsiders, though residually *there,* is blurred, not laughing becomes a nonalternative. That is, even though it seems that the framework of such shaggy dogs might create insiders and outsiders (those who get "it" and those who do not), in this and no-point shaggy dogs generally, almost everyone ends up being included one way or the other since, in effect, there is nothing to get. It is an embodiment of "the exact opposite of what a joke . . . 'ought to be.'"[42]

The apparent absence of the shaggy dog *to mean* something can often impel its audience *to do* something to justify the listening to it. Writing on shaggy dog, the folklorist Brunvand notes, "here we move one more step away from the verbal joke and towards the practical."[43] He identifies the subtype, the no-point shaggy dog.[44] Brunvand explains the subtype more fully: "A completely nonsensical story with a wholly unrelated and pointless punch line is told to a group containing some dupes who believe that they are hearing a genuine joke. When those in-the-know laugh, the suckers wonder what's wrong with their sense of humor; whether they laugh or frown at the punch line, they are funny to behold" (44). In this subtype, the narrative or story is less central than the pressure on the audience who, to paraphrase Brunvand, can defensively collude in the act of nonmeaning and can go on the offensive instead: "[I]n practice listeners tend to fall in with the trick which they know is coming," Brunvand writes, "and to relish the pointless verbosity of shaggy dog stories just as much as they do the pointed gag lines of straight jokes" (44). Overcompensating for an absent pointed narrative, an audience becomes a partner of the teller. A listener is driven both by the self-conscious fear of noninclusion (either by not getting it at all or by pretending the little is more than it is) and by the thrill of immediate self-congratulatory recovery.

As Eric Partridge notes, generally the more "inconsequence,"[45] the better. Those who do not get it may even pretend or, as Brunvand just noted, fall in with what they suspect is coming. While many tall tales, for instance, run the risk of alienating an audience by their regionalism, even there the murky nondescript "pointless" (44) shaggy dog especially can generate consensus among everyone. The laughter of listeners often produces only an *illusion* that there are outsiders or listeners being excluded from the joke. Partridge tells of the shaggy story's adaptability, recounting the arrival of a "very brilliant dog," which belongs to a stranger at "a 'local' in one of the London suburbs"; he observes, "so far as that goes, it might equally well have been a Paris or a New York suburb" (60). The shaggy dog also adapts itself to a relatively young population; it easily accommodates a shift in power from listeners to participants or "leaders," at least co-narrators, without an emphasis on knowledge or the past. The lines between those who laugh and those who find it silly and those who get indignant grow thin, as the swell of tellers rise.[46]

Crucial linkages of misfit insiders, between shaggy dog dead-serious humor and same-language inexpressibility, run in the early nineteenth century (and later). Invitation to self-inclusions, indeterminacy and refittings, collusions between the author and audience grow out of these oral overlays on written texts. The shaggy dog, not to mention the inexpressible, inhabits Charles Brockden Brown's defensive, self-conscious, and periodic interpretation of Jean-Jacques Rousseau: "The character of a rhapsodist may not be well understood; I shall attempt to describe it with that caution and decency becoming one who is painting his own character."[47] The directive to tell in one's own insider-misfit voice orally reminds us of the folk tales. It allows us to understand Wonham's words about oral tall tales, "a concept of truth as what 'works,'"[48] but more particularly the "truth" is what already worked, past tense. In discussions on literature, authors such as Walter Channing or Theophilus Parsons often seem longwinded, but they are efficient from oral perspectives centered around inexpressibility. A written form that both self-consciously describes failures and claims immediate gain can join a felt need for immediate action. The English language, Whitman writes in 1855, "is brawny enough and limber and full *enough*" (25; emphasis added). With regard to the looming impediment of language in the country, Whitman reverses liminal inadequacy ("enough") to declare victory (almost: "shall well nigh"), as we have seen: "It is the medium that shall well nigh express the inexpressible" (25).

The very same frames of inadequacy (the inexpressible, renewed literal language, the no-point shaggy dog) offer options where there has been impasse. Often both are expressed simultaneously. "I dislike inconsistency less than... the fear of giving oneself away," says André Gide, expressing a modern "fear" of "giving oneself away" to the wrong audience, the wrong words, even the idea of consistency. Gide continues, "I think too that here, as always, we are deceived by words, for language imposes on us more logic than often exists in life; and that the most precious part of ourselves is that which remains unformulated."[49] Here desirable narrative inconsistency is linked both to the inexpressible and to an earlier resistance to selecting badly something that is as yet formulated (just out of reach in a more immediate context), thereby equally resisting any acts of identification (always premature or falsely contextualized). In "Desultory Thoughts on Criticism," Washington Irving explains:

> Seriously speaking, however, it is questionable whether our national literature is sufficiently advanced, to bear this excess of criticism; and whether it would not thrive better, if allowed to spring up, for some time longer, in the freshness and vigor of native vegetation. When the worthy Judge Coulter, of Virginia, opened court for the first time in one of the upper counties, he was for enforcing all the rules and regulations that had grown into use in the old, long-settled counties. "This is all very well," said a shrewd old farmer; "but let me tell you, Judge Coulter, you set your coulter too deep for a new soil."[50]

Associated with perpetual freshness and nonformulation,[51] modern self-conscious writing is often grounded historically in the topos of inexpressibility.

The inexpressibility Irving talks about runs in a line, as we have seen in chapter 2, for example, from St. Augustine to Chaucer to Milton to Eliot (though their concern is the failure of the human effort to match divine or perfected experience). This topos, again, generally begins with the inadequacy of words to express something transcending words. Ann Chalmers Watts notes that in "its pure form inexpressibility centers on language, not the speaker: the point is not that the speaker fails, though the speaker does, but that any tongue fails." She adds that "it acknowledges a struggle between word and not-word."[52] In the modern era, it makes a general break to nothing but people, that is, words, discourse, and discontinuity (all is a matter of distances). Referring to Samuel Beckett's *Endgame,* Theodor W. Adorno, for example, densely explains one of the more recent endpoints: "Thought becomes both a means to produce meaning in the work, a meaning which cannot be rendered directly in tangible form, and a means to express the absence of meaning."[53]

When unreliability of narration occurs in modern texts (for example, *The Waste Land*), the boundary between audience and speaker, "you" and "I," diminishes in a characteristic of oral humor: "'Are you alive, or not? Is there nothing in your head?' / But // O O O O that Shakespeherian Rag—It's so elegant / So intelligent / 'What shall I do now? What shall I do?'"[54] An explicit example of this topos in the early modern period, Nathaniel Hawthorne's highly wrought "Wakefield," makes the author and listener interdependent: "If the reader choose, let him do his own meditation; or if he prefer to ramble with me through the twenty years of Wakefield's vagary, I bid him welcome."[55] "Wakefield" frames and twists the kind of rhetoric that was described in *The Massachusetts Quarterly Review* in 1847: "Every material organization exists to a moral end, which makes the reason of its existence."[56] In Hawthorne's story, the narrator, self-consciously throwing meaning to the wind, invites the reader's participation in the writer's own efforts toward the determination of what is perversely expressed—"done up neatly, and condensed into the final sentence"[57]—while remaining ultimately inexpressible, unreadable, cooperatively underdetermined. Usually the procedure is less explicit. In a much later instance, Raymond Carver, for example, begins his story "Cathedral": "This blind man, an old friend of my wife's, he was on his way to spend the night. His wife had died. So he was visiting the dead wife's relatives in Connecticut. He called my wife from his in-laws.' Arrangements were made."[58] The opening word "This" is exemplary. The tone is conversational; a reference has been made to a statement presumably already articulated. But "this" also presumes an intimacy with the audience that predates any possible kind of narrative divulgence. It establishes an initial collusion with the audience that can never be satisfied because, as a demonstrative adjective inside a repeating subject (one that doubles self-referentially as the pronoun "he") it has no prior referent, depending on the detail of its elaboration. The diction of funereal culmination—"Arrangements were made"—literally buries the joke. In both "Wakefield" and "Cathedral," highly self-conscious writing turns, in a word, from narrative to rhetoric, from statement to humor, and (in terms of performance) from telling to receiving.

Like shaggy dogs of oral participation, this writing concerned with an inconsequential core and an audience's crisis, adapts to both fear and self-assertion. In summary, written texts that surround a self-consciously "inadequate" core with rhetoric make the audience a participant by acting oral. These written texts exploit regionalism, commonly and integrally linked with oral rendering, by denaturalizing it. "The individuality of the artist and his understanding of local norms and lore become factors in understanding performance," notes Augustine Okereke of oral performance. "The creativity, achievement, and realized element in narration interpret the behaviours of the locality in which the story originates."[59] The topical allusions in oral tales allow a regional audience to feel included. Wonham, who catalogued other trappings of oral tall tales and shaggy dogs, notes the frequency of "weather conditions, the habits of animals, or the hardships of life that are peculiar to a given region."[60] Regional experience is a determinant in what Wonham also calls "communal repudiation of alien points of view" (28). "Wakefield" and "Cathedral" are tentatively tied to regions, London, Connecticut, Seattle, for example. But summoning geography and oral traditions, both modern and extremely self-conscious texts repudiate self-identified outsiders, and identify place, much like their predecessors, as a means now to *de*naturalize, universalize, and potentially *re*naturalize character. Wakefield is framed "as it were, the Outcast of the Universe" (71), and the narrator's eyes in "Cathedral" are open only to an inner common landscape of a universal, still inexpressible, home: "My eyes were still closed. I was in my house. I knew that. But I didn't feel like I was inside anything" (228).

In the oral strategies disadvantage is transformed into a passing fiction of advantage. Before the disadvantage is sent packing, it resumes what it never was, enabling its audience to collude in assenting to a self-declared nonfiction. Whitman's Preface dramatizes this sequence toward the end: "The poems distilled from other poems will *probably* pass away" (26; emphasis added)—if the listener participates in original ones and makes it so. The opening declaration of the Preface of 1855 itself, "America does not repel the past ... perceives that the corpse is slowly borne from the eating and sleeping rooms of the house" (5), declares the deed as good as done. Of course, it is here addressing the commonly expressed fear articulated in *The Port Folio* in 1807 that "[w]hatever benefit, moreover, we may, originally, have derived from our intimate connexion with Europe, it seems probable that it was ultimately injurious. The facility with which it procured us foreign literature, and particularly that of the parent state, so well adapted to our taste and our wants, may be supposed to have repressed the exercise of our own genius."[61] In a long framing footnote inside the 1876 Preface to the two-volume Centennial Edition of *Leaves of Grass* and "Two Rivulets," the Preface's discourse in another carryover from the oral traditions turns disadvantage to advantage, and values in particular what never "was" by convincing readers that it is now so, and has enough left to turn modern "utterance" out of the ineffable "clue": "Thus, for *enclosing clue* of all . . . 'Leaves of Grass' entire is not to be construed as an intellectual or scholastic effort or poem mainly, but more as a radical *utterance* . . . adjusted to, perhaps born of, Democracy and the Modern—in its very nature regardless of the old conventions, and under the great laws, following only its own impulses" (1011; emphasis added). The spoken ineffable is not immune to parody, as Henry James shows in "The Figure in the Carpet": "Drayton Deane's want of voice, want of form" is not insurmountable, just more literally unpracticed; "He simply hadn't the art to use what he knew; he literally was incompetent. . . . "[62] Therefore, James's narrator finally says as a dead serious joke on the ineffable, "I told him in a *word* just what I've written here" (400; emphasis added).

If framing fictions of the Middle Ages, as Judith M. Davidoff notes, have "an interesting capacity to transform an essentially non-narrative core into narrative,"[63] so the linked tradition of the inexpressible and the no-point shaggy dog has an "interesting capacity" to transform an essentially narrative core of circular meaninglessness into participatory nonfiction: the discourse of inadequacy is turned into a dead-serious action. Beginning in religion and politics, the inexpressible, premised in language's inadequacy, becomes common and popular through humor and dead seriousness. The ground beneath it changes: no longer is inadequacy commonly measured in terms of attempted flourish and failure. Its journey finds instead participation in the misfit-insider to the self-conscious outsider and then back: to participation through self-translation. Although this transformation is flanked with a fear of imitation on the one side and of ventriloquism on the other, neither fits easily. This adaptation of the inexpressible is a search to find a beginning from inside the perceived dead end (where no achievement is possible with the language). Thus it turns back time in orally acting collusions, while making language a physical matter of *written* characters (capable of being exported) and *future* character (capable of being imported) on the page.

In oddities such as "Wakefield" or "Bartleby," readers find a thick shaggy dog—a story that ought to be told if only it can be, and thin characters. Despite the appearance of super self-conscious writing, "Bartleby" yields, on the flip side of the coin, wide results of written texts acting oral. My aim is not to engage in a close reading of every aspect of "Bartleby," but to include another context and direction in particular on the story's structures. Todd F. Davis points to an important change of emphasis when he writes, "I agree with Liane Norman's contention that the story 'insists on the reader's implication in a puzzling, disturbing, and even accusing experience,' that the reader is both participant and judge. Yet this kind of participation and the judgments that inevitably follow, seem to tell readers more about their own individual struggles than the struggles of the lawyer in 'Bartleby.'"[64] The dead serious rebound of this collaborative audience points in part to a parody of a joke recognizable in shaggy dog stories. What inhibits the telling of "Bartleby" is a central fear about having a story to tell in the first place, a fear delivered by the lawyer's stated insecurities about even beginning what he has to say: "While of other law-copyists I might write the complete life, of Bartleby nothing of that sort can be done."[65] Davis still attempts, however, to prop up the lawyer through more standard characterization: "If we are to understand Bartleby or Nippers or Turkey or Ginger Nut or even the lawyer himself, we may do so only through the words of the lawyer."[66] This desire to "understand" presumes that the lawyer, in relatively traditional narrative terms, can "learn" or "see" or change. But that is not necessarily so. Although claiming that Bartleby has little to offer for identification, the lawyer himself hardly does much better; Bartleby presents an enigma restrained exactly by what the lawyer names as "safe" (14), where readers look to explore narrative change in character. The lawyer's own safety ("All who know me, consider me an eminently safe man," 14) gives, of course, an improper and conservative context to Bartleby's literal utterances of refusals to *copy* or mimic. It sets up a demand for the translation of Bartleby's English back to another English, as it already is, even if unrecognized and effectively inexpressible in the contexts that the lawyer provides. To expect Bartleby or the lawyer to change insists on certain traditions or stakes of narrative: but no change of character is necessarily demanded of the lawyer from the perspective of a tale that acts oral, for he offers a foil that frames the story's move toward the oral. That suggests a joke and, again, a serious one. A joke structure, in particular the no-point shaggy dog structure, undergirds the tale. This opening is a set-up, and it is similar to a no-point shaggy dog that exemplifies nothing *but* a frame for what is already there (Bartleby, say)—there is no "meaning"—if not *yet* called its "proper" name. Therefore, as in oral delivery, important time frames of instantaneousness are at stake in the reader's participation.

In the lawyer's mouth Bartleby is a dead metaphor, or what is called a "safe" metaphor,[67] and appropriately his history ends up in the dead letter office. Again while narrative interpretations of "Bartleby" commonly depend on change (in the lawyer's awakening, or absence of it, for instance, at the end of the tale), the seriousness of the no-point shaggy dog and its dead metaphors defy time and pursue "presentness"—what Michael Fried calls a "continuous and entire *presentness*" or the "perpetual creation of itself, that one experiences as a kind of instantaneousness."[68] Similar to the inexpressible, metaphor in Aristotle's designation is improper naming, which suggests current inadequacy, or lack.[69] Karsten Harries says, "refusal of metaphor is inseparably connected with the project of pride, the dream of an unmediated vision, a vision that is not marred by lack, that does not refer to something beyond itself that would fulfill it."[70] Like the inexpressible, it also resists paraphrase, as Bartleby himself resists the lawyer's paraphrase of himself. Under this rubric, metaphor pursues presentness and is inimical to paraphrase or mimicry, and again, like the inexpressible, it stimulates perpetual "corrective action" that cannot be achieved since, as an "erroneous statement," it immediately conflicts with expectations.[71]

Dead metaphors, though, are special, closer to certain kinds of jokes, where listeners encounter, as Ted Cohen explains, "first the realization that it *is* a joke."[72] Referring to Cicero, Doreen Innes explains that dead metaphors, as part of customary speech, can seem a proper term, short of the usual notion for a metaphor in movement to "different" place (11). These metaphors, in addition, thus need translation *back* to a point of what Cohen calls again a "special invitation" in which the speaker and receiver "actively engage one another in coping with a piece of language." The piece, he continues, must be penetrated "in order to grasp the import, for that import is not exactly *in* the remark itself." He points out that both the speaker and receiver engender a "cooperative act of comprehension" (9) since there is "no real point in forcing the connections" (10); dead metaphors, all the more, have long-lost threads of original movement or alienation. Such metaphors, Cohen says tellingly, cultivate intimacy *"all at once"* (11; emphasis added).

If metaphor may be "improper naming," perpetually inexpressible in its pursuit of presentness, a dead metaphor does something different in relation to the inexpressible: it puts the inexpressible—what is not exactly *in* the remark itself—into a time frame that is as yet unfinished. A dead metaphor does not improperly name, but it *frames* "improper naming" for the purpose of re-alienation and ultimately complicity in the recognition. It defies time. It dares time to deliver, not a noted change in character, for instance, but to use Cohen's word, the "intimacy" that legitimizes a character of response already on hand, but so far perceived as lacking. There need not be change, just instantaneousness; "all at once" is how Cohen puts it, a collective self-recognition can offer intimacy "without any exegesis." "Jokes of this kind," he adds importantly, "are the ones most clearly undermined by any need for instruction in the background material" (11). Thus Bartleby's background material, from this direction, is *by definition* immaterial, irrelevant. What is not immaterial is daring time to frame instantly what Cohen calls "intimacy," along with Bartleby's inexpressibility; that is, what already exists in a moment of initiation, if unencumbered by changing character or exegesis.

Daring time, "Bartleby" aims at fusing two jokes. The first is the lawyer's obvious attempts to impose a frame of character in his world; its inconsequence is also part of the second joke, his forcing what Partridge calls "a *non sequitur*, not of faulty logic, but of attitude and response"[73] that is not connected (nor, in Welsch's words, "all that funny"[74]). The structure of "Bartleby" dares the reader as listener to pick the *less offensive* of the two such jokes: Bartleby is immaterial or Bartleby is unoriginal. The lawyer's reasonable response to Bartleby's being immaterial, however, is mocked by his melodramatic recognition at the end that he may have seen too late "some strange magic" (44), a magic and "grass-seed" (44) surrounding Bartleby that he himself did not "select." Among other things, that is a joke. There is not enough there, of course, to make such a selection; Bartleby's actual "magic" is absent to anyone, since Bartleby stands in as an inexpressible; his is also, therefore, a stand-in for complicity, and the lawyer engages only in the *kind* of complicity that points to Bartleby's death, not the kind of complicity that brings him through participation to life. This second joke concerning complicity around the inexpressible or "unmeaningful" suggests a weird and parodic echo of the desire for "originality of character": the appeal of the story can be leveled to the dreaded "absence" of character and writing. That is, in contrast to merely the mundane and quotidian presence of the lawyer, Bartleby is a dead metaphor (transferred from the Dead Letter Office). But in relation to the inexpressible, he is even one tier above that: he is *at least* an absent character. In the rubric of inexpressibility, immateriality trumps unoriginality. His absence means that a character *could be* present at that moment, or later, if recognized. This is exactly a dramatization of the inexpressible as it appears in "Bartleby." Just as "rude" was a derogatory comment for Edward Channing in 1816 and becomes transformed into a virtue, so Bartleby's absence is really a new possibility of an inexpressed figure who could not only materialize, but for the first time do so originally. It is no longer a dead metaphor; it offers the possibility of generation; as Innes explains, a "dead metaphor remains latent metaphor and may be revived" (27).

Such a sequence of response is akin to what happens in the shaggy dog. Unlike the laughter in the written tale (tied to the characters), this laughter in "Bartleby" is relevant to what happens in the shaggy dog. To be joined to the teller, the audience who does not get the joke responds as if it does. In this context, Bartleby is like the aspirin in Brunvand's shaggy dog. The fusion of jokes is present because of the exploitation of dead metaphor, the hovering shaggy dog outline, the translation of language, and the inexpressible.

To see this even more fully, it is necessary to purposefully meander a bit. In "The Negative Structures of American Literature," Terence Martin finds the rhetorical achievement of "absence"[75] a mixed bag. An "enduring signature" of American literature, "the promise of an original world," he argues, is an active "negative impulse" in fiction (22). His classic "overblown" and "serious" example is taken from Sylvester Judd's *Margaret: A Tale of the Real and the Ideal* from 1845. It includes this scene, firing up New England from the ashes of old England: "'We have no monarchical supremacy, no hereditary prerogatives, no patent nobility, no Kings'" (1). From this rhetoric of negation and clarification emerges promise, as Martin write, though it also "suggests the potential terror of absence" (22). He names both "The Beast in the Jungle" and "Bartleby, the Scrivener" as "stories that court terror and enigma by making the confrontation of nothing a subject in itself" (19).[76] Of course this points as well to what Philip Fisher calls a "loose-fitting, minimal identity" or "thinness of character," [77] relevant to "Bartleby."[78] The more Bartleby himself is described, the more he disappears as an overwritten character, and the more he reappears as the shaggy dog's fizzle. His famous line, "I would prefer not to,"[79] as in oral tall tales, massages "the same spot as long as . . . listeners can stand it." J. Russell Reaver continues that it "indulges in this vertical vertigo of story structure," in which the story stretches "upward from its base in a remarkable event, on top of which equally extraordinary events are piled."[80] Only here the "remarkable" events are not remarkable, and the "spot" of Bartleby is just that, a point of no origin. So the parody on the tall tale, stretched to shaggy dog limits, makes a double-edged absence serve as its fizzle. A frame in a tall tale conventionally "prepare[s] the audience for the transition to a fantastic world" (374), Reaver points out, suggesting that it is "where the imaginary hypotheses are respected" (373). The no-point shaggy dog structure of "Bartleby" respects the parody, wherein Bartleby's "lack of origin" is both parodied and "respected."

Although Bartleby is designed to remain shadowy, the narrative and written self-consciousness do not rescue the story. They practically, or more precisely in oral practice, sink it. Once more, we listen, "While of other law-copyists I might write the complete life," the narrator says, "of Bartleby nothing of that sort can be done."[81] The lawyer writes the story, of course, but "Bartleby" is full of exactly these qualifying statements that, in the story's frame, give the details of the story depth or, at least, breadth. Speaking of the tall tale, Ariane Dewey writes, "the fight [in it] was so desperate, to take it seriously was to surrender."[82] Yet writing a spontaneity of time (that never was) does take a fight for retrieving what the oral more traditionally offers over time, what Okereke calls indisputable "communicative competence." He cautions: "Folklore texts are, in most cases, tedious to read."[83] As these frames might seem to sound like (rhetorically) oral texts, their transcriptions are frequently tiresome to read. But this is not the case when they are heard out loud, oral. These frames highlight rhetorical practices that are more auditory in practice. Focused on persuasion and dissent, they have their origins in talking.

"Bartleby" is a very slippery construction. The tale, among its many rolls and roles, is not *about* a character, but *about* character. This distinction is important. A response to anxiety and self-distancing, for one, "Bartleby" concerns among other things articulation of a received English language. Although it has common figurative techniques of fiction, they are but red herrings from this perspective, a perspective that Partridge identifies as one of the many "cosy human" touches that shaggy dogs set into motion.[84] Bartleby's character or "being" can be seen in an entirely different register.[85] This, precisely, is where the desire for intimacy, a spontaneity, an adaptation to constraints—all linked to characteristics of the oral, and voice in particular—come in. Considered especially in light of what Elizabeth Tonkin calls the "oral narrative's character of time unfinished,"[86] Bartleby's "character" comes out. Since "time is one of the essential things [oral] stories are about" (3), so is order as it relates in "the promise of an original world" to an "all at once" history and demand of intimacy without exegesis in "Bartleby." Sorting out "history-as-lived" and "history-as-recorded" is difficult. As Tonkin says, "It is easy to slip from one meaning [of history] to another" (2). The fact of a few written scraps as Bartleby's background seems a hindrance to the story (just as Bartleby himself is characterized by the narrator as a hindrance in his office). Heard differently it is the point of an oral strategy that puts pressure on ordering "what comes first." A typical shaggy dog, according to Partridge, needs to have an ending or *dénouement*, again, of inconsequence: "a gaily illogical psychological inconsequence."[87] Order and the instantaneous initiation of it is all there is, if it is there at all.

This combination of Bartleby's measly written origins along with the joke practices on dead metaphors (making that intimacy and order of origins all there is) puts extraordinary pressure on readers to locate beginnings and endings, or, as Wonham vividly describes it, a "collaborative game" in assimilating a yarn spinner from an audience (23). This fundamental desire to make a speaker from a hearer is antithetical to how such disorientation is sometimes read. For example, on the continuum with modernism's famous loss of the temporal, postmodernism is often described as "bottomless fragmentation" and the "collapse of time horizons and the preoccupation with instantaneity."[88] While these identifications of time only point to the rhetorical complexity of effects, they do not tell us much about what happens in "Bartleby" (59).[89] In acting oral, commensurate with joke structures and the lost point of dead metaphors, all the "story" wants (and that is a wry but damned serious "all") is for the readers, first as listeners and then as yarn spinners, to *order* the elusive "first" from the measly written *origins* of Bartleby to the inevitability of *originality* and written character. In 1809 Ames took a stab at order, resorting to presence in the present (notwithstanding genius, originality, national literature, or language): "Our honors have not faded—they have not been won. Genius no doubt exists in our country. . . . "[90] Bartleby, then, does not, for example, substantially refigure Jesus denied by Peter, though Jesus as a figure of the inexpressible frames and transposes perceptions of time: ". . . though now ye see *him* not, yet believing, ye rejoice with joy unspeakable and full of glory: Receiving the end of your faith, *even* the salvation of *your* souls."[91] Bartleby does not essentially represent an idea of imaginative purity wasted by pragmatism. He is, to add a metaphor, essentially nonrepresentative. This helps to encircle why "Bartleby" has stated trouble in its beginning and ending.[92] The narrator's movement—from the first word in the story ("I," 13) to the last word ("humanity," 45)—takes place as a sequence importantly by having the first word "I" literally precede the last word "humanity." In practice such a sequence gives birth in narrative to a "before" and an "after." But it is not so in "Bartleby." Voice and a desired original "character," epitomized in Bartleby who likes "to be stationary" (138), remain inaudible; and without translation there is no defining point of origin. Translation—the slide or movement in time of one language (and character) from underneath the other—is thus initiated, attempting to forego exegesis. Literally there is no irony to this written frame that acts oral. Irony suggests perception of a gap or distance, but "Bartleby" includes the act of founding, distancing, a characteristic gap, separation of character from (a perceived nonoriginal) character.

From the perspective of the inexpressible and dead metaphor, "Bartleby," then, has little that resembles a conventional narrative's beginning, middle, or end. It never loses sight of its thematic, desired "originality": Bartleby's famous refusal to copy in "I'd prefer not to." But in order to be heard, originality in a very specific sense has itself to be reinitiated. In many ways, finally, the order in "Bartleby" is not a story of perceived originality, but of translated "originals" in speakers. Stripped to its bones, it is a tall order. Like a tall tale (which generally is funny) and a shaggy dog (which is not), this kind of story, in effect, demands to lack consequence.

Replicating the dilemma of an identical or doubled English, either every speaker is perceived as original, or no speaker is perceived as original. Or, as matter of proof, all (another matter) are. This is akin to the special advertisement for the missing dog that helped to define the early shaggy dog tale—a story that also should always be told in one's own words. This condition is exacerbated when the language spoken and heard is perceived to be identical with another's, and painfully so since the "other" English is the "original." In "Bartleby," characters translate the expressible backwards and forwards into the (as yet) inexpressible; they show the force of dead metaphor; they dramatize the vitality of the literal; and they frame the tale so results can be named, without knowing, a fait accompli.

I am not done with "Bartleby." The eponymous hero is a subject who frames the possibility of a "selectable" character. Poised for narrative the reader finds a vanishing point of character, initiation without origin; Bartleby is more literal than the usual "character," and the story of his mark on the world, all but absent, builds self-dramatizing humor. Unlike modes that depend upon preventing "the self from an illusory identification with the non-self, which is now fully, though painfully, recognized as a non-self,"[93] as Paul de Man puts it, this kind of inexpressible, pulling back from narrative, creates a double that destroys narrative. Bartleby epitomizes, then, John Miles Foley's evocation of an oral tradition: a "lack of textual tidiness" (4), often "unnerving" to trace (4), a process rather than a product (23), a series of enactments (22), "[a]lways different and yet always the same ... *implied and instanced*" (23; emphasis in original), and therefore canonically impossible to recover: "We cannot file it, title it, edit and translate it as we would a papyrus manuscript....."[94] Bartleby's apparent lack of province appears up front, especially if eyed, or *abduced* by the lawyer (André Kukla's term): "I believe that no materials exist for a full and satisfactory biography of this man." "Bartleby," the lawyer continues, "was one of those beings of whom nothing is ascertainable, except from the original sources, and in his case those are very small."[95] The story "Bartleby" suggests a frame moving very quickly to give itself the textual vestiges of an oral culture by *acting out* some oral patterns, but the oral qualities only *embody* character traits. Bartleby is not a clever hero, not a decision maker, not a problem solver. This element of performance in the text does more than simulate oral delivery: oral strategies are brought to written texts. The frame of the story, as we have seen, features a man who, not coincidentally, lacks identifiable origins. It pinpoints, as will be shown, a culture of order by dramatizing, instead, a sequence *for* being able to order.

In this frame story the narrative maps "character," while holding back its character; it maps a desire to equate character with origins, originality, point zero, rebirth itself. This can be seen sharply if we glance at Pip in *Great Expectations,* narrated by middle-aged, sad and wiser, Pip. Pip is born in first-person narrative between two identifiable, and inevitably hostile, cross-purposed identities: "My father's family name being Pirrip, and my Christian name Philip, my infant tongue could make of both names nothing longer or more explicit than Pip. So, I called myself Pip, and came to be called Pip."[96] (Actually there are more than two names.) With his two p's Pip is obviously funny but thick with irony of birth, the price of human and social emergence. Bartleby has two b's and only an air of confidence; he is unlike Pip, a character who negotiates his name. Spreading out possibility for himself, Bartleby is more a placeholder for teleology and ideas of origin and plurality than a character like Pip trying to understand tombstones and his own origins. Therefore, though young Pip's uncertainties, even including revenge, can be laughed at and withstand it, paradoxically Bartleby's lack of sureness cannot be; his literal and self-conscious thinness, held together by the mechanics of oral underpinnings, prevents it. And that is due to the written frame that distinguishes "Bartleby" from an oral shaggy dog story. Indeed, the written frame defies the oral laughter in the name of character that it initially engages.

It is difficult to characterize the tale's shape, and that includes its title character: "Bartleby is not a character in *the manner of the usual, imaginative, fictional construction,*" Elizabeth Hardwick writes. "He is indeed only words, wonderful words, and very few of them."[97] Sometimes the tale is understood as a corporate parable, negotiating its Wall Street trappings or questions of the Dead Letter Office in Washington. From a certain perspective, there is keen interest in the lawyer's story, if not more than in Bartleby's, in part because the story is told from the lawyer's point of view; yet the lawyer's character also cedes narrative integrity to the dare of a joke structure, as "Bartleby" paradoxically attempts to generate a more literal and plural "character" than a narrative character. Specifically, the frame presumes an accomplishment that has yet to be resolved, character in a missing "canon" of figures for which, potentially, there is *merely* a missing narrative. In "Bartleby," the designated narrator-*writer* proposes a biography of one of the "singular set of men, of whom as yet nothing that I know of has ever been *written* . . ." (13; emphasis added). Bartleby himself is literally thin in body and recognizability:

> I was quite sure he never visited any refectory or eating house; while his pale face clearly indicated that he never drank beer like Turkey, or tea and coffee even, like other men; that he never went any where in particular that

I could learn; never went out for a walk, unless indeed that was the case at present; that he had declined telling who he was, or whence he came, or whether he had any relatives in the world. (28)

The narrator reiterates that his sources for this particular biography are likewise thin: Again, "I believe that no materials exist for a full and satisfactory biography of this man" (13). Usually the subject precedes the biography; here biography attempts to elicit the subject or character or both simultaneously. Attempts to draw out Bartleby, the man, pin "unabducibility" (the inability, in Kukla's words, to express something because "no suitable sentence for it ever comes to mind for consideration as a possible speech act"[98]) at best to the lawyer's inadequate characterizations; attempts to elicit Bartleby the self-conscious subject of biography identify inadequacy in, more literally, the character of the lawyer, fading in its way from written narrative to joke structure: ". . . my first grand point," the lawyer admits (according to the late John Jacob Astor) is "prudence; my next, method" (14), especially when that method is immediately underscored by "babble" and "doggerel," a "creative process," Northrop Frye notably explains, "left unfinished through lack of skill";[99] the lawyer persists to pronounce "a name [John Jacob Astor] which, I admit, I love to repeat, for it hath a rounded and orbicular sound to it, and rings like unto bullion."[100] While this babble has what Frye names a "prose initiative" in position and greed, it pointedly "tries to make itself associative by an act of will, and it reveals the same difficulties that great poetry has overcome at a subconscious level."[101] Bartleby of this thin and inexpressible singular biography, in contrast to the lawyer's gigantic acts of will, literally stands in for this "great literature" or character, already having overcome such difficulties of babble. The narrator's doggerel and self-disqualifications are framed by certain joke structures. Characteristic of long jokes that build on babble and non sequitur of response (not of logic),[102] they denote an absence of a dénouement, destroy pompousness of reception as well as delivery, and make room for the presence of "'unexpectedness'"[103] itself. The narrator's self-consciousness makes already too clear a lack of qualifications for writing in particular *nonfiction* (a "biography") of this man and province. As a frame, the story shifts this utterance back into (a different) nonfiction: that is, it turns an "expressed inability to express" into the very fiction, or joke, of the lawyer's own narrative character—not the lawyer *as* a character, even ironically. It dares, therefore, a new, "cleaner" nonfiction from inside its own action of plurality. It demands putting into order exactly what is not there, replacing the inconsequential and "minute details, repetitions, and elaborations."[104]

"Cathedral," again, is an example of just this kind of frame that really works entirely neither as a story nor as irony, but equally as something akin to the shaggy dog story in which the story presents and underscores a non sequitur. In a more conventional frame, you might judge which character—one or the other or both or neither—can see. But in "Cathedral" neither character can be judged separately from the joke strategy. One needs to hear Carver's story and, through its frame, the playfulness and deadly seriousness—again, the parody of the joke. "However absurd it may be," as Partridge says, "a 'shaggy dog' must never be silly."[105] This kind of story can be considered not so much a written story as a particular kind of performance. In this frame, like many older ones, the speaker is reluctant, or refuses to make a claim at all. The opening to "Cathedral" may not appear to generate a frame from that "loss" of character. It is worth pausing before it. The doubling between the blind man and the speaking "I" does something in addition to setting up redemptive symbolism.[106] It resequences the story as having at least one voice more than the speaking character's voice for narration. Once more, here is the opening: "This blind man, an old friend of my wife's, he was on his way to spend the night."[107] The narrator, like a tall-tale spinner, "projects multiple verbal meanings at once by addressing at least two audiences," Wonham notes, "and his utterance is calculated to mean something different to each."[108] The "he" is a placeholder, a grammatically unnecessary unit. Its grammatical inaccuracy points to a double start, a natural frame. The sentence is technically compromised, suggesting an oral gesture of composition from inside a written one. It "demands," as Partridge says about the shaggy dog story, "an apt and imperceptible mingling of narrative and dialogue."[109] The second lead, "he," with its redundancy, identifies the speaking "I" as (only) one narrator, opening up the "I" as the "he" that the "he" is simultaneously recording as an "I"/eye. The humor of narration is blatant in the need to make clear which man/narrator is spending the night with the wife: who is on his way to spend the night? Closer now to the parody of a joke, the shaggy dog (sometimes called a "'groaner'") is like the narrators themselves who are "laughing their heads off."[110] If we are not sure of the actors, we are equally not sure what is narrated. Partridge explains, "the 'lead-in' and the 'lead up' have had to be deceptively leisurely and almost diffuse."[111] This kind of frame leads in from a single hoop, with an oral nod to the audience, "by which the audience, the performer, and the performance world are united in the event, while retaining their distinct identities"[112]; the performance identifies two disqualified narrators: the speaking "I" with clear written defects and the blind man with obvious physical ones.

Considered as a performance, these elements of the shaggy dog make sense as a sequence of discursive framing. Further, these disqualifications are meant to be literal, in which exaggeration "begins to act literally" and makes an incongruous picture.[113] The story's symbolism, despite attempts to overread it, paradoxically flattens. Even though "Cathedral" lacks the differentiation attributable, say, to frames such as "The Ant and the Grasshopper" by Somerset Maugham or "The Turn of the Screw" by Henry James, it is still characterized by framing that is particularly conjoined to the topos of the inexpressible. It is put into motion by the "character" that Channing might have described as "absent," now humorously and literally so, splitting that absent character minimally into two false starts, that is itself the initiation. This story puts into immediate effect two simultaneous openings, at least two narrators, each undermining, not corroborating, the authority of the other. The story rejects conventional narrator and subject; it does not accept the commonly used gap of irony within a conventional frame (there is not, "Perhaps I could have saved him, with only a word, two words, out of my mouth. Perhaps I could have saved us all. But I never spoke them," as in Alan Paton's *Too Late the Phalarope*[114]). The discourse impatiently and effectively (defined by outcome) creates stages of narrative, as frames, by which to challenge unqualified success from qualified statements. From an opening and acknowledged defeat, these frames turn out written declarations, which bear an uncanny resemblance to frames themselves. Both defensively refuse meaning in favor of action. Both are dependent conditions of writing, not speaking, for acting in oral ways, while acting out the gap. In statement they explicitly refuse change, but rhetorically predicate changelessness on syntactically complex acts of perceptual change. Both rely upon non-oral origins for temporal complexities of revisited verbs built from seemingly progressive and simple statements.

My comments on "Bartleby" and "Cathedral" and "Wakefield" and "Homage to Mistress Bradstreet" and shaggy dogs and no-point shaggy dogs and tall tales should fold back to encircle a temper and rhetoric I have tried to map. I do not want to blur important differences in works or in genres and subcategories or time. "Bartleby" has a different voice and energy from "Cathedral." No one would confuse Berryman's cadences and crossovers for Hawthorne's formal labyrinths. Yet in each of them, frames (again what Tannen names *"structures of expectations"* (24; emphasis in original) or the "footing" (26) between speaker and hearer (26), dramatize the problem of distancing English from English. In this rhetoric, the reemergence of the topos of the inexpressible utilizes other local traditions, such as shaggy dog and no-point shaggy dog humor to turn passive listeners into active participants. For written frames of rhetorical and historical complexity, strategies of orality help to allow them to make sense. Bonnie D. Irwin notes that the "frame tale depicts these [oral] storytelling events in all their variety and in the process carries many of the keys to oral performance onto the printed page."[115] The oral approach to this kind of framing discourse can retrieve the humor and desire for inclusion of each single listener from the rhetorical and temporal complexity of a topos often linked, in traditions of the divine, to the atemporal. As John Miles Foley explains, oral approaches to *"the degree to which the text promotes—and its readership continues—a tradition of reception,"* and, again, "[t]o the extent that an audience is able to co-create the work by enriching its textual integers and bridging its gaps of indeterminacy according to the rules of the idiom."[116] This framing discourse uses overstated and, in particular, overwritten disadvantage (such as the now familiar perceived language doubled with England's) straight to performed, oral strategies of advantage.

A small poem from *The Dial* in 1841, called "The Future is better Than the Past," captures both the temporal complexity and simple impatience framing the present moment and perceived missing "voices"[117] of the landscape. Framed and opened instead by where it is not, "*Not* where long-passed ages sleep" (1.1; emphasis added), the "real Eden" (1.16) is still "afar" (1.33), yet in persistent unity, with the inexpressible present, ultimately untouched and untouchable by either toil, hope, or time: "It is coming, it shall come, / To the patient and the striving. . . . Stir nor toil nor hope shall mar / Its immortal unity" (lines 17–18; 35–36).[118]

CHAPTER 5

THE INEXPRESSIBLE
AND THE THING ITSELF

A discourse of inadequacy, delivered through frames built around the inexpressible, combines written and oral discourse. It has the former's organization and complexity, the latter's economy. It has, moreover, discursive links to modern preoccupations with the center that cannot hold, the elusive "Thing Itself." Wallace Stevens famously calls it that and self-consciously frames it as a set-up: "Not Ideas about the Thing but the Thing Itself." Robert Pogue Harrison puts the self-conscious, modern desire this way: "The craving for the thing itself, for reality in its first idea, is impossible to satisfy except in a self-consuming anticipation of that which has already happened yet which has not yet happened." He adds, "The beginning 'of that which is always beginning, over and over,' to quote from Stevens's poem 'St. Armorer's Church from Outside' (*CP,* 530), never really begins, for the moment it begins it has already fallen away from the beginning."[1] There are familiar chords: the inexpressible "first idea," or birth, or demarcation of origin that modernism relegates as "itself a myth" (671) playing out in recognizable and longstanding frames of inexpressibility, redundancy of language in relation to strains of teleology, ideas of "originality," and, in particular, time sequences relegated to failed "latecomers." For instance, when Harrison writes regarding Stevens's poem, "It means that from the moment we became historical we have been latecomers, and that nature in its first idea always comes too early for us" (671), we hear a modern dictum that for earlier self-designated "latecomers" is experienced and laid out, as we have heard, literally and defensively. *The Port Folio* (1807) puts it grandly tongue-in-cheek: "If the ancients have got the start of us in point of time, it must be granted that we moderns have far exceeded them in almost every other respect."[2] And forty-three years later the reviewer from *Harper's Monthly Magazine* explicitly labels the American shortcomings: "After the Americans had established their political nationality beyond cavil, and taken a positive rank among the powers of the civilized world, they still remained subject to reproach . . . in the worlds of Art, Science, Literature."[3] The politics of seeming to appear late to the English language, late to literature, late to genius (in each instance, not "first") puts pressure on the same topos of inexpressibility to present what "comes too early" as inevitably yet to come. Looking at written frames that act oral, built on an atypical discourse of the ineffable, is just the beginning of thinking about what happens when a self-conscious self-promotion emerges from commercial, religious, and choral roots of the inexpressible.[4]

Multiple starts toward the "thing itself" (toward an imagined literature, for example) can be defensively organized after political independence around a perceived inexpressibility. Attempts to express an inexpressible English inside English are nudged, in Kukla's philosophical language, into a temporal world of unabducibility and unselectability by the topos of the inexpressible, and the discursive results frequently predate the historical indeterminacy and reformulated inadequacies commonly found in modernist expressions of the latecomer, as in the following from Ezra Pound: "For three years, out of key with his time, / He strove to resuscitate the dead art / Of poetry; to maintain 'the sublime' / In the old sense. Wrong from the start—// No, hardly, but seeing he had been born in a half savage country, out of date."[5] While just what cannot be expressed changes ideologically, there is common ground in a preoccupation with an absent "center."[6] Earlier, the center is linked to what is specifically and potentially "dead" in the same-English language, fingering a perceived inferiority. This American self-promotion is transmogrified into a temporal matter, certain if elusive: "America has a great and noble task *before her* in literature," notes the *American Review* in 1845, "and we firmly believe the power and capacity to do it. The beginnings are faint and scattered, but the elements *are here*."[7] From the same journal four months later we hear, "surely we ought to be wiser than to plume ourselves yet upon our literary position. We need have no doubts of our destiny in this respect."[8]

Such self-conscious concern with progress rears its head early and often. It is acknowledged, and defended, in *The Democratic Review* in 1847:

> A writer in the last Oct. number of the North American Review, says, that "an intense national self-consciousness, though the shallow may name it patriotism, is the worst foe to the true and generous unfolding of national genius." Against the opinion of this learned Theban, we set the high authorities we have already cited; we set the fact, that Greece, Rome and England, the nations which have possessed the most intense self-consciousness, whose writers have been most penetrated by the sense of nationality, and with whose people patriotism has risen almost into a religious sentiment,—have excelled all the other states of the world in their literature, no less than in their physical prowess.[9]

Defensiveness about failures to identify *the* (translated to the *as yet*) inexpressible idiom is a forerunner of the modern era's self-consciousness and plurality, what William James calls the "interrupted and discontinuous" nature of consciousness.[10] In the rise of international modernism with its profound ethos of self-consciousness it is important not to miss the important historical continuity of discourse on the topos of the inexpressible. Modern frames often embody an earlier self-consciousness that would appear in an equally elusive "thing itself" (if named more particularly, such as "National Poetic Literature"). In the earlier period this elusive demand is perceived more literally than the modern "first" instance or a dreaded (too) late one; nineteenth-century complaints concerning authorship and genius illuminate a perceived hole in "our native country, whose genius, hitherto, has not been that of [literary] invention."[11] Discourse of the inexpressible finds acts of language that frame as already achieved what is manqué, both lacking and dearly missed or lost.

Often the ideological and philosophic principles of writers, such as those loosely grouped around the Bergsonian nexus of flux, perception, and duration, are said to epitomize modernity without recognizing in particular longstanding historical and rhetorical practices. Discussing a threshold for humanism in modernist thought, Michael Levenson writes, "subjectivity will become the foundation and support for a range of threatened institutions."[12] Art critic Michael Fried alights on immediacy: "Authenticity" in the modern period pertains, if it exists at all, to "continuous and entire presentness... that one experiences as a kind of instantaneousness."[13] Joseph Frank writes, for instance, that in T. S. Eliot's "The

Waste Land," "syntactical sequence is given up for a structure depending on the perception of relationships between disconnected word-groups. To be properly understood, these word-groups must be juxtaposed with one another and perceived simultaneously," all in all an example of "the internal conflict between the time-logic of language and the space-logic implicit in the modern conception of the nature of poetry."[14] Such descriptions in tune with modernism, however, are not formally in touch with the heritage of the inexpressible topos and frames, with which they are often elided, and in particular the attempts to frame and stabilize instantaneously—and with impatience—the inexpressible, without naming in particular, the desired "result": again, "Now he has passed that way see after him!" (10).[15] Whitman says of the coming and already past, missing and passing and simultaneously present poet.

Framing evolves across literary and same-language anxieties, making texts modern in practice; by the same token, in modern texts that same set of framing strategies around the "thing itself" point to a fundamentally historical lineage. In an era of radically absent centers, therefore, it is easy to miss a common history of poetics, proposed around same-language questions not in terms of (commonly expressed and modern) "loss," but instead (nothing but) gain. Its footing remains pragmatic, adapted from a topos that by definition traditionally excludes human beings, since language remains continuously inadequate. The earlier frames emerging from this topos are often self-consciously bent on naming not just an authority but a root author (if moment-to-moment falling short). More modern and international works, such as "The Love Song of J. Alfred Prufrock," bend against any such centralized and authoritative gestures (instead tracking all failed attempts to recover them): "And I have known the eyes already, known them all— / The eyes that fix you in a formulated phrase / . . . / Then how should I begin / To spit out all the butt-ends of my days and ways? / And how should I presume?"[16] However, a conflict in consciousness (in David Spurr's words), of an embattled sensibility, between what he now calls intellect and imagination,[17] points to an earlier discourse. Prufrock's defensiveness ("In short, I was afraid") combines with a counterpart on the offensive by a change both of perspective and pronoun; "It is impossible to say just what I mean! . . . / If *one* . . . should say: / 'That is not it at all, / That is not what I meant, at all.'"[18] This familiar pairing refits inadequacy and inexpressibility to yet-to-be expressed superiority. When Denis Donoghue notes that Eliot does not want any "particular emotion" to "exceed the situation that provoked it,"[19] he is talking about modern objective correlatives. But the longstanding politics of renaming, which turns offensive-out-of-defensive, is evident in Hugh Henry Brackenridge's tongue-in-cheek introduction of his satire *Modern Chivalry* in 1815:

> I shall consider language only, not in the least regarding the matter of the work; but as musicians, when they are about to give the most excellent melody, pay no attention to the words that are set to music, but take the most unmeaning phrases, such as sol, fa, la; so here, culing [*sic*] out the choicest flowers of diction, I shall pay no regard to the idea.[20]

Particulars can sink a speaker, opening the door to criticism; conversely, nonparticularity or what Brackenridge called "unmeaning" phrases, if vague, keep the frame of the door wide open and invite compromised insiders to become inventive outsiders. Listen again to Brown in *The Rhapsodist:* "It is a very whimsical situation when a person is about to enter into company, and is at a loss what character or name to assume it in."[21] What separates this Rhapsodist from Prufrock is a twist on self-consciousness, a replacement of frames to a degree more literally bound with those of inevitably late "arrivals" ideologically to any modern scene. At the same time, a felt loss of an original, expressible, authoritative language and literature generates, past its inception, a discourse of framing (and renaming) that picks up more modern circlings of absent authorities, self-division, fissures, and loss. Speaking of the poems of Eliot and Ezra Pound, for example, Robert Crawford writes, "Their poetry registers longing, and a jagged sense of pain."[22]

Tellingly, Charles Isenberg describes the frame narrative as a text that is exactly about, again, what it "cannot name,"[23] pointing to the ineffable. In discursive framing, with its emphasis on precision, no response is ever perceived as adequate; it is not surprising, thus, that a ubiquitous cultural fear and parody accompany a stretched self-confidence: in 1845 it is proclaimed, "America has a great a noble task before her in literature, and we firmly believe the power and capacity to do it."[24] These frames, further, do what Isenberg says they do. Defensive and rooted in performance, they emphasize the "reader's activity" (16), multiplying possibilities or candidates by refusing to name. Whitman in 1888 describes the as-yet unnameable "poet": "One needs only a little penetration to see, at more or less removes, the material facts of their country and radius, with the coloring of the moods of humanity at the time, and its gloomy or hopeful prospects, behind all poets and each poet, and forming their birthmarks."[25] In this frame, potential failure is deflected, leaving room for the unnamable birthmark: "In estimating first-class song, a sufficient Nationality, or, on the other hand, what may be call'd the negative and lack of it (as in Goethe's case, it sometimes seems to me) is often, if not always, the first element" (661).

Framing the inexpressible, here an unnameable "poet" or "first-class song" defined by what Whitman calls the "negative and lack of it" (661) can buy time. It can allow time for changes in perception about *how* to reconstitute what is perceived as not there from what may already be there. This discourse of the inexpressible, here Whitman's rhetoric of a national "birthmark," anticipates a modern call to name the missing authors in a still imperfectly mapped America. On this imperfect map, framing the inexpressible persists as useful: for Judith Fetterley, for example, this frame of *never naming* persists: "I seek thus to join the effort to identify the naming of the field of 'American' literature as itself a site of contestation."[26] Earlier, "America"'s expressiblity had a different job: for instance, in Whitman's hands it is designed to *hold back* the naming of any single author for fear of getting it wrong. Yet, in Fetterley's modern version of the frame, the inexpressible site of "America" may be said instead to *generate* authors: it educates and makes room for the inclusion of more authors, built on an anxiety of leaving them out: "I seek nothing less than the creation of a citizenry committed to the values of *inclusion,* empathy, diversity, and community, and the cultural change which would follow upon the creation of such a citizenry" (21; emphasis added).

Thus, the persistent frame of the inexpressible holds hope for both periods: an anxiety of *not saying* (bent earlier on a fear of *letting in* the "wrong" author) lends itself in a modern vision to an anxiety still of *not saying,* but now it frames the possibility of *leaving out* the so-far unrecognized authors. In both instances, holding open the frame more widely still to a desire for naming exactly *which* author or authors demand recognition also persists. For example, this comment from *The Port Folio* in 1807, in its fear of naming the wrong author, might well be a reversed echo from the modern challenge to name the right one: "Genius is a common inheritance."[27] Here is already the recognizable language and action of framing around the inexpressible, reeducating speakers and "citizenry" to uncover values and authors that are already passing right in front of them.

In both versions of reeducation, these frames bracket "missing" authors. The frames evolve from early promotional and colonial rhetoric (constructing *the* missing and ideal "American" author in the English language) to recent empowering social cause (missing the actual plurality of authors in an "American" construct). In each case, the frame effectively draws out more time from cul-de-sacs of "conventional" wisdom. In each case there is an impasse of contemporary "conventional" wisdom, one that fingers an absence or denial of an author or authors, or at least a yet-to-be-expressed recognition of them. In particular, both frames exhibit an acute sensitivity to judgments of inadequacy, and an equally sensitive hope in yet-to-come recognition of the "author" not yet fully expressed. These frames overlap in a poetics of the inexpressible and framing, unfolding perceived high expectations and restricted acts of inclusion.

The demand for inclusion of the "denied" author for William Dunlap, for example, is based on the English inheritance and language. In 1798 he writes, "any deviation from what [the audiences] remember to be fact, appears to them as a fault in the poet; they are disappointed, their expectations are not fulfilled, and the writer is more or less condemned."[28] Dunlap himself points to a fear of "typing" that gets the "poet" wrong in any given instance; this fear of the wrong capture of the American author leads to making time to "express" what is condemned as inexpressible. Dunlap, as with Brown, restricts condemnation, allowing expectation for "national" character, and time for the making of a "character" and poet. Samuel Miller's following statement epitomizes the widening of the time frame to include American authors:

> Such are some of the causes which have hitherto impeded the progress of American Literature. Their influence, however, is gradually declining, and the literary prospects of our country are brightening every day.... and when the time shall arrive that we can give to our votaries of literature the same leisure, and the same stimulants to exertion with which they are favoured in Europe, it may be confidently predicted, that letters will flourish as much in America as in any part of the world; and that we shall be able to make some return to our trans-atlantic brethren, for the rich stores of useful knowledge which they have been pouring upon us for nearly two centuries.[29]

This statement self-consciously takes note of the insufficiency of American authors. Yet, its outline of an exclusion of them, built on the topos of the inexpressible, paradoxically will admit even the "lowest" to be included as possibilities: "In Europe, we meet kings, nobles, priests, peasants," says William Ellery Channing in *The Christian Examiner* in 1830. "How much rarer is it to meet men.... The institutions of the old world all tend to throw obscurity over what we most need to know."[30] Exclusion of "what we most need to know" can, therefore, link itself to fears of a potentially incorrect "selection" or identification of the poet (for instance, in kings or nobles) in the search for what the editor of the *The American Review* in 1845 proceeds to call "a rock or two": "But surely we ought to be wiser than to plume ourselves yet upon our literary position. We need have no doubts of our destiny ... and as to poetry and poets, notwithstanding many delicate effusions, who does not know, that a National Poetic Literature was never yet built on fugitive pieces. A rock or two is generally found necessary for a corner stone."[31]

Like many others in the period, Dunlap develops these rhetorical patterns of framing, for example, that serve at once as an authorial "give" (allowing leeway and room for the poet) and critical "take" (protecting the so-to-speak "character" or author that has yet to be heard). Declaring his work a "free poetical picture," Dunlap in his introduction to *Major André* proceeds, "The subject necessarily involves political questions; but the Author presumes that he owes *no apology* to any one for having shown himself an American."[32] These frames from Dunlap are specifically concerned with renaming or refiguring, from inside expectation to the contrary, the "poet" himself as already recognizable, if recognized.

In other words, this rhetoric of the inexpressible frames a margin, a "marginalized" author who has taken up the challenge, been missed; a new challenge is opened to refigure what has been overlooked. Melville also challenges in 1850 not to miss this figure: "The great mistake seems to be, that even with those Americans who look forward to the coming of a great literary genius among us, they somehow fancy he will come in the costume of Queen Elizabeth's day...."[33] Again, the Preface picks up and frames the missing celebrated author: "The presence of the greatest poet conquers ... there is not left any vestige of despair ... " (10).

Charles Isenberg reminds us frames "do not so much demonstrate a truth as narrativize a desire."[34] This reminder points to a familiar paradigm of inexpressibility. As we have seen, the paradigm entails a long, complex history of the inexpressible deriving values from an act of "naming" or renaming: as Gertrude Stein's super-self-conscious *The Making of Americans* makes inexpressible phrases nearly meaningless by framing them with inadequacy spread over time that can fold back inadequacy into exactly "what I mean," without naming it: "I mean, I mean and that is not what I mean, I mean that not any one is saying what they are meaning, I mean that I am feeling something, I mean that I mean something and I mean that not any one is thinking, is feeling, is saying, is certain of that thing ... I mean, I mean, I know what I mean";[35] or the earlier Frost, whose oven bird knows "not to sing";[36] or with Stevens, where the terms of framing are never as simple as "influence," just as "voice" remains doubtlessly insufficient for Whitman.

Stevens's poems, for example, can be said to typify what earmarks modern and self-conscious poetics. What goes on in them, Joseph Riddel explains in an earlier view, has "everything to do with defining man ... in his consciousness of the paradox of consciousness."[37] Similarly, Michael Heller observes that "it may well be that he [Stevens] inaugurates (to use Derrida's term) a mode of writing which already sees the fictive nature of the philosophical, which takes this fiction for granted, which loves the jouissance of rubbing one philosophical idea against another, is unrelentingly skeptical of philosophy's urge toward certainties."[38] Helen Vendler sees this, but also one of the paradigms for the topos of the inexpressible, in her discussion of Stevens's "prevalent voice of hesitation and qualification": "even the title of 'Not Ideas about the Thing but the Thing Itself' embodies one of Stevens' typical formulas, 'not X but Y,' which appears in a frequency far beyond the normal throughout Stevens' work, and seems to be another case of the left hand subtracting what the right hand gives."[39] Vendler rightly sees Stevens's lack of assertion. It is apparent in the following examples:

> It was not the shadow of cloud and cold,
> But a sense of the distance of the sun—
> The shadow of a sense of his own,
>
> A knowledge that the actual day
> Was so much less. Only the wind
> Seemed large and loud and high and strong.
> (from "Two Illustrations That the World Is What You Make of It"[40])
>
> Opusculum paedagogum.
> The pears are not viols,
> Nudes or bottles. . . .
>
> They are yellow forms
> Composed of curves
> Bulging toward the base.
> They are touched red.
> (from "Study of Two Pears"[41])

Attempts to define Stevens's famous "Thing Itself" are alive with skepticism, what Jacqueline Brogan calls "assertions, modulated with their own contradiction."[42] Analogues are engaged and avoided, therefore, not for their ultimate insufficiency (this is a common observation)—in this history of eking out the expressible through temporal engagement with the inexpressible, such analogues frame and remove their own absurdity.

None of the following trio, for example, can be presumed to exist from the get-go: the "Thing Itself" (from Stevens's poem), an indigenous language of "genius" (articulated in the nineteenth century), and the modern and postmodern analogue (in relation to "truth"). To quote Paul A. Bové, such informed skepticism celebrates "the increasing impossibility of defending 'truth' in any metaphysical way."[43] Many openings in Stevens's poems suggest, but more crucially and simultaneously frame, an analogic world—frame it as already a lost cause, as in the nineteenth-century identification of the desired and "unique" language, which is as good as inexpressible at any given moment in time. The framer is earmarked as antimimetic or, to a degree, purposeless, unable to narrate.

Critics often link this indeterminancy to the moderns who, as Clive Bloom says, are "determined by the defining struggle with structure."[44] Alan Filreis is on the mark to note the importance of pronouns in Stevens's defensiveness. In Stevens's poems, pronouns await in self-deprecating hope the arrival of a hero, a language, and mock-pronouns: "If the poetry of X was music, / So that it came to *him* of its own, / Without understanding . . . ." begins "The Creations of Sound" (310; emphasis added). In "The Idea of Order at Key West": "*She* sang beyond the genius of the sea. / The water never formed to mind or voice . . ." (128; emphasis added). She—the figureless woman—is defenseless, thus defensive. Filreis, again, writes of the "meditative *I*, quietly confessing to an eerily unimportant American life."[45] But he does not connect Stevens's defensiveness to earlier and unquiet discursive framing, as in Brown or Whitman. Making inexpressibility important, Stevens's dramatic "he" or "she" is fall-out from the perceiving, framing "I."[46] Such pronouns, moreover, have their rhetorical roots in frame structures and longstanding defensiveness.

For example, in "The Poem That Took the Place of a Mountain" (512), an "unexplained completion," which comprises a "unique and solitary home," contradicts "How he had recomposed the pines" to get there. The poem does not primarily reiterate ironic awareness (central to modernism). It is historically more artless than that. The obsession with uniqueness and language jokingly dares the frame to yield consensus. Whether as a modern (or a colonial) or a metaphor, "he" is denied an intersection of language and uniqueness. Here is the entire poem:

> There it was, word for word,
> The poem that took the place of a mountain.
>
> He breathed its oxygen,
> Even when the book lay turned in the dust of his table.

> It reminded him how he had needed 5
> A place to go to in his own direction,
>
> How he had recomposed the pines,
> Shifted the rocks and picked his way among clouds,
>
> For the outlook that would be right,
> Where he would be complete in an unexplained completion: 10
>
> The exact rock where his inexactnesses
> Would discover, at last, the view toward which they had edged,
>
> Where he could lie and, gazing down at the sea,
> Recognize his unique and solitary home. [line numbers added]

In relation to point of view, "could" in the penultimate line (13) dangles. It is either redundantly "stupid" from the perspective of "he," thereby dismissed. Or it is the mark of a framer's consensus: "Where he could lie and gazing down at the sea, / Recognize his unique and solitary home" (13–14). But the framer does not use this structure to reveal consensus regarding the obvious; if so, two previous "would[s]" would suffice: "For the outlook that would be right" (9); "The exact rock where his inexactnesses / Would discover, at last, the view toward which they had edged" (11–12). Against the frame, the framer, and the framed, the determinism of "could" juts out self-consciously and inconsistently. It preserves itself as a word out of place, a nonjoking necessity to make a mark against history. It does not concede to narrative and judgment, but dares its existence.

The inability to narrate identifies an old gap between what has been controversially named constative and performative language.[47] "Behind every poem is there not an implicit narrative giving the voice an occasion," asks Daniel R. Schwarz, "a context of experience, in which it speaks?"[48] He contends, "Because his [Stevens's] poems are arenas in which to render acts of perception rather than to record prior reality, the spectator is rhetorically urged to act upon the poem in his act of reading" (15).[49] He summarizes that "we may find it helpful . . . to abandon the concept of a consistent persona" (7)—and that is a commonplace of poets. It is not surprising, then, that critics label this point of view in Stevens's poetry modern and comic irony.[50] But this characteristic is also consistent with early framers. If abandoning the idea of a consistent persona takes place,[51] Stevens's version of the tragicomic mode is held back by the dispersion through openly self-contemptuous and multiple framers waiting for language in their readers.

In favor of conversation and mutual self-recognition, the frames already make the reading of signs redundant. For example, in "Jouga" (337), "Ha-eé-me is a beast." But the framer's self-realization instantly reinscribes Ha-eé-me as perhaps only one of two beasts, like his guitar, thereby reducing isness to the only thing recognized as possible, likeness: " . . . Ha-eé-me is a beast. // Or perhaps his guitar is a beast or perhaps they are / Two beasts. But of the same kind. . . . " In this depiction the concern of reading turns from questioning the existence of the "thing itself" to inquiring for the poem's point and transforms outsiders to insiders. In "Thinking of a Relation between the Images of Metaphors" (356) the creation of readers as instances of their own language appears once more. The poet first makes a framer, rather than a speaker speaking, unaware of fiction. This occurs precisely when the narrator exposes his own superfluousness: "The bass lie deep, still afraid of the Indians."

The humor demanded by the absurdity of the bass's fear (in the absence of any Indians) reflects the presence of a sane and self-elected narrator whose skepticism reveals what is already known. Any fisherman who is only, that is, "all / One ear" cannot reach the bass either. Like the Indians, the bass themselves no longer exist. More absurdly, the bass are safer. They do not exist for the Indians that are dead, and they are safely "dead" to all the living who believe themselves to be one-eared. Entrusted to fiction for humor the framer informs what listeners already know, that they are not one of the one-eared fishermen, hearers of a "deep" that does not exist. This narrator's superfluousness is not directly part of the poem's subject or doctrine. Instead it is a revelation of a character's irrelevance. He chooses to tell a story that is but fact and therefore does not need to be told. The humor—the structure and not the statement often emphasized by modernists—is deadly serious. For instance, the following openings, which are frequently taken to be self-reflexive poems of process, reveal historical frames:

> On her side, reclining on her elbow.
> This mechanism, this apparition,
> Suppose we call it Projection A.
> (from "So-And-So Reclining on Her Couch," 295)

> The night knows nothing of the chants of night.
> It is what it is as I am what I am:
> And in perceiving this I best perceive myself.
> (from "Re-Statement of Romance," 146)

The poem must resist the intelligence
Almost successfully. Illustration:

A brune figure in winter evening resists
Identity. The thing he carries resists

The most necessitous sense. . . .
(from "Man Carrying Thing," 350)

Diction gives away the frames. In the first example "Suppose" (line 3) after "apparition" (line 2) ridicules both the language of determination and absence of language. "We" (line 3) adds a third voice to the common framer's "I." Multiple masks of humor, which are really backtrackings of self-doubt, proliferate where the letter "A," for instance, is tried. The first letter, "A" (line 3), already a projection, requires no final dismissal; the "unpainted shore" (line 25) in the poem's final stanza is anticipated for its obviousness, not its irony. The restatement of romance, indeed, is just that, heard, rather than seen, in the word "only," repeated for the third time in the last stanza: "The night is only the background of our selves," less invisible than inaudible next to the repetitions of what it cannot, by loss of contrast through repetition, foreground: "our selves." In "Man Carrying Thing," we hear again the humor of the "bright obvious" in contrast to the "brune figure in winter" who, of course, in the long tradition of frames, "resists / Identity" (capital "I"). The most bright adjective points to its joke of obscurity, just as the "thing" is by the end finally identified as precisely and literally, the "obvious" itself, no more identified, or not, than the more descriptively bound "brune" figure. I could go on with such instances of obviousness and frames that refuse revelation or are designated meaningfulness.

The humor in Stevens's poems is that of the tall tale, and more pointedly, the no-point shaggy dog. They too are self-evident—so much so that they are encapsulated in the shaggy dog (especially the no-point shaggy dog) or in the very titles of Stevens ("So-And-So Reclining on Her Couch," "The Poem That Took the Place of a Mountain"). One of the forms taking roots in the United States, shaggy dogs,[52] as we have seen, makes room, and in particular time, given their verbosity, for imminent "origin" replacing a perceived and designated one. Partridge explains one source of that in the Greek phrase, *para prosdokian,* that is, contrary to expectation; "usually," he says, this is of the form "of an unexpected word whimsically substituted for an apparently inevitable word."[53] Again, here is the beginning: "The poem must resist the intelligence / Almost successfully. Illustration:

// A brune figure in winter evening resists / Identity. The thing he carries resists // The most necessitous sense . . . ." (350). The ending of "Man Carrying Thing" with an adjectival noun "obvious"—"We must endure our thoughts all night, until / The bright obvious stands motionless in cold" (351)—suddenly substitutes an unexpected noun for the "thing." The "thing" is now not only "obvious," but the obvious: it is transformed from an inexpressible, the "thing," into nothing but the "obvious"; and it is the pronoun "we" that makes it available, if available at all. This oral move is long in the tooth, reframing what is there, "the thing," as not only the "obvious" for all to get, but "motionless" unless "we" make a move. Just so, "So-And-So" on her couch, reclined and fetal, "Born, as she was, at twenty-one, / Without lineage or language," is reborn in the paradigmatic fizzle ending, complete with substitution of name from "So-And-So" to "Mrs. Pappadopoulos": "Good-bye, / Mrs. Pappadopoulos, and thanks," the framer adds at the very end (295–96). The question often is "for what?" (commonly probed for its philosophical tendrils). A telling question might be "by whom?" The poem early sets out, again, "we": "Suppose we call it Projection A." But this time it comes to an end with "one": "one confides in" and "[o]ne walks easily." Pontification occurs at the very expense of the subject of the frame, Mrs. Pappadopoulos. By the end, she is not only dismissed but even more absent as a character than when she began as Projection B in an attempted verbal identification of object: "Let this be called / Projection B." Just her name (chiming "Mrs." with "Pappadopoulos") remains at the end, orally brimming, while she remains inexpressible, both past, gone ("Good-bye") and unexpectedly available, only when under direct address: ("Good-bye . . . and thanks"), now and as yet without "lineage or language" (line 7).

Many of Stevens's poems, then, are exploiting earlier frames that depict such still births of one kind or another, and at the same time resist them formally. Stevens's poetics of inexpressibility is inextricably tied to them. A good way to stand between these discursive patterns of nineteenth-century and twentieth-century frames is through Harold Bloom's proverbial comment, which flags tell-tale "self-consciousness": "Poetic Influence is thus a disease of self-consciousness."[54] He continues to explain: a "strong" poet identifies "a young man in the horror discovering his own incurable case of continuity. By the time he has become a strong poet, and so learned this dilemma, he seeks to exorcise the necessary guilt of his ingratitude by turning his precursor into a fouled version of the later poet himself." He concludes, importantly, "But that too is a self-deception and a banality, for what the strong poet thus does is to transform himself into a fouled version of himself, and then confound the consequence with the figure of the precursor" (62).

Based largely in Freud's family romance, Bloom's statements emphasize, as he acknowledges, priority, "for the commodity in which poets deal, their authority, their property, turns upon priority. They own, they are, what they become first in naming" (64). This is especially crucial for these frames that are coextensive with the topos of the inexpressible. An author such as Brown or even a critic such as Walter Channing articulates the "incurable case of continuity," especially since in this family romance, language is perceived simultaneously as both identity and identical. So the precursor English and the later American are felt as inseparable, making priority moot. Minimizing priority, framing strategies began under unusual conditions of influence, perceived and simultaneous doubling. But where identity is perceived as doubled, rather than linear, influence is especially complex. In Bloom's terms it produces literally overwritten models that reproduce an oral affect. That is, without conditions of priority, what Bloom calls "misprision" by a later author has no space (here precisely time) for "reducing" the precursor, thereby instituting a reduced self. What emerges is that time is luxury. Whitman and others who desire a more instantaneous and less risky version of what Bloom would call a "strong poet" are not faced with the reduction or the ultimate self-reduction that Bloom points to, where the poet transforms "himself into a fouled version of himself," confounding the result with the precursor. Discursive frames, where there is no prioritizing, join a past authorship with a forthcoming one, calling for the same as ever-present. These frames yield no ground to mistaken identity: the "author" was (and so remained unnoticed) or will eventually come. The present is cradle to all possibilities. "What is 1845 to do for us in literature?" asks *The American Whig Review*. "It has at least good opportunities of its own. . . . There is a new year opening of the Christian Era;—let it be so indeed, and like Boniface's ale, savor of the Anno Domini!"[55] Nature itself, *The American Whig Review* continues, guarantees it:

> In these dim attempts at American literature, in the mere fact that people read and write at all, taken in connection with the natural scenery and adaptation of the soil, and the character of the people destined to fill the land, we read the sure elements of a glorious future. With such a people and such a soil—given, as in ancient Greece, simply the letters of Cadmus—and we are sure of the result. It is morally certain.[56]

The strategies of reduction by poets or authors, what Bloom calls "fouled" versions of themselves, and the intimate cooperation of the audience in written feats that act oral often entail risk. Early authors commonly substitute overwritten (and humorous) self-deflation, and the resulting oral action of overwritten texts turns the fear of reduction on its head: Bloom focuses on "I," but if every pronoun can be a subject, which pronoun—"I," "he," "she," "they"—is not eligible in this simultaneity for mastery? Bloom links Whitman and Stevens as examples of this phenomenon, claiming that "Stevens antithetically completes Whitman" (68); at the same time he admits that Stevens, like any British revisionary, will "reduce in regard to the precursors," correcting the earlier "over-idealizer" (68, 69). Bloom's argument follows: "Source study is wholly irrelevant here," and a poet need not have read a precursor for such studies to hold (70). With a new understanding of simultaneity and same-language discourse of framing, defensiveness in Stevens's poems in that context can just as well be read as what is offensive, and that changes the terrain of defensiveness.

Stevens's poems, therefore, offer resonance as well to those narratives that formally frame inadequate beginnings and inexpressibility, and the act of renaming and uttering them. This is exactly what Margaret Fuller, like␣Whitman a few years later, depicts as in 1846 she stages the nation's difficult birth. First she thumps Great Britain's "insular position" as a "parent" England in relation to the development of its "child": "We use her language, and receive, in torrents, the influence of her thought, yet it is, in many respects, uncongenial and injurious to our constitution." Then she renames such a constitution in terms of "forms" yet to be filled: "Nor then shall it be seen till from the leisurely and yearning soul of that riper time national ideas shall take birth, ideas craving to be clothed in a thousand fresh and original forms. Without such ideas all attempts to construct a national literature must end in abortions like the monster of Frankenstein, things with forms, and the instincts of forms, but soulless, and therefore revolting. We cannot have expression till there is something to be expressed."[57] What appears, then, rhetorically is a framing around the topos of the inexpressible that Whitman or Stevens shares. And in between, at an edge of modernism in 1917, Amy Lowell reiterates that inexpressible "difference" ("We are no more colonies of this or that other land, but ourselves, different from all other peoples whatsoever"[58]) that still calls for time: "An individual brought up in one of the small towns scattered over the country was therefore obliged to reproduce suddenly in himself the evolution of three hundred years" (9). She concludes: "It takes the lifetime of more than one individual to throw off a superstition, and the effort to do so is not made without sacrifice" (10). On the defense against inferiority and universalism, for what Lowell calls a "native school" (v): no one can say that what is found in "the seething of a new idealism . . . *hidden away* in the dreams and desires of unknown men" (vi; emphasis added) is wrong any more than Brackenridge's earlier "unmeaning phrases" of musical diction, sol, fa, la, can miss an unnamed target; so the speaker remains invulnerable. On the offense, the speaker's lack of explicitness allows it to pertain to everyone; no speaker or listener or unknown dream is let down. A framing practice, then, that evolves not to name, but to rename all as eligible for naming, found its centering practices of the inexpressible as equally eligible for imminent decentering practices of the modern "throwing off of superstition." As Lowell advises, "Sudden change can never accomplish the result of a long, slow process" (10), even when the frame to do so persists.

The ineffable and the inexpressible, by convention, are on the edge of language, their contours and configurations difficult to see, locate, describe. Framing is easily recognized in narrative and to a certain degree in the topos of the inexpressible, but takes more sorting out when it appears temporal—we are not as used to it appearing that way. The important oral strategies of framing, relocated to the shaggy dog tale and especially the no-point shaggy dog, can be elusive since they can concern nonmeaning itself: their point, at least on the surface, is that there is no point. And the writers themselves, even well-plumbed Whitman, can appear convoluted and obscure.

An effort to distance English from English, a late construing of a longstanding topos, is itself a construct and itself twisted. To imagine a language to be something other than it is while expressing the distance between the two simultaneously means relying on complex formal mechanisms first for creating the distance from itself, and secondly for crossing that distance as the expectation of the expression itself. In *Distancing English,* I have shown that the first distance is formed by engaging the inexpressible, noting the gap between expectation and expression. The second is bridged by the frames that are forged by the inexpressible and mark the distance as itself a set-up. The strategic use of frames that we have seen for shaking a language loose from itself refocuses a perceived statement in a received language that can appear at first to offer little.[59] Remaking the same inexpressible words as bound to expressibility, deriving power from the topos of the ineffable, frames hold off anxiety by formalizing it.

Thus, the absence of a felt language within the very terms of presence in a received same language lends itself to an already long history of self-promotion, recorded self-consciousness, and high expectations. Political severance and surprising successes of the War of 1812 add to the momentum and to anxieties of perfectibility. We hear it building between these dates when a writer for *The Port Folio* in 1807 exclaims, "Till we exhibit a work which the verdict of scholars shall enrol with the great efforts of genius of other countries, the truth of the criticism I have delivered, harsh as it appears, is unimpeachable."[60]

Finding the exact words for that "work" suggests patterns of expectation and discourses of propagation, rather than of course the achieved. We have seen how that discursive framing develops around the inexpressible. Publicity of productivity, suppression of hardships (for attracting further emigration from England), along with a developing religious "laboratory" of perfection in non-Anglican denominations produce expectations and self-promotion where "nothing" is guaranteed but self-revision to advantage. Whether in Whitman's Preface, or in the critical debates on language, or the no-point shaggy dog, there exists simultaneously a rousing defensiveness, matching anxieties of insufficiency and critical attacks regarding degeneration, an adapted inexpressibility in the core of language's perceived doubling. This intersection in frames of the offensive and defensive traces a reinterrogated line of inexpressibility. My aim in this study has been to recover a specific lineage of a topos, the topos of the inexpressible, and a series of opportunistic adaptations of that topos that straddle confidence and anxiety, while suggesting temporal amendments that fit eras of growing possibilities, at least, of expressibility and self-inclusion on a human scale of time.

This study is suggestive. Many other contemporary critics and journals could have been cited; many other writers could be included at length (such as James Kirke Paulding, Edgar Allan Poe, Henry David Thoreau, Emily Dickinson, Henry James, or John Ashbery). Every reader will think of a poem or story that contains the inexpressible and wonder how I could have overlooked it. This study, nevertheless, suggests contexts and a frame for understanding that is important. It brings together much that has been peripheral or outside of critical discussion; it ties earlier discursive demands on expectation, hyperbole, and inexpressibility to major contributions; it enables us to hear anew the language of Whitman's Preface and contemporaries; and it restores early discursive roots to self-conscious discourse in the modern era.

Notes

INTRODUCTION

1. Walter Channing, "Essay on American Language and Literature," *North-American Review and Miscellaneous Journal* 1, no. 3 (September 1815): 307–8.
2. David Cressy, *Coming over: Migration and communication between England and New England in the Seventeenth Century* (Cambridge: Cambridge University Press, 1987), 4.
3. *A Voyage into New England: Begun in 1623. and ended in 1624* (London: William Jones, 1624), 1.
4. *Sea Changes: British Emigration and American Literature* (Cambridge: Cambridge University Press, 1992), 46; emphasis added.
5. *To Begin the World Anew: The Genius and Ambiguities of the American Founders* (New York: Knopf, 2003), 3, 4.
6. David McCullogh, *1776* (New York: Simon & Schuster, 2006), 77.
7. "Dallas' Reports," *The American Review and Literary Journal for the Year 1802* 2, no. 1 (1802): 27
8. Examples of what Mencken calls "surviving differences" can be found, for instance, in *The American Language: An Inquiry into the Development of English in the United States* (New York: Knopf, 1967), 275–301.
9. Walt Whitman, *Walt Whitman: Complete Poetry and Collected Prose* (New York: Library of America, 1982), 5.
10. "Hawthorne and His Mosses: By a Virginian Spending July in Vermont," *The Literary World* VII (July–December 1850): 147.

11. "The Man on the Dump," *The Collected Poems of Wallace Stevens* (New York: Vintage, 1982), 203.

CHAPTER 1

1. Norman Pettit, "Subjects of the Crown: in Exile: Aliens in a Strange Land," in *Declarations of Cultural Independence in the English-Speaking World: A Symposium,* ed. Luigi Sampietro (Milan: D'Imperio Editore Novara, 1989), 27, 30. Pettit critiques attempts (by Sacvan Bercovitch or Patricia Caldwell, for instance) to construct emerging American "voices" in the colony because the examples point more notably, he says, to situations in which *"all* the speakers are English" (26). Cressy concurs, saying the "colonists referred to themselves as 'the English,' as distinct from the Dutch or the native Americans. It was to England that they looked for their history, their cultural lifeline, and for many of their future expectations." David Cressy, *Coming Over,* viii.

2. Pettit argues, "Few scholars of North American birth, it would seem, are able adequately to deal with the reluctance of English Puritans to sail for New England's shore" (24).

3. Stephen Fender adds that the complexities of this regard extend past the revolutionary period in self-debate "the very medium of which—the English language itself—originated in the metropolis from which young country had fought to be free." *Sea Changes: British Emigration and American Literature* (Cambridge: Cambridge University Press, 1992), 95.

4. In an initial light of continuity with England, America finds its place among former British settler colonies, such as Australia and New Zealand, which in a recent symposium have been given attention. As Douglas Gray suggests for New Zealanders, for instance, "What has actually happened is rather a gradual realization of a separate identity—an identity still deeply involved with Britain and with British literary tradition, but different," 70. See "Sailing in Another Direction: Some Early New Zealand Writing," in *The Declarations of Cultural Independence in the English-Speaking World: A Symposium: Università degli Studi di Milano,* ed. Luigi Sampietro (Novara: D'Imperio, 1989). That slow separation is matched with a residual feeling of fear and potential irrelevance; Gray quotes from the writer Allen Curnow, "'our presence in these islands is accidental, irrelevant; ... we are interlopers on an indifferent or hostile scene'" (69). So in "The Australian Declaration of Independence," John McLaren emphasizes Australia's early and long tradition of ties with England, ultimately fraught with terror and marginality as well. He writes of Australia's initial attempts to establish a "new Britain": "in this golden dream Australia did not so much declare an independence of Europe as provide a place where Europeans, and particularly English-men with their wives and children, could fulfil the hopes that Europe had frustrated" (*Declarations,* ed. Sampietro, 101). Even so, and at increased distances from England, the presence of savagery at the heart of the civilization, and especially colonization, inevitably takes hold, paradoxically pointing back again to the country's colonial history and to oppressive ties with England. The original prison colony and its political practices, where Australians "both as individuals and as a society, were at the mercy of forces outside themselves," continue to suggest "terror which lies at the heart of the colonial society" (106).

5. "American Poetry," *The Knickerbocker Magazine* XII, no. 5 (November 1838): 386.

6. "Lack of Poetry in America," *Harper's New Monthly Magazine* 1 (August 1850): 403. This is echoed in "American Poetry," *Littell's Living Age* VI (July 1845): 85.

7. Rev. Sidney Smith, *Edinburgh Review* 33 (January 1820): 79.

8. Edmund Morris, *The Rise of Theodore Roosevelt* (New York: Ballantine, 1979), 468.

9. Walter Channing, "Essay on American Language and Literature," 309.

10. "A Vocabulary, or Collection of Words and Phrases Which Have Been Supposed to Be Peculiar to the United States of America," review by Sidney Willard, *North-American Review* III, no. 9 (September 1816): 355.

11. The debate emerges from a historical lineage grounded in Thomas Hobbes's "sense of connection between an ordered language and an ordered state" (33) traced by David Simpson in *The Politics of American English, 1776–1850*. Focusing on questions of language, social contract, and ideas of "improvement" of the English language (conventions that will be adapted to local debates on a self-translated English in America), Simpson cites Thomas Hobbes as well John Locke, David Hume, Adam Smith, Samuel Johnson, and Edmund Burke. Simpson concludes, "it was to prove more difficult to declare independence from Samuel Johnson than it had been to reject George III" (33). See *The Politics of American English, 1776–1850* (New York: Oxford, 1986), 3–51.

12. "A Statistical View of the Commerce of the United States of America," *North-American Review* III, no. 9 (September 1816): 347.

13. "Lack of Poetry in America," *Harper's New Monthly Magazine* 1 (August 1850): 404.

14. Noah Webster, *Sketches of American Policy* (Hartford: Hudson and Goodwin, 1785), 47.

15. Webster, Preface, *An American Dictionary of the English Language* (New York: Converse, 1828), unpaginated.

16. For an analysis of the complexity of Webster's politics, see Simpson, 24, 52–56. For a detailed look at his complex and important position to the national language argument (48), noted here, see "Noah Webster" (52–90): "As 1776 did not usher in a new language, so neither did it invent a new literature or a new philosophy. It did, however, impose the demand that these prospects be examined and worked for, and it determined that the traditional Enlightenment preoccupations persisting or arising in the early years of independence should take on a consciously national resonance, whether for or against innovation and novelty. Thus, although ambitions for changing, fixing, or analyzing to its roots the quixotic spirit of language had been commonplace in the eighteenth century, they become focused as part of the *American* ideal after 1776" (24).

17. Fisher Ames, "American Literature," in *Works of Fisher Ames with a Selection from His Speeches and Correspondence by His Son Seth Ames*, vol. II (Boston, MA: Little, Brown and Company, 1854), 430.

18. S. Willard, "A Vocabulary," *North-American Review* III, no. 9 (Sept. 1816): 355.

19. John C. McCloskey, "The Campaign of Periodicals After the War of 1812 for National American Literature," *PMLA* 50, no. 1 (March 1935): 262.

20. Donald R. Hickey, *The War of 1812: A Forgotten Conflict* (Chicago: University of Illinois Press, 1995), 2.

21. Walter R. Borneman, *1812: The War That Forged a Nation* (New York: Harper Collins, 2004), 7–53.

22. Quoted by Hickey, *The War of 1812*, 15.

23. Attributable in the records to John Randolph of Virginia by Richard M. Johnson of Kentucky: *Annals of Congress,* House of Representatives, 12th Congress, 1st session, 459.

24. "A National Literature, 1837–1855," *American Literature* 8, no. 2 (May 1936): 125.

25. Hickey, *The War of 1812*, 3. As Harry L. Coles in an earlier work also notes, "Though each side was able to win minor victories on its opponent's soil, neither was capable of carrying out a large-scale, decisive offensive" (255). At the same time, he notes, "The War of 1812 has sometimes been called the Second War of American Independence and, rightly understood, this concept has merit ... the war did mark the end of American dependence on the European system.... From the Revolution onward a basic aim of American statesmen had been to achieve freedom of action so that the United States could choose war or peace as its interests might dictate. With the settlement of 1815 this aim became a reality to a degree

that the early statesmen had hardly dared to hope" (270–71). Harry L. Coles, *The War of 1812* (Chicago: University of Chicago Press, 1965). See also Borneman, *1812,* 304.

26. The journal, founded by William Tudor, Edward Channing, and Richard Henry Dana (the elder), known for its "enlightened conservatism," was grounded in an anti-Malthusianism bent toward America's civilization and its progress, and founded among many competing desires: a desire to resist the cultural dominance of England, along with a concomitant desire to resist radical French influences or emerging movements of "nature" in the United States by writers such as Henry David Thoreau.

27. Francis C. Gray, "An Address Pronounced Before the Society of Phi Beta Kappa," *North-American Review* III, no. 9 (September 1816): 301.

28. Simpson, *The Politics of American English,* 24.

29. Henry N. Day, "Taste and Morals:—The Necessity of Aesthetic Culture to the Highest Moral Excellence," *American Biblical Repository and Classical Review,* Third Series, 3 (July 1847): 525.

30. Simpson, *The Politics of American English,* 53.

31. Benedict Anderson, *Imagined Communities: Reflections on the Origin and Spread of Nationalism* (London: Verso, 1983), 48, 61–63. This subject continues to provoke debate. For another account of the public sphere and the "nation that imagined its inception as an effect of linguistic action," see Christopher Looby, *Voicing America: Language, Literary Form, and the Origins of the United States* (Chicago: University of Chicago Press, 1996), 2.

32. Philip Spencer and Howard Wollman, *Nationalism: A Critical Introduction* (London: Sage, 2002), 30. This conclusion is part of the ongoing debate, referenced above.

33. Homi K. Bhabha, *Nation and Narration* (London: Routledge, 1990), 2; emphasis in original.

34. Joyce Appleby, *Inheriting the Revolution: The First Generation of Americans* (Cambridge, MA.: Harvard University Press, 2000), 5, 11.

35. Edmund S. Morgan, *The Genuine Article: A Historian Looks at Early America* (New York: W. W. Norton & Company, 2004), 251, 252. As Morgan notes, this creation of character is clearly sketched by Paul Longmore, who explores Washington's self-conscious development of reputation and roots in his English ideals: "He [George Washington] would never entirely let go of English ideals, but he *would* labor to redefine his identity in American terms. Ultimately, he would conduct that redefinition publicly in collaboration with his countrymen. They, in turn, would make him the exemplar of the new nation's values." See *The Invention of George Washington* (Berkeley: University of California Press, 1988), 10; emphasis in original.

36. Richard Jenkins, *Rethinking Ethnicity: Arguments and Explorations* (London: Sage, 1997), 10.

37. *Sea Changes,* 67, 66.

38. See, for example, Stuart Hall, "The Local and the Global: Globalization and Ethnicity," in *Culture, Globalization and the World-System: Contemporary Conditions for the Representation of Identity,* ed. A. D. King (Minneapolis: University of Minnesota Press, 1997), especially 35–39. See also Ernest Gellner, *Nations and Nationalism* (Oxford: Blackwell, 1983); Tom Nairn, *Faces of Nationalism: Janus Revisited* (London: Verso, 1997).

39. In a further twist, Cressy adds that such a view of New England was one "some New Englanders were happy to encourage, if it meant they would be left alone" (32).

40. Robert Pinsky, "Poetry and American Memory," *The Atlantic Monthly* (October 1999): 64.

41. Morgan, *Genuine Article,* 257. On the development of deportment in early America, see Richard L. Bushman, *The Refinement of America: Persons, Houses, Cities* (New York: Knopf, 1992), 61–99.

42. Charles Brockden Brown, Preface, *American Review and Literary Journal for the Year 1801,* First Edition (1802), iv.

43. *The Monthly Magazine and American Review* 1, no. 1 (April 1799): 1. In 1801, the journal became *The American Review and Literary Journal*.

44. Edward Cahill, "Federalist Criticism and the Fate of Genius," *American Literature* 76, no. 4 (December 2004): 687. Such an odd position of the Federalists looks ahead a few decades to the situation of the Whigs, well described by Simpson, echoing Arthur Schlesinger: "the whigs began to realize that Jackson's campaigns had profited considerably by a popular interest, or at least a populist rhetoric, that could no longer be ignored. The way to fight Jackson was not to stand forth on the explicitly argued doctrines of a necessary elitism, as the old Federalists had done, but rather to begin to claim that the whigs themselves were the genuine party of the people. Thus, an explicit recognition of class distinctions and differences of interest, in Federalist discourse, is replaced by a disingenuous rhetoric of equality in which there are no workers and no employers, and in which all have the same interests and the same opportunity for profit and progress" (145–46).

45. Ames, "American Literature," 432–33.

46. This study proceeds under the assumption well articulated by Benedict Anderson that "[i]n fact, all communities larger than primordial villages of face-to-face contact (and perhaps even these) are imagined. Communities are to be distinguished, not by their falsity/genuineness, but by the style in which they are imagined." Anderson's emphasis on "style" has particular applicability to Whitman's poetics and strategies in the Preface, as will become clear. See *Imagined Communities: Reflections on the Origin and Spread of Nationalism* (London: Verso, 1983), 15.

47. See Fender, *Sea Changes: British Emigration and American Literature* (Cambridge: Cambridge University Press, 1992), 60.

48. Cressy, *Coming Over,* 1–2.

49. Ernst Robert Curtius, *European Literature and the Latin Middle Ages,* trans. Willard R. Trask (London: Routledge & Kegan Paul, 1953), 160.

50. Whitman, *Complete Poetry and Collected Prose,* 25. The topos of the inexpressible is of course also relevant to Whitman's poems, a subject for another study.

51. Channing, "Essay," 307.

52. Harold Bloom, *The Western Canon: The Books and Schools of the Ages* (New York: Riverhead Books, 1994), 247.

53. Philip Fisher, *Still the New World: American Literature in a Culture of Creative Destruction* (Cambridge, MA: Harvard University Press, 1999), 56. Fisher relates "Song of Myself" to the Constitution, as an outline, and immediately links Whitman's poetics to "Lincoln's political idea," emphasizing "unity" (see 56–57).

54. *Poets Thinking: Pope, Whitman, Dickinson, Yeats* (Cambridge: Harvard University Press, 2004), 37, 38. Vendler's descriptions of Whitman's "reprise-poem" (39) trace not only another important rebuttal to what she calls "Whitman's apparently 'spontaneous' language" (39), but also a map for framing: "Whitman repeats, in his second-stanza reprise, almost all the elements of the first scene. But this time those elements are named by a speaker who has placed himself in a markedly altered relation to the scene" (41). In his "process of thinking as a form of transmutation" (60), she points to Whitman's decisions of order in the reprise (59), along with the interrogations of his own "compositional impulses" (62).

55. Kenneth M. Price, ed., *Walt Whitman: The Contemporary Reviews,* American Critical Archives 9 (New York: Cambridge University Press, 1996), 8.

56. Price, *Walt Whitman,* 10.

57. Oscar Wilde, "The Gospel According to Walt Whitman," in Price, *Walt Whitman,* 321.

58. Williams, "An Essay on *Leaves of Grass,*" in *Leaves of Grass: One Hundred Years After,* ed. Milton Hindus (Palo Alto: Stanford University Press, 1955), 22.

59. Charles A. Dana, "New Publications: *Leaves of Grass,*" in Price, *Walt Whitman,* 5; emphasis added.

60. Betsy Erkkila, "Introduction: Breaking Bounds," in *Breaking Bounds: Whitman and American Cultural Studies,* eds. Betsy Erkkila and Jay Grossman (Oxford: Oxford University Press, 1996), 8.

61. Erkkila, *Whitman the Political Poet* (New York: Oxford University Press, 1989), 292.

62. "Whitman's *originality* has less to do with his supposedly free verse...." See Bloom, *Western Canon,* 248; emphasis added.

63. In the former, R. W. French also summarizes a common trajectory of reception (see above); the latter reflects his conclusions regarding the need to understand his still "elusive" (79) art. See "Reading Whitman," *Essays in Literature* 10.1 (April 1983): 78, 79.

64. An exceptional chapter, which discusses the Preface of 1855 directly, is Paul A. Bové's "*Leaves of Grass* and the Center: Free Play or Transcendence." See *Destructive Poetics: Heidegger and Modern American Poetry* (New York: Columbia University Press, 1980), 131–79. "Whitman's 'Preface' to the 1855 edition of *Leaves of Grass* remains the most important single document in American poetics" (133), he writes. I will discuss this work later. Two other essays that directly address the Preface are Chaviva M. Hosek's "The Rhetoric of Whitman's 1855 Preface to *Leaves of Grass,*" *Walt Whitman Review* 25 (1979): 163–73; and Donez Xiques, "Whitman's Catalogues and the Preface to *Leaves of Grass,*" *Walt Whitman Review* 23 (1977): 68–76. More recent books and articles that follow ideas of reception, the performative element, and nationalism more generally in Whitman's body of work include the following: Kerry C. Larson, *Whitman's Drama of Consensus* (Chicago: University of Chicago Press, 1988); James Perrin Warren, *Walt Whitman's Language Experiment* (University Park: Penn State University Press, 1990); Mark Bauerlein, *Whitman and the American Idiom* (Baton Rouge: Louisiana State University Press, 1991); Vincent J. Bertolini's "'Hinting' and 'Reminding': The Rhetoric of Performative Embodiment in *Leaves of Grass,*" *ELH* 69 (2002): 1047–82, in which the "idea of intersubjectivity in lyric reading intended to have particular extratextual effects within the active, sensual subjectivities of readers and within the social and political worlds which they inhabit" (1048–49) is examined; and Scott MacPhail's "Lyric Nationalism: Whitman, American Studies, and the New Criticism" *TSLL* 44, no. 2 (Summer 2002): 133–60, in which Whitman's broad, even literal appeal as an Adamic figure is critically traced and questioned: he writes that "we need to first acknowledge the powerful authority of Whitman to give national legitimacy to those to whom he speaks and who speak through him, and then we should begin to consider for whom he speaks in this instance, and how" (152).

65. Ferguson, "'We Hold These Truths,'" *Reconstructing American Literary History,* ed. Sacvan Bercovitch, *Harvard English Studies* 13 (Cambridge: Harvard University Press, 1986): 25.

66. For this quotation by Boucher in the context of competing English voices such as Henry Kett's, heard, for example, in "The United States of America cannot fail to perpetuate the language of their parent country," see Allen Walker Read, "British Recognition of American Speech in the Eighteenth Century," *Dialect Notes* VI, part VI (1933): 317–20. Read notes that although Boucher's comments appear in a Preface to his *Glossary* published in 1807, it appears from Boucher's editors that the preface was itself written in 1800.

67. William Ellery Channing, "National Literature," *The Christian Examiner* XXXVI, no. VI (January 1830): 270.

68. The historical juncture of the text is underscored by Paul A. Bové: "Considered historically, Whitman's 'Preface' faces a unique situation: he cannot directly call for a more creative understanding of the past since the habitual mode of then current American poetry, in fact, stands in an imitative, derivative relationship to old British forms. As a result of the paradoxical situation in which Whitman finds himself, a direct request for an authentic look at or interpretation of the past would be misinterpreted, misconceived as further support for the already entrenched conservatism of American letters which Whitman propagandistically attacks elsewhere." See *Destructive Poetics,* 143. Michael P. Kramer puts it differently: Whit-

man's "act of projection must also be seen to occupy a particular, adversarial position within the discourse on American English in mid-nineteenth-century America.... Whitman's denial is itself a mode of contestation...." (92–93). In particular, he notes, Whitman can take on the "role of redactor, gathering passages and ideas from a variety of writers representing different discourses and assembling them into a whole intended to be more than the sum of its parts" (105). In this light, Kramer focuses more largely on Whitman's participation in the "complex history of American English and the difficult synthesis that faced the American linguist" (105). See *Imagining Language in America: From the Revolution to the Civil War* (Princeton: Princeton University Press, 1992).

69. "On American Literature," in *Essays by a Citizen of Virginia: Essays on Various Subjects of Taste, Morals, and National Policy by a Citizen of Virginia* (Georgetown, D.C.: Published by Joseph Milligan; Jacob Gideon, Junior, Printer, Washington, 1822), 42, 66.

70. "American Poetry," *The Knickerbocker* XII, 386.

71. Mary Thomas Crane records the history of the "frame" in the lyric, implying control but also carrying "connotations of shaping by experience, and even of fiction or feigning," potentially in a favorable light. *Framing Authority: Sayings, Self, and Society in Sixteenth-Century England* (Princeton, NJ: Princeton University Press, 1993), 180.

72. See Fender, *Sea Changes*, 29.

73. Cressy, *Coming Over*, 10. Stephen Railton notes a similar action regarding rhetoric of literature authorship involving a combination of understatement, hyperbole, and self-consciousness predicated on statements of anxiety (rather than fear). See *Authorship and Audience: Literary Performance in the American Renaissance* (Princeton: Princeton University Press, 1991), 20.

74. "An Oration on American Literature" (January 1840), in *The Early Works of Orestes A. Brownson, Volume V: The Transcendentalist Years, 1840–1841*, ed. Patrick W. Carey, Marquette Studies in Theology No. 38, Andrew Tallon, Series Editor (Milwaukee: Marquette University Press, 2004), 201. See also "American Literature" IV (January 1839): 133–52.

75. Without discussing at length formal histories of framing, David L. Minter's work on "interpreted design" suggests an action tantamount to framing, with a focus on American prose and a "juxtaposition of two characters" (3); he writes that the first character, a "man of design," offers the "means of assuring success," while the second character, a "man of interpretation," offers a "means of taming unexpected and unacceptable failure" (6). His analysis focuses on what he calls a "defining problem of our time" (27), suggesting a "[t]ension between imagination and reality" (27). See *The Interpreted Design as a Structural Principle in American Prose* (New Haven: Yale University Press, 1969).

76. Stephen Fender notes a standing preoccupation with national character, originating in a narrative of emigrants, a narrative "by which the country has come to define itself—even the assumption of American exceptionalism and the recurrent image of American 'character'...," 9. For an analysis of this standing preoccupation with national character and its early ties to emigration, see *Sea Changes*, 5–16.

77. Robert Weisbuch has described a related phenomenon as "actualism," by which "absences become virtues." He says, "actualism is confident, assertive, and programmatic; but a different, sometimes contradictory attitude develops alongside it, one that is nervous, exploratory, and fragmented. It is an ontological insecurity that, when capitalized upon, becomes an epistemological daring." *Atlantic Double Cross* (Chicago: University of Chicago Press, 1986), xiv.

78. As explained by J. C. Furnas in "Don't Laugh Now," a surprisingly simple ending belies a common time shift in oral shaggy dogs: "by making normal reflex shortcuts between an opening situation and the sort of conclusion one would expect in normal life," a listener is "tricked," exploiting a non sequitur of logic to make room for real-time changes of expectations for survival. See "Don't Laugh Now," *Esquire* (May 1937): 237.

79. Ames, *Works*, 430.

80. Celia Britton, *Edouard Glissant and Postcolonial Theory: Strategies of Language and Resistance* (Charlottesville: University of Virginia Press, 1999); *Edouard Glissant*, 183.

81. *The Port Folio* 4, no. 22 (28 November 1807): 343.

82. This returns, sideways, to an early, and surprising, motive for emigration, as Fender explains: "Of all motives for emigration expressed or implied in the emigrant letters, the most surprising is their hope to find greater leisure in the United States," 60. For further explanation of this expectation, and a "myth" of agrarianism, see Fender, 60–63.

83. For a continuing discussion on inclusion of America in the debate on the "postcolonial," see Peter Hulme, "Including America," *ARIEL: A Review of International English Literature* 26, no. 1 (1995): 119. He says that the "'postcolonial' is (or should be) a descriptive, not an evaluative, term" (120). See Cathy N. Davidson for a perspective that looks at the usefulness of postcolonialism in promoting transnational American studies and the subtle workings of power: *Revolution and the Word: The Rise of the Novel in America, Expanded Edition* (Oxford: Oxford University Press, 2004), 13–24. On the place of postcolonialism in U.S. studies, see Amritjit Singh and Peter Schmidt, "On the Borders Between U.S. Studies and Postcolonial Theory," in *Postcolonial Theory and the United States: Race, Ethnicity, and Literature* (Jackson: University Press of Mississippi, 2000), 3–69. For a consideration of postcolonial status and its relevance to the development of early American literature, see Lawrence Buell, "Postcolonial Anxiety in Classic U.S. Literature," in Singh and Schmidt, 196–219. For a look at how "U.S. imperialism is thus best understood as a complex and interdependent relationship with hegemonic as well as counterhegemonic modalities of coercion and resistance," see Donald E. Pease, "New Perspectives on U.S. Culture and Imperialism," in Amy Kaplan and Donald E. Pease, eds., *Cultures of United States Imperialism* (Durham: Duke University Press, 1993), 22–37. For a survey of how the idea of empire has often been left out of American studies, see Amy Kaplan, "'Left Alone with America': The Absence of Empire in the Study of American Culture," in Kaplan and Pease, 3–21. For a study of how imperialism is "achieved textually" see Eric Cheyfitz, *The Poetics of Imperialism: Translation and Colonization from* The Tempest *to* Tarzan (New York: Oxford University Press, 1991), 10.

84. See Tucker, *Essays,* 42; emphasis added, and Royall Tyler, Preface, *The Algerian Captive, or, The Life and Adventures of Doctor Updike Underhill: Six Years a Prisoner Among the Algerine* (New York: Modern Library, 2002), 6; emphasis added.

85. For resonance, see for example an attempted rhetorical question in *The Port Folio* (new series) 3, no. 25 (20 June 1807): 386–87: "Do the early accounts of any nation comprise more proofs of an ardent, persevering, and aspiring temper, incessantly struggling with difficulties and dangers, unwearied and undismayed; or an intelligence more prolifick in devices to overcome the embarrassments of infancy?" See also "Literary Prospects of 1845," *The American Review: A Whig Journal of Politics, Literature Art, and Science* 1, no. 2 (February 1845): 149; emphasis added: "The beginnings are faint and scattered, but the elements *are here.*" In "American Letters: Their Character and Advancement" the editor of *The American Review* suggests that youth is to be overcome: "Our physical triumphs are acknowledged; and in most of the great departments of intellectual power, we need not hesitate to compare ourselves with other nations. But surely we ought to be wiser than to plume ourselves yet upon our literary position. We need have no doubts of our destiny in this respect; but we are young and can afford to wait a little for a reputation." See *The American Review: A Whig Journal of Politics, Literature Art, and Science* (also cited as *The American Whig Review*) 1, no. 6 (June 1845): 575. And citing a lack of hope in the "rigor of our conventions of religion and education" and "only such a future as the past," Emerson also echoes disadvantages that critics noted; see remarks from "The Editors to the Reader," *The Dial* I, no. 1 (July 1840): 1–4, including twists and turns on "backwardness." Margaret Fuller edited the journal from 1840–1842.

86. *The Port Folio* 4, no. 22, new series (28 November 1807): 343.

87. Richard Shryock, *Tales of Storytelling: Embedded Narrative in Modern French Fiction* (New York: Peter Lang, 1993), 4. For a study of "foregrounding" in American narrative, see Tony Tanner, *City of Words: American Fiction 190–1970* (London: Jonathan Cape Ltd., 1971), 20. For a study of the "envoy" in English and American Literature, see Bernd Engler, "Literary Form as Aesthetic Program: The Envoy in English and American Literature," *REAL: The Yearbook of Research in English and American Literature* 7 (1990): 61–97.

88. See Charles Isenberg, *Telling Silence: Russian Frame Narratives of Renunciation* (Evanston, IL: Northwestern University Press, 1993), 143.

89. While there are often assumptions of popular speech in Whitman, more commonly Whitman's Preface, for example, structurally adapts "high" rhetoric, such as the inexpressible, or even "low" humor, such as the shaggy dog, rather than including popular terms: as H. L. Mencken points out clearly, "not many specimens of the popular speech ever got into his [Whitman's] writings, either in prose or in verse." See *The American Language: An Inquiry into the Development of English in the United States* (New York: Knopf, 1967), 81.

90. Jan Harold Brunvand, "A Classification for Shaggy Dog Stories," *The Journal of American Folklore* 76, no. 299 (January–March 1963): 44. For reference, a classic shaggy dog is recounted by J. C. Furnas in "Don't Laugh Now." Notice that it deals with the tension between American and English points of view, diction, and kinship. "An advertisement appears in a New York paper offering a £500 reward for the return of a certain large, white shaggy dog, marked thus and so, to an address in a London suburb. A New Yorker who has just picked up a big white shaggy stray with the indicated markings, immediately takes ship for England with the dog, goes to the advertised address and rings the doorbell. A man opens the door. 'You advertised about a lost dog.' 'Oh,' says the Englishman coldly, 'not so damn shaggy' and slams the door in the American's face." See J. C. Furnas, "Don't Laugh Now," 237.

91. Eric Partridge, The 'Shaggy Dog' Story: Its Origin, Development and Nature (with a few seemly examples) (Freeport, NY: Book for Libraries Press, 1953), 52.

92. Ted Cohen, "Metaphor and the Cultivation of Intimacy," in *On Metaphor,* ed. Sheldon Sacks (Chicago: University of Chicago Press, 1979), 7.

93. Headnote for Peter Bulkeley, "The Gospel-Covenant," in *The Puritans in America: A Narrative Anthology,* eds. Alan Heimert and Andrew Delbanco (Cambridge, MA: Harvard University Press, 1985), 117.

94. Paul Crowther, "Literary Metaphor and Philosophical Insight: The Significance of Archilochus," in *Metaphor, Allegory, and the Classical Tradition: Ancient Thought and Modern Revisions,* ed. G. R. Boys-Stones (Oxford: Oxford University Press, 2003), 99–100.

95. As many note, the work of naturalists in the eighteenth century, particularly with regard to degeneration and relocation in *Histoire Naturelle* by Comte de Buffon (Georges Louis Leclerc Buffon), following on the heels of growing taxonomies and quantification (including, for example, statistics such as those of Gregory King pointing in the late seventeenth century, as Bill Luckin argues, to "those incapable of securing 'self-sufficiency,'" 242), informed debates about America's self-sufficiency, regarding its separation from its roots in England, including the separation and possible degeneration of its language; Bill Luckin, like many others, also notes developing links between degeneration, Darwinism, eugenics, and what he calls "racially tinged urban tribalism" (243), focusing on the medical and environmental public sphere. For a reading of the complex interrelations, see "Revisiting the idea of degeneration in urban Britain: 1830–1900," *Urban History* 33, no. 2 (2006): 234–52.

96. See Looby, *Voicing America,* 4.

97. Robert Ferguson stresses that "[f]rom the beginning, the North American colonies were text-oriented cultures through written charters, responses to charters, covenants, compacts, and not least, biblical exegesis." He further admonishes that "[w]e have to keep

in mind the whole range of communication" issuing from this textuality. *Reading the Early Republic* (Cambridge, MA: Harvard University Press, 2004), 3, 50.

98. Channing, "Essay," 313.

99. "Essay," 314.

100. Here is another instance of the "complex and ambiguous case of America's postcolonial origins," which includes settler colonialism "based on confiscation of land from its inhabitants" as well as an edge of severed relationships with Britain through "violent revolution" after settler colonialism on behalf of that imperial power (14). Cathy Davidson argues for continuing investigations of postcolonial theory with regard to the United States. See *Revolution and the Word*, 13–24.

101. Edward Channing, "On Models in Literature," *North American Review* 3, no. 8 (July 1816): 208–9.

CHAPTER 2

1. William Shakespeare, *King Lear* 1.i.62, *The Riverside Shakespeare* (Boston: Houghton Mifflin, 1974), 1256

2. William Ellery Channing, "National Literature," *The Christian Examiner* XXXVI (January 1830): 277. All of this, if yet to be "proved," collapses once more into the sum total of what he calls the "condition of our literature" as it is framed to be, shorn of those inadequacies "which obstruct its advancement."

3. St. Augustine, "Book VIII: The Search for God by the Understanding," in *The Trinity*, trans. John Burnaby (Philadelphia: The Westminster Press, 1955), 55.

4. Robert Graves beautifully renders this in parodic form in *Claudius the God: And His Wife Messalina* (New York: Vintage, 1989), 132: "However, the point is that Augustus, whenever he got into a tangle, used to cut the Gordian knot, like Alexander, saying: 'Words fail me, my Lords. Nothing that I might utter could possibly match the depths of my feelings in this matter.' And I learned this phrase off by heart and constantly made it my salvation." The complex history surrounding the term "occupatio," including a possible and early mistaken reading of "occultatio," is outlined by H. A. Kelly. See "*Occupatio* as Negative Narration: A Mistake for *Occultatio/Praeteritio*," *Modern Philology* 74, no. 3 (February 1977): 311–15. Other common terms that mark this history include "praeterition," "paralipsis," "metalepsis," and "prolepsis."

5. Geoffrey Chaucer, "The Squire's Tale," in *The Canterbury Tales*, V.34–41, *The Works of Geoffrey Chaucer*, ed. F. N. Robinson, 2nd ed. (Boston: Houghton Mifflin Company; Cambridge, MA: The Riverside Press, 1957), 128.

6. Ernst Robert Curtius, *European Literature and the Latin Middle Ages*, trans. Willard R. Trask (London: Routledge & Kegan Paul, 1953), 159–62.

7. See Carlos Baker, *Ernest Hemingway* (Harmondsworth, England: Penguin, 1972), 529–46. Baker's reference is to the opening scene of *A Farewell to Arms*: "In the late summer of that year we lived in a house in a village that looked across the river and the plain to the mountains" (Hemingway, *A Farewell to Arms* [London: Arrow, 1994], 3). Hemingway also uses the device in *The Sun Also Rises* (1927) and *For Whom the Bell Tolls* (1941).

8. On the connection between poetry and rhetoric in the Middle Ages, see Curtius, "Poetry and Rhetoric," in *European Literature*, 154–66.

9. Curtius's chapter on "Devotional Formula and Humility" shows how the "medieval formula of submission is dependent on pagan Roman prototypes." See *European Literature*, 411.

10. C. S. Lewis, *English Literature in the Sixteenth Century Excluding Drama* (Oxford: Oxford University Press, 1954), 61.

11. André Kukla explains that the intersection of mathematics with the ineffable points to "relatively arcane foundational issues in set theory and metamathematics." See *Ineffability and Philosophy,* Routledge Studies in Twentieth Century Philosophy, vol. 22 (London: Routledge, 2005), 1.

12. Peter S. Hawkins, "Dante's *Paradiso* and the Dialectic of Ineffability," in *Ineffability: Naming the Unnamable from Dante to Beckett,* eds. Peter S. Hawkins and Anne Howland Schotter (New York: AMS Press, 1984), 5.

13. For this emphasis, see Ben-Ami Scharfstein, *Ineffability: The Failure of Words in Philosophy and Religion* (Albany: State University of New York, 1993), 51.

14. St. Augustine, *De Doctrina Christiana,* I.6, trans. D. W. Robertson, Jr. (Indianapolis: Library of Liberal Arts, 1978), 11.

15. Schotter, "Vernacular Style and the Word of God: The Incarnational Art of *Pearl,*" in *Ineffability: Naming the Unnamable,* 24.

16. Scharfstein, *Ineffability: The Failure of Words,* 188.

17. Hawkins, "Dante's *Paradiso,*" 8.

18. Schotter, "Vernacular Style," 23.

19. Ibid., 32.

20. Book I. 32–35, *The Works of Geoffrey Chaucer,* 389–90; emphasis added. For excellent looks at secular and classical roots of the humility topos and their transformations, see Curtius, *European Literature,* 407–13, and Eric Auerbach, *Literary Language and Its Public in Late Latin Antiquity and in the Middle Ages,* trans. Ralph Manheim (Princeton, NJ: Princeton University Press, 1965), 27–52.

21. Marjorie Garber, "'The Rest Is Silence': Ineffability and the 'Unscene' in Shakespeare's Plays," in *Ineffability: Naming the Unnamable,* 40.

22. Maureen Quilligan, "Milton's Spenser: The Inheritance of Ineffability," in *Ineffability: Naming the Unnamable,* 66.

23. Stanley E. Fish, *Self-Consuming Artifacts: The Experience of Seventeenth-Century Literature* (Berkeley and Los Angeles: University of California Press, 1972), 40.

24. In 1628 we find in a sermon by John Donne an appearance of the word "inexpressible": "Thou shalt feele the joy of his third birth in thy soul, most inexpressible this day." See "Inexpressible," *The Oxford English Dictionary,* vol. VII, 2nd ed. (Oxford: Clarendon Press, 1989), prepared by J. A. Simpson and E. S. C. Weiner: 913. Though the word describing the topos gradually moves in this direction, the gist of the topos remains intact. In practice, both terms continue to appear, as we will see, in primary and secondary texts, though the word "inexpressible" becomes the more common and colloquial choice.

25. For a full reading in the context of autobiography, see Nancy K. Miller, "Facts, Pacts, Acts," *Profession* 92: Presidential Forum, 12.

26. Fish, *Self-Consuming Artifacts,* 70.

27. Ibid.

28. Edmund Spenser, *The Faerie Queene,* lines 28–35 (London: George Routledge, Ryder's Court, 1843), 9; emphasis added.

29. Spenser's "thickest woods" (I.11.97) and "deepe darkness" (I.8.334) are classic allegorical methods for representing the unreadable, opaque signs to human eyes and the peril of an "Errours den" (I.13.114) around every corner of the earthly path. For "The Flower," see *The Works of George Herbert,* ed. F. E. Hutchinson (Oxford: Oxford University Press, 1941), 166.

30. Fish, *Self-Consuming Artifacts,* 75. He notes in more detail: "References backward are not, as in an Anglican sermon, complicating and unsettling, but clarifying and confirming, and repetitions, rather than expanding the area of reference, pin it down and make it manageable" (72).

31. Sacvan Bercovitch, *American Jeremiad* (Madison: University of Wisconsin Press, 1978), 23.

32. The more conventional rhetoric of ineffability, of course, exists on the spectrum for the American Puritans. In "The Augustinian Strain of Piety," Perry Miller notes, for example, Thomas Shepard's words: "we admire the luster of the sun the more in that it is so great we can not behold it" (Perry Miller, *The New England Mind: The Seventeenth Century* [Cambridge, MA: Harvard University Press, 1939], 11). And he underlines at more length that Samuel Willard required "over a thousand folio pages" to "tell what man may comprehend, by declaring that all reason is too finite to comprehend the infinite" (11). Still, Miller adds that the Puritans, unlike their predecessors, leaned in general away from defeat and toward accomplishment; as he says, "they dilated continually upon the balance of the attributes and the impenetrable mystery of the Godhead" (14). Therefore, he writes, the Puritans "insisted that the attributes [of God] are modes of human understanding rather than of the divine nature" (13), though they also in effect "came close to identifying these [selected] conceptions with His essence" (14).

33. Bercovitch, *American Jeremiad*, 29; emphasis added.

34. Miller, *New England Mind*, 13. The point regarding the Puritan perspective pertains to a theological angle conducive to *expressing* the inexpressible. This expression was anything but univocal, to a degree self-persuading. Along these lines, Ann Kibbey emphasizes the Puritans' use of metaphor for generating "a social imperative, one that persuades them of the fixity and certainty of their own system of reference"; see *The Interpretation of Material Shapes in Puritanism: A Study of Rhetoric, Prejudice, and Violence* (Cambridge: Cambridge University Press, 1986), 41. For a look at "a Puritan culture that is contested from within," challenging "the myth of consensus at the center," see Janice Knight, *Orthodoxies in Massachusetts: Rereading American Puritanism* (Cambridge, MA: Harvard University Press, 1994), 2, 4. For a look at "certain fundamental sources of tension within Puritan culture itself," especially "their flight from individualism even as they consecrated the individual in his unmediated relation to God," see Andrew Delbanco, *The Puritan Ordeal* (Cambridge, MA: Harvard University Press, 1989), 22. Delbanco stresses how "the story of seventeenth century New England communities is overwhelmingly one of a falling away from the transplanted ideals with which they were founded" (16). William C. Spengemann emphasizes that the communities of early American literature must be placed in a much larger context than they have been, including "writings from any part of the globe where the language confronted the New World—Shakespeare's London, Aphra Behn's Surinam, Sir Francis Drake's California, Captain Cook's Hawaii, Janet Schaw's Jamaica, Francis Brooke's Montreal." See *A New World of Words: Redefining Early American Literature* (New Haven: Yale University Press, 1994), 50. In the same way, Bernard Bailyn cautions that "Puritanism, we now know, was no unified historical phenomenon, even in its New England form. Up close, it proves to be a range of beliefs, ideas, and attitudes, clustering into shifting and unstable groupings," what he calls "a socio-ecclesiastical program whose promoters gained a precarious ascendancy within a society boiling with 'dissident' beliefs and sects." See *The Peopling of British North America: An Introduction* (New York: Knopf, 1986), 48–49. Here he echoes Philip Gura in *A Glimpse of Sion's Glory: Puritan Radicalism in New England, 1620–1660* (Middletown, CT: Wesleyan University Press, 1984).

35. As the topos of the inexpressible crosses through a time line, so tropes such as "nature" can intersect with stages of their alterations. As Stephen Fender shows, rhetoric of settlement, for example, goes through stages of altering "convention to suit conditions encountered in the New World." See *Sea Changes*, 30. In particular he revisits the trope of "nature." In the period of discovery, he argues, "nature" is inscribed as Edenic, what Fender calls a "beneficent negative catalog of culture" (57), a (good) absence of an already corrupted culture in Europe. In subsequent stages of settlement, however, "nature" in the New World is rewritten in terms of *locus amoenus,* a positive catalogue of abundance for settlement and sales. (29–35). This is just an example of the continuous revisiting of a trope historically: here

one reconceiving nature opportunistically as "full" of raw materials for transport, rather than benignly "empty" of European corruption (29), as new conditions and contexts develop.

36. Richard Henry Dana, Sr., "Review of the Sketch Book of Geoffrey Crayon," *North-American Review* IX (September 1819): 323–24.

37. Kukla, *Ineffability and Philosophy,* Routledge Studies in Twentieth Century Philosophy, vol. 22 (London: Routledge, 2005), 135; emphasis added.

38. Kukla includes five categories of ineffability in the new taxonomy (135): "unrepresentability," "unabducibility," "unselectability," "unexecutability," and "unreportability." Three of them, including "unabducibility" and "unselectability," are what Kukla calls "species of *unspeakability*" (146).

39. Whitman, "A Backward Glance o'er Travel'd Roads," *Walt Whitman Complete Poetry and Collected Prose,* 660.

40. J. Hector St. John de Crèvecoeur, *Letters From an American Farmer* (Gloucester, MA: Fox, Doubleday, 1968), 50.

41. Jeffrey Richards writes that "*Letters* offers a picture of the good life grounded in liberty and individual autonomy, where personal and familial independence are maintained by honest labor, property ownership, civil rights, mutual respect, peace, and the institution of marriage." As he says, however, the enemies are not outsiders but neighbors—the very whigs whose political doctrine embraces the liberties that the Farmer James undogmatically affirms. "For Crèvecoeur, whig practices defeat whig principles (285–86). So, Richards explains further, Crèvecoeur is the Frenchman, posing as Farmer James, "who gave Americans for many generations the picture of themselves they *most wanted to see*—the tolerant prosperous, land-holding, peaceable, and domestic people outlined in Letter III . . ." (296; emphasis added). In counterpoint, Richards also argues that in the "landscapes" Crèvecoeur gave "the image of its opposite, a nightmare of popular cruelty and personal despair" (296), an image that would take many years to unfold. Jeffrey Richards, "Revolution, Domestic Life, and the End of 'Common Mercy' in Crèvecoeur's 'Landscapes,'" *William and Mary Quarterly,* 3rd Series, LV, no. 2 (April 1998). Similarly, in *Sea Changes* Fender observes in particular Farmer James's "problematic value of leisure" (94), negotiating values of a "rambler" juxtaposed with the hard and often brutal work of settlement (see 92–93). And Eric P. Kaufmann writes regarding the roots and posture of Crèvecoeur's "American": "Notwithstanding the effusiveness of his rhetoric, Crèvecoeur's enthusiasm for the new mixed-origin American was a posture conditioned by both romantic millenarianism and Crèvecoeur's outsider status in his adopted homeland." See *The Rise and Fall of Anglo-America* (Cambridge, MA: Harvard University Press, 2004), 39

42. Webster, Preface, *American Dictionary,* no pagination.

43. Benjamin Franklin, "Proposals and Queries to Be Asked the Junto" (1732), in *The Papers of Benjamin Franklin,* eds. Leonard W. Labaree, Whitfield J. Bell, Helen C. Boatfield, and Helene H. Fineman, vol. 1: 1706–1734 (New Haven: Yale University Press, 1959), 261–62.

44. Marginalia in a Pamphlet by Matthew Wheelock" (1770), in *The Papers of Benjamin Franklin,* eds. William B. Willcox, Dorothy W. Bridgwater, Mary L. Hart, Claude A. Lopez, C. A. Myrans, Catherine M. Prelinger, and G. B. Warden, vol. 17 (New Haven: Yale University Press, 1973), 380.

45. Joseph Addison, "The Vision of Mirzah," *The Spectator,* No. 159 (Saturday, September 1, 1711), in *Addison and Steele: Selections from* The Tatler *and* The Spectator, 2nd ed., ed. Robert J. Allen (New York: Rinehart and Winston, Inc., 1970): 323.

46. Catherine Gore, *Sketches of English Character* (London: Richard Bentley, 1846), 163.

47. Philosophers pick up the thread: Immanuel Kant, Søren Kierkegaard, Ludwig Wittgenstein, and Martin Heidegger, to name a few. Philosophers and critics like Heidegger and George Steiner are noted for linking ideas of the topos especially to poetic language. For

Steiner, light, music, and, more recently, silence epitomize a search for primordial unity. In a reading of *Paradiso,* he writes: "The circle is complete: at its furthest reach, where it borders on light, the language of men becomes inarticulate as is that of the infant before he masters words. Those who would press language beyond its divinely ordained sphere, who would contract the *Logos* into the word, mistake both the genius of speech and the untranslatable immediacy of revelation." See "Silence and the Poet," *Language and Silence,* 41.

48. Steiner, "Silence and the Poet," *Language and Silence,* 51.

49. M. H. Abrams, *A Glossary of Literary Terms,* 8th ed. (Boston: Thomson Wadsworth, 2005): 1; final emphasis added.

50. See *Poetry & Pragmatism* (Cambridge: Harvard University Press, 1992), 134.

51. *The Poetry of Robert Frost: The Collected Poems, Complete and Unabridged,* ed. Edward Connery Lathem (New York: Henry Holt and Company, 1969), 120.

52. Henry Adams, *The Education of Henry Adams,* intro. James Truslow Adams (New York: The Modern Library, 1918 by the Massachusetts Historical Society, 1931 by the Modern Library), 382, 389.

CHAPTER 3

1. There are of course many kinds of frames that are not covered here, especially frames that draw less directly from the topos of the inexpressible (praise and humility), and more directly from the traditional search in frames for human wisdom. A tenuous cohesion and didactic emphasis derived from the frame structure can be seen to vary throughout the world. For example, in contrast with the more indefinite Arabic framing, the Indian inner tales of the *Panchatantra* exhibit greater moral certitude, as in "Grateful Beasts and Thankless Man" or "Ape, Glow-Worm, and Officious Bird." For a collection of the original Hindu tales, see *The Panchatantra,* edited in the original Sanskrit by Dr. Johannes Hertel (Cambridge, MA: Harvard University Press, 1908). In these frames, the search for human wisdom remains, but that quest is not so much unreachable as it is, more simply, flexibly endless, as stories can be moved around or added or deleted. Yet, in common with its counterpart in the topos of the ineffable, human inadequacy is identified through a search for even higher wisdom, indicated by the included quotations from sacred texts (see Katherine Gittes, *Framing the Canterbury Tales: Chaucer and the Medieval Frame Narrative Tradition* [New York: Greenwood Press, 1991], 16–17). In the inner, more completed Indian stories, the various forms of wisdom suggest, still, a tension of perpetuity and discovery.

Historically, then, frames are often concerned with the pursuit of wisdom. Like many medieval "framing fictions" the chanson d'aventure, offers for example, as Judith M. Davidoff points out, a "signal marker pointing the way for all men toward an enlightening experience." See *Beginning Well: Framing Fictions in Late Middle English Poetry* (Rutherford, NJ: Farleigh Dickinson University Press, 1988), 59. This holds true for the structures upon which these chansons are based; for example, the exemplum, which includes the vision-core *moralitas* (63). Poems such as John Lydgate's "Fall of Princes" or Thomas Hoccleve's "Regement of Princes" or "Floure and the Leafe" include imperatives to educate the speaker in faith or learning. In the quest for enlightenment, conventions and formulaic openings of medieval frame structures permit many "signals" for expansions. This predictability, as in oral situations, allows what Davidoff calls "presuppositions about categorizing and making sense of literary works" to move into the foreground (18). The rigid self-referencing of frames, as she notes, allows, then, room for surprising reorganizations of perception. As she explains, the framing fiction "is comprised of a rather fixed structural pattern and is typically cast in predictable diction; and yet, paradoxically, this very conventionality and predictability permitted particularly able writers to anticipate audience recognition of that pattern and ... to manipulate audience response in quite subtle ways" (Davidoff, 35). When Kirsten H. Powell writes about emblem artists and visual frames for literary texts, her views about reinventing an audience's perspective, or even updating material, easily accommodate the didacticism and enlightenment of the ineffable; François Chaveau puts new frames, she explains, around Jean de La Fontaine's fables, "to instruct and please the reader." See *Fables in Frames: La Fontaine and Visual Culture in Nineteenth-Century France* (New York: Peter Lang, 1997), 12.

In "Seeing through Screens: The Gothic Choir Enclosure as Frame," Jacqueline E. Jung unifies the choral function of the screen in the gothic cathedral. Medieval stories have actually included a literal frame around a text box. Surrounded by marginalia, a story inside a manuscript can have its attention shifted from the content to how the story is presented or told or understood. "Seeing through Screens: The Gothic Choir Enclosure as Frame," in *Thresholds of the Sacred: Architectural, Art Historical, Liturgical and Theological Perspectives on Religious Screens, East and West*, ed. Sharon Gerstel (Washington, DC: Dumbarton Oaks Research Library and Collections, distributed by Harvard University Press, 2006), 185–213. The variations on this are wide, including dream visions of the fourteenth century (notably in Chaucer), love visions drawing from *Le Roman de la Rose* that frame a debate or a complaint in the fifteenth century, the commonplace book of the sixteenth century, or popularized gothic tales of transformation.

2. Emily Brontë, *Wuthering Heights*, ed. Heather Glen (London: Routledge, 1988): 119. For a close study of the story within a story and the "embedded narrative," see William Nelles, *Frameworks: Narrative Levels and Embedded Narrative* (New York: Peter Lang, 1997).

3. For an analysis of how "the whole subject of tragedy exists to cope with human nervousness at the fact of indefinition" and further how it puts the audience "through an actual experience of the insufficiency of our finite minds to the infinite universe," see *King Lear, Macbeth, Indefinition, and Tragedy* (New Haven, Yale University Press), 85, 86.

4. From Davidoff, *Beginning Well*, 92.

5. "The Seafarer,"*Old and Middle English Poetry:* based on *Old and Middle English: An Anthology* edited by Elaine Treharne, ed. Duncan Wu (Oxford: Blackwell, 2002), 17 (lines 1–2) and 21 (lines 88–89).

6. *Achilles' Choice: Examples of Modern Tragedy* (Princeton, NJ: Princeton University Press), 7–8.

7. Geoffrey Chaucer, "Troilus and Criseyde," *The Works of Geoffrey Chaucer*, 2nd ed., ed. F. N. Robinson (Boston: Houghton Mifflin Company, 1957), V.1803–4, 479.

8. Larry Scanlon, *Narrative, Authority, and Power: The Medieval Exemplum and the Chaucerian Tradition* (Cambridge: Cambridge University Press, 1994), 5.

9. Writing of medieval English poetry Dana M. Symons notices that the "emphasis on the trickiness of mediation raises the perennial anxiety ... about the status of literary language" (8). See "A Complaynte of a Lovers Lyfe," *Chaucerian Dream Visions and Complaints*, ed. Dana M. Symons (Kalamazoo, MI: Medieval Institute Publications, College of Arts & Sciences, Western Michigan University, 2004), 71–147.

10. *On Christian Doctrine*, I.6, trans. D. W. Robertson, Jr. (Indianapolis: The Library of Liberal Arts, 1978), 10–11.

11. Elaine Scarry, *The Body in Pain: The Making and Unmaking of the World* (New York: Oxford University Press, 1985), 4.

12. Randall Jarrell, "The Woman at the Washington Zoo," *The Woman in the Washington Zoo: Poems & Translations, Selected Poems: including The Woman at the Washington Zoo* (New York: Atheneum, 1966), 2–3.

13. Margaret Atwood, "Siren Song," *Selected Poems: 1965–1975* (London: Virago, 1991), 195, 196.

14. Dante's silences, tied to glory and vision, for example, are marked in contrast to feeble speech: "Thenceforward my vision was greater than speech can show, which fails at such a sight, and at such excess memory fails" (55–57), he writes. "Now will my speech fall short," he continues, "even in respect to that which I remember, than that of an infant who still bathes his tongue at the breast" (106–8). He concludes, "O how scant is speech, and how feeble to my conception! and this, to what I saw, is such that it is not enough to call it little" (121–23). See *The Divine Comedy*, trans. Charles S. Singleton, *Paradiso 1: Text*, Bollingen Series LXXX (Princeton, NJ: Princeton University Press, 1991): 375–79.

15. Edmund Blunden, "Forefathers," *The Oxford Book of English Verse* (Oxford: Clarendon Press, 1939), 1139.

16. Dante Alighieri, *The Divine Comedy*, trans. Charles S. Singleton, *Paradiso, 1: Text*, Bollingen Series LXXX (Princeton, NJ: Princeton University Press, 1991), Canto I.70–1, 7.

17. Samuel Beckett, *Waiting for Godot*, trans. Samuel Beckett (New York: Grove Press, 1982): 10.

18. For a look at this lineage and its transformations, with an emphasis on the work of Eugenio Montale, see Clodagh J. Brook, *The Expression of the Inexpressible in Eugenio Montale's Poetry: Metaphor, Negation, and Silence* (Oxford: Clarendon Press, 2002): "An issue central to Montale's poetry is the place of language in creating something quite different from and perhaps independent of any original state of mind during the process of linguistic expression" (15).

19. The traditionally editorial use of "gathering" and "framing" in sixteenth-century England, for example, in the commonplace book and throughout the texts of this period, is covered in Mary Thomas Crane, *Framing Authority: Sayings, Self, and Society in Sixteenth-Century England*. In particular, she notes in this discursive practice an "uncertainty" (182) of the line between authorship and editing. See especially chapter VIII, "Bend or Frame: Lyric Collections and the Dangers of Narrative, 1550–1590," 162–96. She notes that the "twin discursive practices of 'gathering' these textual fragments and 'framing' or forming, arranging, and assimilating them created for English humanists a central mode of transaction with classical antiquity and provided an influential model for authorial practice and for authoritative self-fashioning" (3).

20. Shryock, *Tales of Storytelling*, 13.

21. A major adversary around the seeming problem of a self-same, English-language exclusion is defensive self-perception. Most "adversaries" are not critics attacking American literature (though there was just enough criticism to feed impatience: "the states of America can never have a native literature any more than they can have a native character." See Inchiquen's "Favourable View of the United States," *Quarterly Review* 10, no. 20 (1814): 494–530 for a favorable take disputing the unfavorable views of the United States.

22. "Original Review," *Analectic Magazine* 1, 2nd ed. (1813): 266; emphasis added.

23. See Theophilus Parsons, "Comparative Merits of the Earlier and Later English Writers," *The North American Review* X, New Series–Vol. 1 (January 1820): 32.

24. To review, André Kukla defines this category of ineffability in this way: "We may, under certain circumstances, come to entertain the possibility of saying an unselectable sentence; but we always decide against it in the end." See *Ineffability and Philosophy*, Routledge Studies in Twentieth Century Philosophy, vol. 22 (London: Routledge, 2005), 146.

25. Whitman, *Complete Poetry and Prose*, 25.

26. Parsons, "Comparative Merits," 32; emphasis added.

27. Whitman, *Complete Poetry and Prose*, 5; emphasis added.

28. This effacement of the middle distance is registered from a different angle when Fender writes of a recurring feature of the literature of initiation; he says that "it tends to elide, or even efface, the middle distance between the individual and the horizon. . . . " See *Sea Changes*, 15.

29. "Frames, Preferences, and the Reading of Third-Person Narratives: Towards a Cognitive Narratology," *Poetics Today* 18, no. 4 (Winter 1997): 448.

30. For a similar take of building "readings" or frames degree by degree around character, see Barbara Johnson's analysis of *Billy Budd:* " . . . the confrontation between Billy and Claggart is built by a series of minute gradations and subtle insinuations. The opposites that clash here are not two *characters* but two *readings.*" See "Melville's Fist: the execution of *Billy Budd*," *Deconstruction: Critical Concerns in Literary and Cultural Studies,* ed. Jonathan Culler, vol. 2 (London: Routledge, 2003), 230.

31. "Nationality in Literature," *The Democratic Review* XX (March 1847): 266.

32. "Defence of Poetry," *North-American Review* 34, no. 74 (January 1832): 74–75.

33. Channing, "Essay," 312, 309.

34. Channing, "Reflections," 36.

35. For an excellent article on the "overdetermined ways" in which national identities take shape, especially in relation to Native Americans, see Carroll Smith-Rosenberg's essay "Surrogate Americans: Masculinity, Masquerade, and the Formation of a National Identity," *PMLA* 119, no. 5 (October 2004): 1325–35. This article clearly illustrates the European Americans' anxiety regarding "their loss of a centuries-old British identity" (1329) as it pertains to their mimicry of Native American practices of song and dance; these exhibitions belied, as explained by Smith-Rosenberg, performances both of power (colonization) and admission of need (for images of nature and virility): "part gentleman, part savage" leaving "an actor without a center, playing a role with no internal coherence" (1332). Interestingly, Smith-Rosenberg calls the European Americans' "desire to incorporate . . . coexisting with a nationalistic need to differentiate themselves from Europe" an *"introjection"* (1330), an emotional self-contradictory state of performance by European Americans that echoes my readings of an equally insatiable desire both to incorporate and differentiate—that is, translate—oneself from within oneself in terms of the shared or "imported" English language.

36. Channing, "Essay," 308.

37. "American Letters—Their Character and Advancement," *The American Whig Review,* 579. The writer E. W. Johnson is identified by Benjamin T. Spencer, who in turn attributes the identification to Dr. F. L. Mott. See "A National Literature," *American Literature,* 153. Again, ironically, many of the classic statements of American literary deficiency come from those who most resisted—and at the same time most craved—an inner dynamic of privilege in America, preserving a much greater connection to the British and often an equally great fear of a misstep toward their own letters. John C. McCloskey implicitly captures the fear (and desire) when he cites a report, from an article in the *North American Review,* of how Federalists, compared to Democrats generally, "believed that American letters 'must wait for decision on its [literature's] merits or demerits, from the higher authorities of London.'" See "Campaign of Periodicals," 262.

38. Ernest Hemingway, *Green Hills of Africa* (London: Vintage, 2004), 14. Hemingway's reference is of course to the Transcendentalists, but he remarks with equal force on what he considers to be "writers of rhetoric" (14), Edgar Allan Poe and Herman Melville.

39. The state of insufficiency has a long history of being grounded paradoxically in what Fender has called, again, a "beneficent negative catalog," one of "nature unforced" (60) aimed in counterpoint to a perceived absence of culture, that is, a view of "nature [a perceived *absence* of culture] unforced"; as he notes further, it has derivation in the "classical trope for the Golden Age and the happy country gentleman's enclosed garden, and a utopian *satire* on the complexity, cupidity and violence of contemporary life," 57 (emphasis added; see also *Sea Changes,* 57–60). Or, as Cressy puts it from another angle, adjectives like "'excellent' and 'abundant' flowed freely" (*Coming Over,* 10) as acts of persuasion back to England for potential emigrants and investors, in counterpoint to the hardships of the New World. This cultivation of letters and tropes around, again, "nature unforced" among what Fender calls

this early "vast middle class" (46) situates a writerly flow of correspondence (54–60), later also prone to attack for inhibiting nature's course in literature. It establishes an early preponderance of written preoccupations with hyperbolic expectations framed both by doubts of insufficiency and commercial enterprise. There are, of course, extensive written accounts of the earlier explorations and settlements, for instance at Roanoke and Jamestown, and the reason for the settlement was not essentially religious but commercial. "The Jamestown colony was an entrepreneurial effort, organized and financed by the Virginia Company of London, a start-up venture...," writes David A. Price. See *Love and Hate in Jamestown: John Smith, Pocahontas, and the Start of a New Nation* (New York: Vintage, 2003), 3. Annette Kolodny adds to this discussion what she identifies as an effectively gendered discourse: "By the time European women began to arrive on the Atlantic shores of what is now the United States, the New World had long been given over to the fantasies of men." She also adds, in the litany of promotional rhetoric, that "[a]t the end of the fifteenth century, Christopher Columbus remained convinced that the biblical Garden of Eden lay further up the Orinoco River than he had been able to explore.... By the beginning of the eighteenth century, it was relatively commonplace for colonial promoters to promise prospective immigrants 'a *Paradise* with all Virgin beauties.'" See *The Land before Her: Fantasy and Experience of the American Frontiers: 1630–1860* (Chapel Hill: University of North Carolina Press, 1984), 3.

40. Webster, *Dissertations on the English Language with Notes, Historical and Critical, to Which Is Added, by way of Appendix, an Essay on a Reformed Mode of Spelling with Dr. Franklin's Arguments on that Subject* (Gainesville, FL: Scholars' Facsimiles & Reprints, 1951), 20.

41. *Harper's New Monthly Magazine* 1 (August 1850): 403–4.

42. "A Conversation," *The Knickerbocker Magazine* II, no. 1 (July 1833): 4.

43. This statement occurs inside a larger enterprise, toward a Christian and democratic literature. See "Prognostics of American Literature," *The American Biblical Repository and Classical Review,* Third Series, III (July 1847): 506.

44. For a reading of Margaret Fuller that echoes the self-consciousness and performance of hyperbole and speciousness, see Railton, *Authorship and Audience,* 20–21.

45. Tucker, *Essays,* 6; emphasis added.

46. "American Poetry," *The Knickerbocker Magazine,* 385.

47. "Defence of Poetry," *North-American Review* 34, no. 74 (January 1832), 67.

48. Of course, in this context, even the import of books took the stage in Irving's comment—"who would pay a half eagle for American poetry, when they could get English, equally as good, for half of the price." See "American Poetry," *The Knickerbocker Magazine,* 385.

49. Channing, "Essay," 309, 311.

50. See Shoshana Felman, *The Literary Speech Act: Don Juan with J. L. Austin, or Seduction in Two Languages,* trans. Catherine Porter (Ithaca: Cornell University Press, 1983), 15. While Austin eventually modified his distinction between performatives and statements, he concludes that the "doctrine of the performative/constative distinction stands to the doctrine of locutionary and illocutionary acts in the total speech-act as the *special* theory to the *general* theory"; see J. L. Austin, *How to Do Things with Words* (Oxford: Oxford University Press, 1976), 148.

51. Jacques Derrida, "Declarations of Independence," *New Political Science* 15 (1986): 9.

52. "Declarations of Independence," *New Political Science* 15 (1986): 9.

53. Ferguson, "'We Hold These Truths,'" 9. For a study of the theory and practice of performative conditions surrounding the American Revolution, see Jay Fliegelman, *Declaring Independence: Jefferson, Natural Language, & the Culture of Performance* (Stanford, Stanford University Press, 1993).

54. Blaise Pascal, *Pensées* (I.7), trans. W. F. Trotter (New York: P. F. Collier & Son, 1938), 12.

55. "An Examination," *The Port Folio* III, no. 25, 385.

56. Samuel Miller, "Nations Lately Become Literary," *A Brief Retrospect of the Eighteenth Century; Part First; in Two Volumes Containing A Sketch of the Revolutions and Improvements in Science, Arts, and Literature During That Period*, vol. 2. (New York: T. and J. Swords, 1803), 394.

57. Preface, *American Review and Literary Journal for the Year 1801*, from first edition (1802), iv.

58. See "Literary Prospects of 1845," *The American Review: A Whig Journal of Politics, Literature, Art, and Science* 1, no. 2 (1845): 150.

59. *Writings of Melville* 5 (Chicago: Northwestern University Press, 1970), 150.

60. Ames, *Works*, 430.

61. See Karl J. R. Arndt, "Introduction: German as the Official Language of the United States of America?," *Die deutschsprachige Presse der Amerikas/The German Language Press of the Americas* 3 (München: K. G. Saar, 1980), 33–35, and, more largely, 19–42.

62. Edward Channing (crying against the "imitator," 204), 205, and Royall Tyler (in his preface to *The Algerian Captive*) set the tone. See the following: "A country then must be the former and finisher of its own genius. It has, or should have, nothing to do with strangers," Channing, 207. From another perspective, Royall Tyler says: "There are two things wanted, said a friend to the author: that we write our own books of amusement, and that they exhibit our own manners." Royall Tyler, Preface, *The Algerian Captive, or, The Life and Adventures of Doctor Updike Underhill: Six Years a Prisoner Among the Algerine* (New York: Modern Library, 2002), 6.

63. Tucker, for example, calls out for a change of behavior: "Though this habitual veneration for the English name is very much diminished, it is far from being extinguished. We still continue to adopt their fashions in dress, their customs and manners, and follow them through all their capricious changes." Tucker, *Essays*, 52.

64. Trying to restore the slide against classical learning, an editor from *The Port Folio* argues rhetorically, "To the puny objections which have been urged against Classical learning, we mean not to reply." *The Port Folio* (new series) 4, no. 23 (5 December 1807): 357. Other projects in language between the Revolution and the Civil War include, in Thomas Gustafson's words, "projects to guard or renovate the language," projects "that range from John Adams's proposal for an 'American Academy for refining, improving, and ascertaining the English language' and Noah Webster's labors on his spellers and dictionary to Ralph Waldo Emerson's condemnation of 'rotten diction' in *Nature* and the efforts of James Fenimore Cooper in *The American Democrat* and of Abraham Lincoln to rectify the meaning of such key political words as 'liberty' and 'equality.' See *Representative Words: Politics, Literature, and the American Language, 1776–1865* (Cambridge: Cambridge University Press, 1992), 2.

65. "Comparative Merits," 29.

66. "Preface to the First Edition," *Poets and Poetry of America*, ed. Rufus Wilmot Griswold (Philadelphia, 1851, 1st ed.1842), 6–7.

67. "Hawthorne and His Mosses: By a Virginian Spending July in Vermont," *The Literary World* VII (July–December 1850): 126. His ideas of authorship, on the one hand suggesting a culmination of literary nationalism (written after Melville was known), of course also harbor under the umbrella of the inexpressible the "death" of the author, that is, under the "ever-eluding spirit of all beauty," in which "all fine authors are fictitious ones" (125). Yet, this topos also traditionally makes room for the trope of "failure" as the "test of true greatness" (146); along these lines, it allows, therefore, a refusal of any single identification of authorship that opens all the more reconsiderations, for example, of Hawthorne's inclusion in the catalogue of authors in this review, and self-inclusion in that lineage.

68. "Editor's Address," *The Massachusetts Quarterly Review* 1, no. 1 (December 1847): 3.

69. Tucker, *Essays*, 42–43.

70. Ibid., 43.

71. Ames, *Works,* 437.

72. This quest for originality has also been seen by historian Edmund S. Morgan in the life of George Washington. Detecting the impulse, Morgan goes as far as to remove altogether the more naive phrasing attached to Washington, "original thinker" or "creative genius," in an effort to identify Washington's strategy of self-recasting as something more practical, in his words, "something much more mundane but at the same time *so elusive, so difficult to define,* that when it emerges in one situation after another, we begin to see what his contemporaries saw and to be overwhelmed by it as they were" (emphasis added). Morgan, *Genuine Article,* 251. Gordon Wood reviews the practice of *recasting* that Bernard Bailyn suggests in his books on the founders. He notes in particular Bailyn's interest in the "recasting of the world of power, the re-formation of the structure of public authority, of the accepted forms of governance, obedience, and resistance, in practice as well as in theory" (38), although Wood adds that, again, "these aspirations had no certain outcomes" (38). See Gordon S. Wood, "Creating the Revolution," *The New York Review of Books,* February 13, 2003, 38.

73. A similar cycle has been recognized by Longmore: "All of this, the imitation the sense of inferiority, the resentment, and finally the assertion of superiority based on native standards marked the social and cultural maturation of colonial America." See *The Invention of George Washington,* 10.

74. Co-authorship entails many ancillary techniques. It, moreover, innately refuses to draw a clear line between editing and authoring. The traditionally editorial use of "gathering" and "framing" in sixteenth-century England, in the commonplace book and throughout the texts of this period, is covered in Mary Thomas Crane, *Framing Authority: Sayings, Self, and Society in Sixteenth-Century England* (Princeton, NJ: Princeton University Press, 1993).

75. Henry Wadsworth Longfellow, "Our Native Writers," *Every Other Saturday* I (April 12, 1884): 116; emphasis added.

76. Ibid.

77. "Nations Lately Become Literary," *A Brief Retrospect of the Eighteenth Century. Part First; in Two Volumes: Containing a Sketch of the Revolutions and Improvements in Science, Arts, and Literature, during that Period,* Vol. II (New York: T. and J. Swords, 1803) [actually published in 1804]), 405.

78. George Steiner leads into this statement, explaining that "it is decisively the fact that language does have its frontiers, that it borders on three other modes of statement—light, music, and silence—that it gives proof of a transcendent presence in the fabric of the world." See "Silence and the Poet," *Language and Silence,* 39.

79. It is necessary to pause here on the crucial word "character." A critical perception of "character," is often construed in relation to a perceived overlapping English, as is "originality," as we have seen. Critics often hold the language to be responsible for the absence of what Walter Channing precisely calls the "national character" ("Essay," 311). Appearing in *The North-American Review* and *The Port Folio* and other early nineteenth-century periodicals, the word "character" is repeatedly and literally linked to the missing ingredient that is absent in the new nation. See Gray, "Address," 289–305. Fender muses about the preoccupation with "character": "If subjects of the United Kingdom wished to refer to themselves in this way [concerning character], they would have to decide which adjective to use.... 'British' is a nationality, not a trait." See Fender, *Sea Changes,* 7. Unlike Aristotle's definition of "character," in which characteristics are ascribable—whether to "bravery, temperance, generosity, magnificence, magnanimity, honor, mildness, friendliness in social intercourse"—this use of "character" is of a different sort. It is made-to-order, a matter of performance, something that designates success or failure. For Aristotle on character formation see "Nicomachean Ethics," in *Aristotle's Ethics,* ed. J. L. Ackrill (London: Faber and Faber, 1973), 61–66.

80. Brown, "The Rhapsodist, *No. II,*" *Columbian Magazine* 3, no. 9 (September 1789): 537

81. See *"The Rhapsodist, No. III," Columbian Magazine* 3, no. 10 (October 1789): 600.

82. Ibid., 598.

83. Nathaniel Hawthorne, "Wakefield," in *Nathaniel Hawthorne: Tales and Sketches,* ed. Roy Harvey Pearce (New York: The Library of America), 290. It is well known that Hawthorne's planned collection "The Story Teller" was a frame narrative. Similarly Poe uses the frame narrative as a device in his early work *The Narrative of Arthur Gordon Pym of Nantucket* (1838).

84. Edgar Allan Poe, "Critical Notices: Drake-Halleck" (review of Joseph Rodman Drake's *The Culprit Fay, and Other Poems* and Fitz-Greene Halleck's *Alnwick Castle with Other Poems*), *Southern Literary Messenger* 2, no. 5 (April 1836): 326; emphasis added.

85. Brown, "The Rhapsodist," No. I, *The Columbian Magazine* 3 (Philadelphia: printed for James Trenchard, August, 1789): 466; emphasis added.

86. Early literature unsurprisingly is full of footnotes, lengthy introductions, long afterwards, and dedications. For example, Charles Brockden Brown includes an "Advertisement" in *Wieland; or The Transformation* (Oxford: Oxford University Press, 1994), 3–4. James Fenimore Cooper opens *The Prairie* with a geological treatise on the great plains (New York: Signet, 1964, v–vii). Herman Melville includes a preface called "EXTRACTS SUPPLIED BY A SUB-SUB-LIBRARIAN" to *Moby-Dick* (New York: Macmillan, 1964), 7–8. In *Revolution and the Word,* Davidson notes in relation to the American novel, a "truism" that "individual action is inseparable from the national." Thus, she argues, there exists "the abundance of prefaces, dedications, and other overt addresses in early novels that underscore the collective (or even national) significance of seduction, picaresque aimlessness or gothic horror.... She summarizes, "Novelists continued to 'amend' the idea of the nation throughout the early national period" (6). She adds, "Understanding how the genre [fiction] defined itself and reached its readership parallel with the creation of the United States helps us to delineate contending forces in the early Republic that are often erased in the heroic historiography of nation building" (8). I would amend and broaden this statement historically, again, to include the established and contested lineage of "gathering" and "framing" practices of the sixteenth century in England informing the lyric, "even as it countered it." It participated, as Crane notes, in a "version of authorship that was collective instead of individualist" and was associated with social mobility "within the changing hierarchies of the early modern state" (*Framing Authority,* 4). All of these are kin to framing. Indeed, Washington Irving's most well-known American tales, "Rip Van Winkle" and "The Legend of Sleepy Hollow," are doubly framed—first, introduced by a gentleman named Geoffrey Crayon (whose name is notably the image of a bold if underdeveloped writing implement), and further framed in a collection where these two stories are the only American ones that appear (the other twelve are British folk tales).

87. *"The Rhapsodist, No. III," Columbian Magazine* 3, 600; emphasis added.

88. Stephen Railton, "The Address of *The Scarlet Letter," Readers in History: Nineteenth-Century American Literature and the Contexts of Response,* ed. James L. Machor (Baltimore: Johns Hopkins University Press, 1993), 158–59.

89. *"The Rhapsodist, No. I," Columbian Magazine* 3, no. 8 (August 1789): 467.

90. Ted Cohen, "Metaphor and the Cultivation of Intimacy," *On Metaphor* (Chicago: University of Chicago Press, 1979), 7. He explains further, "The sense of close community results not only from the shared awareness that a special invitation has been given and accepted, but also from the awareness that not everyone could make that offer or take it up," 7.

91. Whitman, *Complete Poetry,* 5.

92. Barbara Johnson notices a similar effect of oscillations within the text of *Billy Budd*: "The effect of these explicit oscillations of judgment within the text is to underline the *impor-*

tance of the act of judging while rendering its outcome undecidable." She adds, "Judgment, however difficult, is clearly the central preoccupation of Melville's text . . . Melville's seems to be presenting us less with an *object* for judgment than with an *example* of judgment" (235).

93. Stanley Fish, "Authors-Readers: Jonson's Community of the Same," *Representations* 7 (Summer 1984): 52.

94. Discoveries and contentions of pluralities also play a part here. As Anderson argues, utopias are underwritten by the discovery of "irremediable human pluralism," and in particular a thinking of Europe as "only one among many civilizations, and not necessarily the Chosen or the best" (67, 68). A utopian and solitary underpinning of the inexpressible, a single human being attempting to express what cannot be expressed except by God, is in these terms comparably fanned out by its base in a response to the pluralities of human existence. In this sense the inexpressible is a utopian gesture because at its root is human plurality. And in turn here we hear the drive, again as noted above by Cathy Davidson, of the inseparability of the individual action from the national, especially as its pluralities compromise imagined ideas of a community that is "Chosen or the best."

95. W. B. Yeats, "Per Amica Silentia Lunae," *Mythologies* (London: Macmillan, 1959), 331.

CHAPTER 4

1. Preface by editor, "American Letters: Their Character and Advancement," *The American Whig Review*, 575; emphasis in original.

2. James Russell Lowell, "Longfellow's *Kavanagh*: Nationality in Literature," *The North-American Review* 29, no. 144 (July 1849): 211.

3. *The Port Folio* 4, no. 23, new series, 5 (December 1807): 357.

4. Edward Channing, "On Models in Literature," 207.

5. William Cobbett, *A Year's Residence in the United States of America*, 56.

6. *Coherence in Spoken and Written Discourse*, ed. Deborah Tannen (Advances in Discourse Processes 12) (Norwood, NJ: Ablex, 1984), 24. Tannen uses this phrase to define the term "frame." See pages 24–25 for a linguistic analysis of frames in spoken and written narratives.

7. N. P. Willis, "To The Public (the Editor's Preface)," *American Monthly Magazine* 1 (1829): iii.

8. "Sculpture and Sculptors in the United States," *American Monthly Magazine* 1, no. 2 (May 1829): 125.

9. Robin Tolmach Lakoff, "Some of My Favorite Writers Are Literate: The Mingling of Oral and Literate Strategies in Written Communication," in *Spoken and Written Language: Exploring Orality and Literacy*, ed. Deborah Tannen (Advances in Discourse Processes 9) (Norwood, NJ: Ablex, 1982), 241.

10. "American Poetry," *The Knickerbocker Magazine*, 387.

11. "Defence of Poetry," *The North-American Review*, 66.

12. G. M. Wharton, "Literary Property," *The North American Review* 52, no. 111 (April 1841): 403.

13. "American Poetry," *The Knickerbocker Magazine*, 385–86.

14. Spencer, "A National Literature," 131.

15. Ralph Waldo Emerson, "Editor's Address," *Massachusetts Quarterly Review* I (December 1847): 2–3.

16. Tannen, *Coherence*, 29.

17. Ernest J. Smith in his archival work on *The Dream Songs* found this comment from 1955–56 notes by Berryman in the Berryman Papers, Box 5, folder 5, labeled "Published

Poetry: *77 Dream Songs*," University of Minnesota Libraries Manuscripts Division. See his article: "John Berryman's 'Programmatic' for *The Dream Songs* and an Instance of Revision," *Journal of Modern Literature* 23, nos. 3–4 (Summer 2000): 430.

18. From the Preface to Dryden's translation of *Ovid's Epistles*, 1680, rpt. in *Essays of John Dryden*, ed. W. P. Ker, vols. 1 and 2 (New York: Russell, 1961), 237; emphasis added.

19. "The Task of the Translator," *Theories of Translation*, eds. Rainer Schulte and John Biguenet (Chicago, IL: University of Chicago Press, 1992), 74.

20. D. S. Carne-Ross, "Translation and Transposition," in *The Craft of and Context of Translation: A Symposium*, eds. William Arrowsmith and Roger Shattuck (Austin: The University of Texas Press, 1961), 6.

21. Edward Channing's phrase is "borrowers and imitators." See "Models in Literature," 205.

22. Gabór Bezeczky, "Literal Language," *New Literary History* 22, no. 3 (1991): 609.

23. Channing, "Models in Literature," 208.

24. John Berryman, *The Freedom of the Poet* (New York: Farrar, Straus, and Giroux, 1976), 328.

25. *John Berryman: Collected Poems: 1937–1971*, ed. Charles Thornbury (New York: FSG, 1989), 133. (I will refer to this edition in the text as *CP*.)

26. The inexpressibility topos, by contrast, is noteworthy here as well. As Ann Chalmers Watts says, "Defined in its pure form inexpressibility centers on language, not the speaker: the point is not that the speaker fails, though the speaker does, but that any tongue fails." She adds that "it acknowledges a struggle between word and not-word"—which is obviously a relevant but different struggle between word and word. See Ann Chalmers Watts, "*Pearl*, Inexpressibility, and Poems of Human Loss," *Publications of the Modern Language Association of America* 99, no. 1 (1984): 27.

27. Pascal Covici, Jr., *Humor and Revelation in American Literature: The Puritan Connection* (Columbia: University of Missouri Press, 1997), 3.

28. "The Editor's Table," *American Monthly Magazine* 1 (January 1830): 730.

29. Berryman, *CP*, 135.

30. Berryman, *The Dream Songs* (London: Faber and Faber, 1969), vi.

31. *The Literary World: A Journal of Science, Literature and Art* VII (July–December 1850): 146; emphasis added. (Original publications appeared on August 17 and August 24, 1850.)

32. Berryman, *CP*, 133.

33. Lowell, "Nationality in Literature," 202–3.

34. Joseph Mancini, Jr., "A Hearing Aid for Berryman's *Dream Songs*," *Modern Language Studies* 10, no. 1 (1979–80): 58.

35. Berryman, *CP*, xxxv.

36. Henry B. Wonham, *Mark Twain and the Art of the Tall Tale* (New York: Oxford University Press, 1993), 27.

37. Evert Duyckinck, "Authorship," *Arcturus* 1, no. 1 (December 1840): 23.

38. Wonham, *Mark Twain*, 24.

39. Ibid., 24. See also Jennifer Andrews, "Reading Toni Morrison's *Jazz*: Rewriting the Tall Tale and Playing with the Trickster in the White American and African-American Humor Traditions," *Canadian Review of American Studies* 29, no. 1 (1999): 3.

40. Roger L. Welsch, "Of Light Bulbs and Shaggy Dogs," *Natural History* 102, no. 2 (1993): 20.

41. Jan Harold Brunvand, "A Classification for Shaggy Dog Stories," *The Journal of American Folklore* 76, no. 299 (January–March 1963): 68. Shaggy dogs are sometimes cited in the category of "dialect humor," but especially so when related to regional tall tale humor. While drawing from regional detail, the emphasis, however, in the shaggy dog, continues to

be on a combination of verbal effusion with boiled-down inclusion of every listener, as the tale in its fundamental inconsequentiality resists the punch line that commonly separates "insiders" and "outsiders." As Walter Blair writes about "Hezekiah Bedott" in the *Widow Bedott Papers,* "it merits reprinting chiefly because it is a fine example of what today would be called a shaggy-dog story, still a favorite among American humorists. Max Eastman admiringly described tales of this sort as "loose, rambling, fantastically inconsequential monologues" whose appeal derives in part from their "'total want of structure,' 'a mess, the messier ... within the limits of patience, the better'" (xiv–xv). For a look at how "dialect humor" in the antebellum period generally played up the "incongruity" between "'ideals of freedom'" and "'ordinary people who speak, think and act in ordinary terms,'" see *The Mirth of a Nation: America's Great Dialect Humor,* eds. Walter Blair and Raven I. McDavid, Jr. (Minneapolis: University of Minnesota Press, 1983), xi. For a collection of humor, including jokes, tall tales, and selections from Mark Twain, from colonial to modern times, see *America's Humor: From Poor Richard to Doonesbury,* eds. Walter Blair and Hamlin Hill (Oxford: Oxford University Press, 1978). For a study of humor and Mark Twain, focusing on the gaps between his early idealism and America's imperial directions, see James M. Cox, *Mark Twain: The Fate of Humor* (Columbia: University of Missouri Press, 2002).

42. Welsch, "Light Bulbs," 20.

43. Brunvand, "Shaggy Dog Stories," 44.

44. Shaggy dogs come in many breeds: one kind exploits punning; another, the logical non sequitur; another large category, stories about animals, to name three. Six major categories have been expertly identified by Brunvand in his classic 1963 summary "A Classification for Shaggy Dog Stories."

45. Eric Partridge, *The 'Shaggy Dog' Story: Its Origin, Development and Nature (with a few seemly examples)* (Freeport, NY: Book for Libraries Press, 1953), 43.

46. Of course, the no-point shaggy dog, like its umbrella of the tall tale, has other important facets besides its audience that account for its longevity. For example, the core, though inconsequential, is different in each tale. Even synopses or titles make this clear: a shaggy dog about a dog that is shot in the bar is more grotesque than a more silly groaner about a Man Who Walked on the Walls and Ceiling. The listener's role, however, remains fundamental. Regardless of perspective on the shaggy dog story, whether Partridge's classical emphasis or Rapkins's homespun leanings or Welsch's angle on humor, the teller's drawn-out embellishment, a mix of bravado and smallness, increasingly constituted the "shaggy dog" and its meaninglessness; specifically, the final "groan" depends on the pull in a local audience to ape relevancy, only to defuse it and dismember it for redistribution of self-applause throughout the listeners.

47. Brown, "The Rhapsodist, No. I," *Columbian Magazine* 3, no. 8 (August 1789): 467.

48. Wonham, *Mark Twain,* 8. We hear a reverberation of Nancy K. Miller's reading of the autobiographical impulse, which, as she argues, "stages a meeting with the symmetrical desire in the other constituted by readers." If "autobiography" can be said to name an aspect of the nationalist discourse, then this line of interdependence offers an interesting direction to pursue. See "Facts, Pacts, Acts," *Profession* 92: Presidential Forum, 12.

49. André Gide, "The Value of Inconsistency," in *The Modern Tradition: Backgrounds of Modern Literature,* eds. Richard Ellmann and Charles Feidelson Jr. (New York: Oxford University Press, 1965), 699.

50. Washington Irving, "Desultory Thoughts on Criticism," *The Knickerbocker Magazine* 14 (August 1839): 175.

51. Richard Poirier, in his studies on the "vague" (chapter 3, 129–168) in a line of Emersonian pragmatism, notes how "language itself remained the one unavoidable cultural inheritance ... the one that could not be dispensed with. However, a felt need to dispense with it became, for those of an Emersonian inclination, unremitting, not to be assuaged...."

Why then was it not possible to escape from language? Because it remained the necessary medium by which to talk about efforts to get out of it or beyond it.... It could be said, then, that insofar as America is represented by Emersonian pragmatists it has always been what is called postmodernist. That is, Emerson's America is a place that from the outset recognized the contingency of all institutions and recognized language as a form of knowledge that was also a form of repressive power." See *Poetry & Pragmatism*, 134–35.

52. See Ann Chalmers Watts, "*Pearl*, Inexpressibility, and Poems of Human Loss," *Publications of the Modern Language Association of America* 99, no. 1 (1984): 27.

53. Theodor W. Adorno, "Trying to Understand *Endgame*," in *Notes to Literature*, ed. Rolf Tiedemann, trans. Shierry Weber Nicholsen, vol. 1 (New York: Columbia University Press, 1991), 242.

54. Eliot, *Collected Poems* (London: Faber and Faber, 1963), 40.

55. Nathaniel Hawthorne, "Wakefield," in *Nathaniel Hawthorne: Tales and Sketches*, ed. Roy Harvey Pearce (New York: The Library of America), 290.

56. *The Massachusetts Quarterly Review* 1, no. 1 (December 1847): 3.

57. "Wakefield," 290–91.

58. Raymond Carver, "Cathedral," *Cathedral* (New York: Vintage, 1989), 209.

59. Augustine Okereke, "The Performance and the Text: Parameters for Understanding Oral Literary Performance," in *Across the Lines: Intertextuality and Transcultural Communication in the New Literatures in English*, ed. Wolfgang Klooss (Amsterdam: Rodopi, 1998), 41.

60. Wonham, *Mark Twain*, 24.

61. *The Port Folio* 4, no. 22 (28 November 1807): 344.

62. Henry James, *The Figure in the Carpet, and Other Stories*, ed. Frank Kermode (London: Penguin, 1986), 397.

63. Judith M. Davidoff, *Beginning Well: Framing Fictions in Late Middle English Poetry* (Rutherford: Fairleigh Dickinson University Press, 1988), 18.

64. Todd F. Davis, "The Narrator's Dilemma in 'Bartleby the Scrivener': The Excellently Illustrated Re-statement of a Problem," *Studies in Short Fiction* 34, no. 2 (1997): 183–84. See also William Vaughn, "Moving from Privacy: 'Bartleby' and Otherness," *Centennial Review* 43, no. 3 (1999): 535–64.

65. Herman Melville, *The Piazza Tales and Other Prose Pieces, 1839–1860*, ed. Harrison Hayford (Chicago, IL: Northwestern University Press, Newberry Library, 1987), 13.

66. Davis, "Narrator's Dilemma," 184.

67. Doreen Innes, "Metaphor, Simile, and Allegory as Ornaments of Style," in *Metaphor, Allegory, and the Classical Tradition: Ancient Thought and Modern Revisions*, G. R. Boys-Stones, ed. (Oxford: Oxford University Press, 2003), 11. A "safe" metaphor, with reference here to Demetrius, only seems the proper term in relation to "customary speech"; the lawyer's English is a point of reference to such relations, even to the point of his self-description as a "safe" man. What is called a "necessary" metaphor, in contrast, looks as an alien to migrate, according to Cicero, "'into its own'" place (Innes, 7); so Bartleby as necessary, and as an "alien" to such "safe" ground, looks to migrate (in the case of self-distancing) by *staying* in his "own place."

68. Michael Fried, "Art and Objecthood," in *Minimal Art: Essays and Reviews* (Chicago: University of Chicago Press, 1998), 166.

69. Innes notes metaphor's roots in relocation, "'carrying across,'" what Aristotle calls the "'the introduction of an alien term.'" "Metaphor, Simile, and Allegory," 7.

70. Karsten Harries, "Metaphors and Transcendence," *Critical Inquiry* 5, no. 1, *Special Issue on Metaphor* (Autumn 1978): 84.

71. Don R. Swanson, "Toward a Psychology of Metaphor," in *On Metaphor*, ed. Sheldon Sacks (Chicago: University of Chicago Press, 1979), 162.

72. Ted Cohen, "Metaphor and the Cultivation of Intimacy," *Critical Inquiry* 5, no. 1, Special Issue on Metaphor (Autumn 1978): 10.

73. Partridge, *'Shaggy Dog' Story,* 87. Cohen's essay on the figurative, the literal, and jokes provides a good general background. See Cohen, "Metaphor and the Cultivation of Intimacy," in *On Metaphor,* 1–10.

74. Welsch, "Light Bulbs," 20.

75. Terence Martin, "The Negative Structures of American Literature," *American Literature* 57, no. 1 (March 1985): 22.

76. Martin's conclusion for Bartleby's existence, however, moves from rhetoric and takes a thematic turn toward something he calls "pure existence": "His [Bartleby's] death in prison signals Melville's concern with the fate of pure existence as well as society's increasing failure to acknowledge it at all." See "Negative Structures," 19.

77. Philip Fisher, *Still the New World: American Literature in a Culture of Creative Destruction* (Cambridge, MA: Harvard University Press, 1999), 157.

78. On the point regarding character, Alan Singer suggests that the "aesthetic enterprise" of "Bartleby" is made "into a practicable métier of human character—one that outstrips the devices of characterization. . . ." See this argument embedded in *Aesthetic Reason: Artworks and the Deliberative Ethos* (University Park: Penn State University Press, 2003), 171. More largely, David S. Reynolds has a good sense of the formal admixture of elements of character and plot in "Bartleby": "None of the elements in "Bartleby, the Scrivener," therefore, were new to American fiction—they were a direct inheritance from the dark city-mysteries fiction of the late 1840s. What is new about Melville's story is its formal innovations: the skilful use of the flawed narrator; the symbolic setting; the psychological and metaphysical suggestions." See *Beneath the American Renaissance: The Subversive Imagination in the Age of Emerson and Melville* (Cambridge, MA: Harvard University Press, 1988), 296.

79. Melville, *Piazza Tales,* 20.

80. J. Russell Reaver, "From Reality to Fantasy: Opening-Closing Formulas in the Structures of American Tall Tales," *Southern Folklore Quarterly* 36, no. 4 (1972): 372.

81. Melville, *Piazza Tales,* 13.

82. Ariane Dewey, "Comic Tragedies/Tragic Comedies: American Tall Tales," in *Sitting at the Feet of the Past: Retelling the North American Folktale for Children,* eds. Gary D. Schmidt and Donald R. Hettinga (New York: Greenwood Publishing Group, 1992), 196.

83. Okereke, "Performance," 44.

84. Partridge, *'Shaggy Dog' Story,* 36.

85. "Bartleby was one of those beings . . . ," Melville, *Piazza Tales,* 13.

86. Elizabeth Tonkin, *Narrating Our Pasts: The Social Construction of Oral History, Cambridge Studies in Oral and Literate Culture 22,* eds. Peter Burke and Ruth Finnegan (Cambridge: Cambridge University Press, 1992), 67.

87. Partridge, *'Shaggy Dog' Story,* 43.

88. David Harvey, *The Condition of Postmodernity: An Enquiry into the Origins of Cultural Change* (Oxford: Blackwell, 1989), 59.

89. The anticipatory complexity of frames toward what Jürgen Wolter calls twentieth-century "metafictional narrative" ("metafiction as self-conscious narrative," 67), is relevant, and he has written, for example, "Brown and Irving were among the first American writers to pave the way toward twentieth-century metafictional narrative." See Jürgen Wolter, "'Novels are . . . the most dangerous kind of reading': Metafictional Discourse in Early American Literature," *Connotations: A Journal for Critical Debate* 4, nos. 1–2 (1994/95): 78. While I do not agree on the emphasis by which they "paved the way," I think that the practice, if founded in different contexts, is important to recognize.

90. Ames, *Works,* 431.

91. 1 Peter 1.8–9 Authorized King James Version. There are many other views to this

position. For an earlier and excellent review and analysis, see Dan McCall's *The Silence of Bartleby* (Ithaca: Cornell University Press, 1989). Also see Gillian Brown's *Domestic Individualism: Imagining Self in Nineteenth-Century America* (Berkeley: University of California Press, 1990). Brown looks at "Bartleby" in contemporary literary contexts, while anticipating "contemporary accounts of both agoraphobia and anorexia" (8); she writes, "By maintaining the integrity of the private sphere, this opposition [between home and market] sustains the notion of a personal life impervious to market influences, the model of selfhood in a commercial society. In his propinquity to walls and his preference for his own wall-like impenetrable postures, Bartleby presents an extreme version of such a model...." (174). Alan Singer sees Bartleby's "character" as a site of knowledge without intelligibility, putting the "reader" and the narrator in terms of interpretation on a "continuum of action." See *Aesthetic Reason*, 153–59. In Jane Desmarais's look toward an "understanding of his [Bartleby's] character" (26), there is "a story about the failure of modern social life" (30) in which she uses "political and psychological notions of stoicism" (35) to examine the state of democracy and rights of the individual. See "Preferring Not To: The Paradox of Passive Resistance in Herman Melville's 'Bartleby,'" *Journal of the Short Story in English* 36 (April 2001): 25–39. For a look at a "'sublime' ethics" in "Bartleby," in which the text effectively, like the character Bartleby, "says more than it seems" (558), see William Vaughn, "Moving from Privacy: 'Bartleby' and Otherness," *Centennial Review* 43, no. 3 (Fall 1999): 535–64.

92. Along the same lines of framing, Barbara Johnson argues about the ending of *Billy Budd* that it "problematizes the very *idea* of authority by placing its own reversal in the pages of an 'authorized' naval chronicle" (215).

93. Paul de Man, "The Rhetoric of Temporality," in *Blindness and Insight: Essays in the Rhetoric of Contemporary Criticism* (Minneapolis: University of Minnesota Press, 1983), 207.

94. John Miles Foley, "The Impossibility of Canon," *Teaching Oral Traditions*, ed. John Miles Foley (New York: Modern Language Association, 1998), 22.

95. Melville, *Piazza Tales*, 13.

96. Charles Dickens, *Great Expectations* (Harmondsworth, England: Penguin, 1985), 3.

97. Elizabeth Hardwick, from "Bartleby in Manhattan," in *Melville's Short Novels*, ed. Dan McCall (New York: W.W. Norton & Company, 2002), 261, 262; emphasis added.

98. Kukla, *Ineffability and Philosophy*, xii.

99. Northrop Frye, *Anatomy of Criticism* (Princeton, NJ: Princeton University Press, 1973), 277.

100. Melville, *Piazza Tales*, 14.

101. Frye, *Anatomy*, 277.

102. Partridge, *'Shaggy Dog' Story*, 87.

103. Ibid., 51.

104. Brunvand, "Shaggy Dog Stories," 44. Evan Esar suggests "the most plausible guess" for origins of shaggy dog jokes as "verbal transference, since drunks and tramps were often described as shaggy, and sometime called ragshags, shagnasties, etc. The shift from shaggy to shaggy dog resulted from the popularity of one of these 'alcohological' stories which actually dealt with a shaggy dog." See *The Humor of Humor* (New York: Horizon Press, 1952), 255–56. But Brunvand suggests the still problematic nature of shaggy dog jokes, including Esar's theory of origins, which he believes still remains "insufficiently documented" (45).

105. Partridge, *'Shaggy Dog' Story*, 52.

106. The following two examples point toward redemption. "In the moment when the blind man and the narrator share an identical perception of spiritual space, the narrator's sense of enclosure—of being confined by his own house and circumstances—vanishes as if by an act of grace...." Mark A. R. Facknitz writes. See "'The Calm,' 'A Small, Good Thing,' and 'Cathedral': Raymond Carver and the Rediscovery of Self Worth," *Studies in Short Fiction* 23 (1986): 295. The symbolism continues to follow lines of revelation and the ineffable:

"The confrontation with language has led him [narrator] into the realm of the ineffable 'something' beyond a linguistic register, beyond the power of words to inhibit, to the point at which they shatter" (38–39), Nelson Hathcock writes. This tracing of the ineffable still connects to the more traditional and symbolic search beyond words for "meaning." As Hathcock says, "The nihilism that many readers have faulted Carver for espousing is successfully deflected by these two narrators; through language, through the engaged imaginative act of 'telling,' they are granted a new vision of their lives and, in the process, a re-vision of meaning" (31). See *Studies in Short Fiction* 28 (1991): 31–39.

107. Carver, "Cathedral," 209.
108. Wonham, *Mark Twain*, 31.
109. Partridge, *'Shaggy Dog' Story*, 52.
110. Welsch, "Light Bulbs," 20; Partridge, *'Shaggy Dog' Story*, 22.
111. Partridge, *'Shaggy Dog' Story*, 52.
112. Stephen Belcher, "Framed Tales in the Oral Tradition: An Exploration," *Fabula* 35 (1994): 1; Nancy Mason Bradbury, "Traditional Referentiality: The Aesthetic Power of Oral Traditional Structure," in *Teaching Oral Traditions* (New York: Modern Language Association, 1998), 137.
113. Wonham, *Mark Twain*, 19.
114. Alan Paton, *Too Late the Phalarope* (New York: Scribner, 1953), 1.
115. "The Frame Tale East and West," *Teaching Oral Traditions*, 391.
116. *The Singer of Tales in Performance* (Indianapolis: Indiana University Press, 1995), 137; emphasis in original.
117. "The Future Is better Than the Past," *The Dial* 2, no. 1 (July 1841): 57–58, line 2.
118. *The Dial* 2, no. 1 (July, 1841): 57–58.

CHAPTER 5

1. Robert Pogue Harrison, "Not Ideas about the Thing but the Thing Itself," *New Literary History* 30, no. 3 (1999): 668. See Wallace Stevens, *The Collected Poems of Wallace Stevens* (New York: Vintage, 1982).
2. "*The Port Folio* 3, no. 26 (27 June 1807): 401.
3. "Lack of Poetry in America," *Harper's New Monthly Magazine*, 403.
4. The religious and choral roots of the inexpressible I have already covered in chapter 1, note 6. Commercial, promotional, and rhetorical roots of the inexpressible are also crucial and longstanding. As Cressy in *Coming Over* writes of this rhetoric of unreachable perfectibility, the "reports of their [the sea captains'] voyages, often written to gain funding for future expeditions, presented America as a land of . . . immeasurable promise. The stony reality was often obscured in these first flickerings of the American dream" (2). He explains, further, how John Smith "actually coined the name 'New England' and did everything in his power to promote 'this unregarded country,'" emphasizing that rhetoric: the "potential of New England lay as much in its *mystery* as in its proven resources" (Cressy, 4; emphasis added). Thus, although the English had made several probing voyages, according to the words of Smith, "'The coast is yet still even as a coast unknown and undiscovered. . . .'" (Cressy, 4).
5. Ezra Pound, "Hugh Selwyn Mauberly,"1.1–6, *Ezra Pound: Selected Poems, 1908–1959* (London: Faber and Faber, 1975), 98.
6. Further evidence of this common ground can be heard in Fender's comment regarding T. S. Eliot, who "applying the sense of loss to the condition of being modern rather than American, would express something of [Washington] Irving's anxiety in his essay, 'Tradition and the Individual Talent'" (97). David S. Reynolds in *Beneath the American Renaissance*

notes how Horace Bushnell, in his "Dissertation on Language" (1849), can sound "like a precursor of Jacques Derrida" in that he "multiplied paradoxical, figurative expressions of a truth that remains forever indecipherable" (444–45). Regarding Whitman, he notes that "'The Sleepers' might indeed be described as presurrealistic, but, far from being unusual for its day," it employs "common devices of the American Subversive Style" (518). He suggests resistance to "oppressive literary influence" in the importance of "popular culture" and especially "a large variety of popular cultural voices" (5).

7. "Literary Prospects of 1845," *The American Review*, 149; emphasis added.

8. "American Letters: Their Character and Advancement," *The American Review*, 575.

9. "Nationality in Literature," *The Democratic Review*, 269.

10. William James, *Principles of Psychology*, vol. 1 (New York: H. Holt and Company, 1890), 238.

11. *The Monthly Magazine and American Review* 1, no. 1 (April 1799): 3.

12. Michael H. Levenson, *A Genealogy of Modernism: A Study of English Literary Doctrine 1908–1922* (Cambridge: Cambridge University Press, 1984), 13.

13. Michael Fried, "Art and Objecthood," *Minimal Art,* ed. Gregory Battock (New York: E. P. Dutton & Co, 1998), 146.

14. Joseph Frank, *The Idea of Spatial Form* (New Brunswick, NJ: Rutgers University Press, 1991), 14.

15. Richard Poirier names this resonance in relation to James's program of "vagueness," an aspect of what he calls "Emersonian pragmatism": "to a wholly unusual degree it [Emersonian pragmatism] never allows any one of these terms [such as "nature" or "action"] to arrive at a precise or static definition." See *Poetry & Pragmatism,* 129.

16. Eliot, "The Love Song of J. Alfred Prufrock," *Collected Poems: 1909–1962* (London: Faber and Faber, 1963), 16.

17. David Spurr, *Conflicts in Consciousness: T. S. Eliot's Poetry and Criticism* (Urbana: University of Illinois Press, 1984), xviii–xix.

18. "Prufrock," 16–17; emphasis added.

19. Denis Donoghue, "T. S. Eliot and the Poem Itself," *Partisan Review* 67, no. 1 (Winter 2000): 20.

20. Hugh Henry Brackenridge, "Introduction," *Modern Chivalry,* rpt., gen. ed., Harry Hayden Clark (New York: American Book Company, 1937), 3. As Davidson notes, this "ambiguous voice" in Brackenridge's comic epic points to compromised insiders in postrevolutionary America, inclusive of the new democracy and its defects. See *Revolution and the Word,* 20.

21. Brown, "The Rhapsodist, No. I," *Columbian Magazine* III, no. 8 (August 1789): 466.

22. Robert Crawford, *The Modernist Poet: Poetry, Academia, and Knowledge since the 1750's* (New York: Oxford, 2001), 170.

23. Charles Isenberg, *Telling Silence: Russian Frame Narratives of Renunciation* (Evanston, IL: Northwestern University Press, 1993), 143.

24. "Literary Prospects," 149.

25. Whitman, "A Backward Glance O'er Travel'd Roads," *Complete Poetry,* 661.

26. "Not in the Least American," in *Nineteenth-Century American Women Writers: A Critical Reader,* ed. Karen L. Kilcup (Oxford: Blackwell Publishers, 1998), 20.

27. *The Port Folio* 3, no. 25 (June 20, 1807): 386.

28. William Dunlap, "Preface," *André: A Tragedy in Five Acts,* 1st ed. (New York: B. T. & J. Swords, April 4, 1798), iii.

29. Samuel Miller, "Nations Lately Become Literary," 409–10.

30. "National Literature," *The Christian Examiner* (January 1830), 286.

31. Editor in a preface to the following: E. W. Johnson, "American Letters: Their Character and Advancement," *The American Review: A Whig Journal of Politics, Literature, Art and Science,* 575.

32. Dunlap, "Preface," iii; emphasis added.

33. Melville, "Hawthorne and His Mosses," 126.

34. Isenberg, *Telling Silence,* 17.

35. *The Making of Americans: Being a History of a Family's Progress* (Normal, IL: Dalkey Archive Press, 1995), 782.

36. "The Oven Bird" is one of Frost's most anthologized poems.

37. Joseph N. Riddel, "The Contours of Stevens Criticism," in *The Act of the Mind: Essays on the Poetry of Wallace Stevens,* eds. J. Hillis Miller and Roy Harvey Pearce (Baltimore, MD: The Johns Hopkins Press, 1965), 273.

38. Michael Heller, "Oppen and Stevens: Reflections on the Lyrical and Philosophical," *Sagetrieb* 12, no. 3 (1993): 26. The essay "What's Historical About Historicism?" importantly tracks more largely the critical reception of Stevens in relation to historicism: "More than a decade ago, then, it seemed necessary to assume that historical approaches to Stevens doubtless led to the conclusion that Stevens was apolitical," Alan Filreis writes. He concludes, "As you will see, I am equally concerned about the reversal of the trend: the assumption that to historicize Stevens is to find him enabling a 'revolutionary' poetic context" (211). See *The Wallace Stevens Journal,* "What's Historical about Historicism?" vol. 28, no. 2 (October 2004): 210–218.

39. Helen Vendler, "The Qualified Assertions of Wallace Stevens," in *The Act of the Mind,* 175–76. According to Schotter the poem suggests "the kingdom of heaven" by using "various analogical devices, while at the same time using a naive dreamer as a warning against taking them literally." She analyzes two theological possibilities for conveying the ineffable: the "positive" method which proposes "analogies for God," and the "negative" which denies "that any analogies are valid." Vendler concludes, "The two ways tend to work in a dialectical manner, the latter continually warning against the idolatry that the former might encourage." See Schotter, "Vernacular Style," 23.

40. Wallace Stevens, *The Collected Poems* (New York: Vintage Books, 1982), 513.

41. Ibid., 196.

42. Jacqueline Brogan, "The 'Form/And Frame' of 'As If' in Wallace Stevens," *American Poetry* 3, no. 3 (1986): 48.

43. Paul A. Bové, "Discourse," in *Critical Terms for Literary Study,* eds. Frank Lentricchia and Thomas McLaughlin (Chicago: University of Chicago Press, 1990), 55.

44. Clive Bloom, "Preface," *American Poetry: The Modernist Ideal,* eds. Clive Bloom and Brian Docherty (London: Macmillan, 1995), 7.

45. Filreis, *Modernism from Right to Left: Wallace Stevens, The Thirties & Literary Radicalism* (Cambridge: Cambridge University Press, 1994), 4.

46. Samuel French Morse is one of the few critics who tries to address directly this question of point of view. About "The Comedian as the Letter C," he says, "The most surprising thing about this poem is its point of view." Although Morse's emphasis is a deflection of autobiographical readings—"No poem by a writer of such great detachment is likely to be purely autobiographical"—his recognition of the tendency of Stevens's critics to allow for only a single, if self-countering, voice remains important. See Samuel French Morse, "Some Ideas about the Thing Itself," in *Critics on Wallace Stevens,* ed. Peter L. McNamara (Coral Gables: University of Miami Press, 1972), 24, 25. The poem "The Comedian as the Letter C" has often been the focus for those who look politically and thematically at postcolonial issues; for a direct pairing see J. E. Elliott in "What's 'Post' in Post-Colonial Theory," *Borderlands: Negotiating Boundaries in Post-Colonial Writing,* ed. Monika Reif-Hülser (Amsterdam: Rodopi 1999), 50, or for a look at Crispin and more widely at Stevens's "postcolonial imagination,"

see Anna Boyagoda's "'Being There Together': Stevens and the Postcolonial Imagination," *The Wallace Stevens Journal* 29, no. 1 (April 2005): 62–71.

47. Austin's definition sets the stage:

> To name the ship *is* to say (in the appropriate circumstances) the words "I name, &c." When I say, before the registrar or altar, &c., "I do," I am not reporting on a marriage: I am indulging in it. What are we to call a sentence or an utterance of this type? I propose to call it a *performative sentence* or a performative utterance, or, for short, "a performative." ... The name is derived, of course, from "perform," the usual verb with the noun "action": it indicates that the issuing of the utterance is the performing of an action—it is not normally thought of as just saying something.

See *How To Do Things With Words,* 2nd ed. (Oxford: Oxford University Press, 1975), 6–7.

The words "just saying something" mark one major ambiguity, as they are considered more recently, and even by Austin himself at the end, also "discourse-specific." The links, however, between the aggregate of terms that Austin applies to the performative and a comparable action of frames will be explored further.

48. Daniel R. Schwarz, *Narrative & Representation in the Poetry of Wallace Stevens: 'A Tune Beyond Us, Yet Ourselves'* (London: St. Martin's Press, 1993), 3.

49. Mark Halliday observes that "we can credit Stevens with a kind of interactive power beyond ... the capacity for interpersonal caring whose effects I have described in this essay. We can thus acknowledge that there seem to be moments in reading Stevens when 'difference disappears' (*CP* 454) and indeed *we* become the interior paramour" (166), if "moments are only moments" (167), he qualifies. See Mark Halliday, *Stevens and the Interpersonal* (Princeton, NJ: Princeton University Press, 1991). Shoshana Felman puts succinctly one of Austin's precepts of *act* and participation in "performatives": the function of the performatives is "not to inform or describe, but to ... accomplish an *act* through the very process of their enunciation" (15).

50. For one good reading of Stevens in the ironic mode, see Marjorie Perloff, "Irony in The Rock," in *Critics on Wallace Stevens,* 101–12.

51. If it does so, it is at the expense of fictions that are often described as autotelic, able to assimilate the ruptures.

52. See Partridge, *'Shaggy Dog' Story,* 54. For a type index of the shaggy dog story, see Brunvand, "Classification," 47–67.

53. Partridge, *'Shaggy Dog' Story,* 13.

54. Harold Bloom, *The Anxiety of Influence: A Theory of Poetry* (New York: Oxford University Press, 1973), 29.

55. *The American Whig Review* 1, no. 2 (February 1845): 147.

56. Ibid., 149.

57. Margaret Fuller, "American Literature; Its Position in the Present Time, and Prospects for the Future," *Papers on Literature and Art* (London: Wiley and Putnam, 1846), Part II, 123–24.

58. Amy Lowell, *Tendencies in Modern American Poetry* (New York: Macmillan Company, 1917), v.

59. Interestingly, Stephen Booth, in a more general context of "nonsense" writes, " ... I celebrate the poem's ability to deafen us to the illogic of its assertion about the sheep, the poem's ability to let us understand something that does not make sense as if it *did* make sense.... " See Stephen Booth, *Precious Nonsense: The Gettysburg Address, Ben Jonson's Epitaphs on His Children, and Twelfth Night* (Berkeley: University of California Press, 1998), 5.

60. *The Port Folio* (new series) 4, no. 23 (5 December 1807): 385.

Selected Bibliography

Ackrill, J. L. *Aristotle's Ethics*. London: Faber & Faber, 1973.
Adams, Henry. *The Education of Henry Adams*. Boston: Massachusetts Historical Society, 1918. Reprint edition, New York: Random House, Modern Library, 1931.
Addison, Joseph."The Vision of Mirzah." In *Addison and Steele: Selections from* The Tatler *and* The Spectator. 2nd ed., edited by Robert J. Allen. New York: Rinehart and Winston, Inc., 1970. Originally published in *The Spectator*, No. 159 (Saturday, September 1, 1711).
Adorno, Theodor W. "Trying to Understand *Endgame*." In *Notes to Literature*, edited by Rolf Tiedemann, translated by Shierry Weber Nicholsen, vol. 1. New York: Columbia University Press, 1991.
"American Epics." *Putnam's Monthly Magazine* 3, no. 18 (June 1854): 639–48.
"American Poetry." *Littell's Living Age* 6 (July 1845): 85–87.
Ambrisco, Alan, S. "'It Lyth Nat in My Tonge': *Occupatio* and Otherness in the Squire's Tale." *Chaucer Review: A Journal of Medieval Studies and Literary Critcism* 38, no. 3 (2004): 205–28.
Ames, Fisher. "American Literature." In *Works of Fisher Ames with a Selection from His Speeches and Correspondence by His Son Seth Ames*, vol. 2, 428–42. Boston: Little, Brown and Company, 1854.
Ammons, Elizabeth and White-Parks, Annette. *Tricksterism in Turn-of-the-Century American Literature: A Multicultural Perspective*. Hanover: University Press of New England, 1994.

Anderson, Benedict. *Imagined Communities: Reflections on the Origin and Spread of Nationalism.* London: Verso, 1983.

Andrews, Jennifer. "Reading Toni Morrison's *Jazz:* Rewriting the Tall Tale and Playing with the Trickster in the White American and African-American Humor Traditions." *Canadian Review of American Studies* 29, no. 1 (1999): 87–107.

Annals of Congress, House of Representatives, 12th Congress, 1st session, 459.

Appleby, Joyce. *Inheriting the Revolution: The First Generation of Americans.* Cambridge, MA: Harvard University Press, 2000.

Arac, Jonathan. *The Emergence of American Literary Narrative, 1820–1860.* Cambridge, MA: Harvard University Press, 2005.

Archibald, Elizabeth. "Declarations of 'Entente' in *Troilus and Criseyde.*" *The Chaucer Review* 25, no. 3 (1991): 190–213.

Aristotle. "Nicomachean Ethics." In *Aristotle's Ethics,* edited by J. L. Ackrill. London: Faber and Faber, 1973.

Armstrong, Paul B. "Reading James's Prefaces and Reading James." In *Henry James's New York Edition: The Construction of Authority,* edited by David McWhirter, 125–37. Stanford: Stanford University Press.

Arndt, Karl J. R. "Introduction: German as the Official Language of the United States of America?" In *Die deutschsprachige Presse der Amerikas/The German Language Press of the Americas.* 3rd ed., vol. 3, 19–42. München: K. G. Saar, 1980.

Atwood, Margaret. *Selected Poems: 1965–1975.* London: Virago, 1991.

Augustine. *The Trinity.* Translated by John Burnaby. Philadelphia: Westminster, 1955.

———. *De Doctrina Christiana.* Translated by D. W. Robertson, Jr. Indianapolis: Library of Liberal Arts, 1978.

Austin, J. L. *How to Do Things with Words.* Oxford: Oxford University Press, 1976.

Austin, William. *Peter Rugg: The Missing Man. New-England Galaxy* VII, no. 361 (10 September 1824), serialized.

Auerbach, Erich. *Literary Language and Its Public in Late Latin Antiquity and in the Middle Ages.* Translated by Ralph Manheim. Princeton, NJ: Princeton University Press, 1965.

Bailyn, Bernard. *The Peopling of British North America: An Introduction.* New York: Knopf, 1986.

———. *To Begin the World Anew: The Genius and Ambiguities of the American Founders.* New York: Knopf, 2003.

Baker, Carlos. *Ernest Hemingway.* Harmondsworth, UK: Penguin, 1972.

Bassett, John E. "*Roughing It:* Authority through Comic Performance." *Nineteenth- Century Literature* 45, no. 2 (1988): 220–34.

Bauerlein, Mark. *Whitman and the American Idiom.* Baton Rouge: Louisiana State University Press, 1991.

Bauman, Richard. "Verbal Art as Performance." *American Anthropologist,* New Series, 77, no. 2 (June 1975): 290–311.

Beckett, Samuel. *Waiting for Godot.* Translated by Samuel Beckett. New York: Grove Press, 1982.

Belcher, Stephen. "Framed Tales in the Oral Tradition: An Exploration." *Fabula* 35 (1994): 1–19.

Benaziza, Lahsen. *Romancing Scheherazade: John Barth and The One Thousand and One Nights.* Université Ibn Zohr, Publication de la Faculté des Lettres et des Sciences Humaines, Agadir, Maroc, Série: theses et mémoires 2001.

Benjamin, Walter. "The Task of the Translator." In *Theories of Translation,* edited by Rainer Schulte and John Biguenet. Chicago: University of Chicago Press, 1992.

Bercovitch, Sacvan. *American Jeremiad.* Madison: University of Wisconsin Press, 1978.

Berryman, John. *The Freedom of the Poet.* New York: Farrar, Straus, and Giroux, 1976.

———. *John Berryman: Collected Poems: 1937–1971.* Edited by Charles Thornbury. New York: Farrar, Straus, and Giroux, 1989.

Bertolini, Vincent J. "'Hinting' and 'Reminding': The Rhetoric of Performative Embodiment in *Leaves of Grass.*" *ELH* 69, no. 4 (2002): 1047–82.

Bezeczky, Gábor. "Literal Language." *New Literary History* 22, no. 3 (1991): 603–11.

Bhabha, Homi K. *Nation and Narration.* London: Routledge, 1990.

Blair, Walter, and Hamlin Hill, eds. *America's Humor: From Poor Richard to Doonesbury.* Oxford: Oxford University Press, 1978.

Bloom, Clive, and Brian Docherty, eds. *American Poetry: The Modernist Ideal.* London: Macmillan, 1995.

Bloom, Harold. *The Anxiety of Influence: A Theory of Poetry.* New York: Oxford University Press, 1973.

———, ed. *Walt Whitman,* ed. New York: Chelsea House, 1985.

———, ed. *The Western Canon: The Books and Schools of the Ages.* New York: Riverhead Books, 1994.

Bogdanos, Theodore. *Pearl, Image of the Ineffable: A Study in Medieval Poetic Symbolism.* University Park: Pennsylvania State University Press, 1983.

Bolwell, Robert Whitney. "Concerning the Study of National Ism in American Literature." *American Literature* 10, no. 4 (January 1939): 405–16.

Booth, Stephen. *King Lear, Macbeth, Indefinition, and Tragedy.* New Haven: Yale University Press, 2002.

———. *Precious Nonsense: The Gettysburg Address, Ben Jonson's Epitaphs on His Children, and Twelfth Night.* Berkeley: University of California Press, 1998.

Borneman, Walter R. *1812: The War That Forged a Nation.* New York: Harper Collins, 2004.

Bové, Paul A. *Destructive Poetics: Heidegger and Modern American Poetry.* New York: Columbia University Press, 1980. See esp. pp. 131–79, "*Leaves of Grass* and the Center: Free Play or Transcendence."

———. "Discourse." In *Critical Terms for Literary Study,* edited by Frank Lentricchia and Thomas McLaughlin, 50–65. Chicago: University of Chicago Press, 1990.

Boyagoda, Anna. "'Being There Together': Stevens and the Postcolonial Imagination." *The Wallace Stevens Journal* 29, no. 1 (April 2005): 62–71.

Boys-Stones, G. R. *Metaphor, Allegory, and Classical Tradition: Ancient Thought and Modern Revisions.* Oxford, Oxford University Press, 2003.

Brackenridge, Hugh Henry. *Modern Chivalry,* edited by Harry Hayden Clark. New York: American Book Company, 1937.

Bradbury, Nancy Mason. "Traditional Referentiality: The Aesthetic Power of Oral Traditional Structure." In *Teaching Oral Traditions,* edited by John Miles Foley, 136–45. New York: Modern Language Association, 1998.

Brereton, Geoffrey. *Principals of Tragedy: A Rational Examination of the Tragic Concept of Life and Literature.* Coral Gables: University of Miami Press, 1969.

Briggs, Charles L. "Poetics and Performance as Critical Perspectives on Language and Social Life." *Annual Review of Anthropology* 19 (1990): 59–88.

Britton, Celia. *Edouard Glissant and Postcolonial Theory: Strategies of Language and Resistance.* Charlottesville: University of Virginia Press, 1999.

Brogan, Jacqueline. "The 'Form/And Frame' of 'As If' in Wallace Stevens." *American Poetry* 3, no. 3 (1986): 34–50.

Brontë, Emily. *Wuthering Heights.* Edited by Heather Glen. London: Routledge, 1988.

Brook, Clodagh J. *The Expression of the Inexpressible in Eugenio Montale's Poetry: Metaphor, Negation, and Silence.* Oxford: Clarendon Press, 2002.

Brown, Charles Brockden. "Preface." *American Review and Literary Journal for the Year 1801,* from first edition (1802): iii–vi.

———. *Wieland; or The Transformation and Memoirs of Carwin the biloquist.* Oxford: Oxford University Press, 1994.

———. *Carwin, the biloquist; and other American tales and pieces.* London: Printed for Henry Colburn and Co., 1822.

———. "The Rhapsodist, No. I." *The Columbian Magazine* 3 (August 1789): 464–67.

———. "The Rhapsodist, No. II." *Columbian Magazine* 3, no. 9 (September 1789): 537–41

———. "The Rhapsodist, No. III." *Columbian Magazine* 3, no. 10 (October 1789): 597–601.

Brown, Gillian. *Domestic Individualism: Imagining Self in Nineteenth-Century America.* Berkeley: University of California Press, 1990.

Brownson, Orestes A. "An Oration on American Literature." In *The Early Works of Orestes A. Brownson, Volume V: The Transcendentalist Years, 1840–1841,* edited by Patrick W. Carey. Marquette Studies in Theology No. 38, edited by Andrew Tallon, 197–214. Milwaukee, WI: Marquette University Press, 2004.

Brunvand, Jan Harold. "A Classification for Shaggy Dog Stories." *The Journal of American Folklore* 76, no. 299 (January–March 1963): 42–68.

Buell, Lawrence. "Postcolonial Anxiety in Classic U.S. Literature." In Singh and Schmidt, *Postcolonial Theory and the United States,* 196–219.

Bushman, Richard L. *The Refinement of America: Persons, Houses, Cities.* New York: Knopf, 1992.

Cahill, Edward. "Federalist Criticism and the Fate of Genius." *American Literature* 76, no. 4 (December 2004): 687–717.

Cairns, William B. *On the Development of American Literature from 1815 to 1833.* Madison: The University of Wisconsin Press, 1898.

Cameron, Sharon. *The Corporeal Self: Allegories of the Body in Melville and Hawthorne.* Baltimore: Johns Hopkins University Press, 1981.

———. *Lyric Time: Dickinson and the Limits of Genre.* Baltimore: Johns Hopkins University Press, 1979.

Carne-Ross, D. S. "Translation and Transposition." In *The Craft & Context of Translation: A Symposium,* edited by William Arrowsmith and Roger Shattuck, 3–21. Austin: The University of Texas Press, 1961.

Casper, Scott E. *Constructing American Lives: Biography and Culture in Nineteenth-Century America.* Chapel Hill: University of North Carolina Press, 1999.

Carver, Raymond. *Cathedral.* New York: Vintage, 1989.

Channing, Edward. "On Models in Literature." *North American Review* 3, no. 8 (July 1816): 202–9.

Channing, Walter. "Essay on American Language and Literature." *North-American Review and Miscellaneous Journal* 1, no. 3 (September 1815): 307–14.

———. "Reflections on the Literary Delinquency of America." *North-American Review and Miscellaneous Journal* 2, no. 4 (November 1815): 38–43.

Channing, William Ellery. "National Literature." *The Christian Examiner* 36, no. 6 (January 1830): 269–95.

Chaucer, Geoffrey. *The Canterbury Tales.* In *The Works of Geoffrey Chaucer.* 2nd ed. Edited by F. N. Robinson. 2 vols. Boston: Houghton Mifflin; Cambridge, MA: The Riverside Press, 1957.

———. "Troilus and Criseyde." In *The Works of Geoffrey Chaucer.* 2nd ed., edited by F. N. Robinson. 2 vols. Boston: Houghton Mifflin, 1957.

Cheever, George B. "American Poets." *North American Review* 33, no. 73 (October 1831): 297–325.

Cheyfitz, Eric. *The Poetics of Imperialism: Translation and Colonization from The Tempest to Tarzan.* New York: Oxford University Press, 1991.

Clark, Harry Hayden. "Nationalism in American Literature." *University of Toronto Quarterly* II (1933): 492–519.
Claybaugh, Amanda. *The Novel of Purpose: Literature and Social Reform in the Anglo-American World.* Ithaca: Cornell University Press, 2007.
Cmiel, Kenneth. *Democratic Eloquence: The Fight over Popular Speech in Nineteenth-Century America.* New York: W. Morrow, 1990.
Cobbett, William. *A Year's Residence in the United States of America.* New York: Printed for the author by Clayton and Kingsland, 1818.
Cohen, Ted. "Metaphor and the Cultivation of Intimacy." In *On Metaphor,* edited by Sheldon Sacks, 1–10. Chicago: University of Chicago Press, 1979.
Coles, Harry L. *The War of 1812.* Chicago: University of Chicago Press, 1965.
Comprehending Oral and Written Language. Edited by Rosalind Horowitz and S. Jay Samuels. San Diego: Academic Press, 1987.
"A Conversation." *The Knickerbocker Magazine* 2, no. 1 (July 1833): 1–13.
Cooper, James Fenimore. *The Prairie.* New York: Signet, 1964.
Covici, Pascal, Jr. *Humor and Revelation in American Literature: The Puritan Connection.* Columbia: University of Missouri Press, 1997.
Cox, James M. *Mark Twain: The Fate of Humor.* Columbia: University of Missouri Press, 2002.
Crain, Patricia. *The Story of A: the Alphabetization of American from The New England Primer to the Scarlet Letter.* Stanford: Stanford University Press, 2000.
Crane, Mary Thomas. *Framing Authority: Sayings, Self, and Society in Sixteenth-Century England.* Princeton, NJ: Princeton University Press, 1993.
Crawford, Robert. *The Modernist Poet: Poetry, Academia, and Knowledge since the 1750s.* New York: Oxford University Press, 2001.
Cressy, David. *Coming Over: Migration and Communication between England and New England in the Seventeenth Century.* Cambridge: Cambridge University Press, 1987.
Crèvecoeur, J. Hector St. John de. *Letters from an American Farmer.* Gloucester, MA: Fox, Doubleday, 1968.
Crowther, Paul. "Literary Metaphor and Philosophical Insight: The Significance of Archilochus." In *Metaphor, Allegory, and the Classical Tradition: Ancient Thought and Modern Revisions,* edited by G. R. Boys-Stones, 83–100. Oxford: Oxford University Press, 2003.
Curtius, Ernst Robert. *European Literature and the Latin Middle Ages.* Translated by Willard R. Trask. London: Routledge & Kegan Paul, 1953.
Cutler, Ed. "Passage to Modernity: *Leaves of Grass* and the 1853 Crystal Palace Exhibition in New York." *Walt Whitman Quarterly Review* 16, no 2 (1998): 65–89.
"Dallas's Reports." *The American Review and Literary Journal for the Year 1802* 2, no. 1 (1802): 27.
Dana, Charles A. "New Publications: *Leaves of Grass.*" In Price, *Walt Whitman,* 3–8.
Dante Alighieri. *The Divine Comedy: Paradiso. Italian Text and Translation.* Translated by Charles S. Singleton, Bollingen Series 80, vol. 3, part 1. Princeton, NJ: Princeton University Press, 1975–1977.
Davidoff, Judith M. *Beginning Well: Framing Fictions in Late Middle English Poetry.* Rutherford, NJ: Farleigh Dickinson University Press, 1988.
Davidson, Cathy N. *Revolution and the Word: The Rise of the Novel in America, Expanded Edition.* Oxford: Oxford University Press, 2004.
———. *The Experimental Fictions of Ambrose Bierce: Structuring the Ineffable.* Lincoln: University of Nebraska Press, 1984.
Davis, Todd F. "The Narrator's Dilemma in 'Bartleby the Scrivener': The Excellently Illustrated Re-statement of a Problem." *Studies in Short Fiction* 34, no. 2 (1997): 183–92.
Day, Henry N. "Taste and Morals:—The Necessity of Aesthetic Culture to the Highest

Moral Excellence." *American Biblical Repository and Classical Review,* 3rd ser., 3 (July 1847): 524–47.
Dean, Susan. "Seeds of Quakerism at the Roots of *Leaves of Grass.*" *Walt Whitman Quarterly Review* 16, no 3/4 (1999): 191–201.
Delbanco, Andrew. *The Puritan Ordeal.* Cambridge, MA: Harvard University Press, 1989.
"Defence of Poetry." *North-American Review* 34, no. 74 (January 1832): 56–78.
Deleuze, G., and F. Guattari *Kafka: Toward a Minor Literature.* Minneapolis: University of Minnesota Press, 1986.
de Man, Paul. *Blindness and Insight: Essays in the Rhetoric of Contemporary Criticism.* Minneapolis: University of Minnesota Press, 1983. See esp. ch. 10, "The Rhetoric of Temporality."
Dennie, Joseph. "An Examination." *The Port Folio* 3, no. 25 (1807): 385–89.
Derrida, Jacques. "Declarations of Independence." Translated by Tom Keenan and Tom Pepper. *New Political Science* 15 (1986): 7–15.
Desmarais, Jane. "Preferring Not To: The Paradox of Passive Resistance in Herman Melville's 'Bartleby.'" *Journal of the Short Story in English* 36 (April 2001): 25–39.
Dew, Thomas R. "An Address." *Southern Literary Messenger* II, no. 24 (1836): 261–82.
Dewey, Ariane. "Comic Tragedies/Tragic Comedies: American Tall Tales." In *Sitting at the Feet of the Past: Retelling the North American Folktale for Children,* edited by Gary D. Schmidt and Donald R. Hettinga, 195–201. New York: Greenwood Publishing Group, 1992.
Dickens, Charles. *Great Expectations.* Harmondsworth, UK: Penguin, 1985.
Dickie, Margaret. *Lyric Continencies: Emily Dickinson and Wallace Stevens.* Philadelphia: University of Pennsylvania Press, 1991.
Donoghue, Denis. "T. S. Eliot and the Poem Itself." *Partisan Review* 67, no. 1 (Winter 2000): 10–37.
Dryden, John. *Essays of John Dryden.* Edited by W. P. Ker. 2 vols. New York: Russell, 1961.
Dunlap, William. *André: A Tragedy in Five Acts.* New York: B. T. & J. Swords, 1798.
Duyckinck, Evert. "Authorship." *Arcturus* 1, no. 1 (December 1840): 20–23.
———. "Literary Prospects of 1845." *The American Review: A Whig Journal of Politics, Literature, Art, and Science* 1, no. 2 (1845): 46–151.
"The Editor's Table." *The American Monthly Magazine* 1 (January 1830): 718–32.
Eliot, T. S. *Collected Poems: 1909–1962.* London: Faber and Faber, 1963.
Elliott, J. E. "What's 'Post' in Post-Colonial Theory." In *Borderlands: Negotiating Boundaries in Post-Colonial Writing,* edited by Monika Reif-Hülser, 43–53. Amsterdam: Rodopi, 1999.
Emerson, Ralph Waldo. "Editors' Address." *The Massachusetts Quarterly Review* 1, no. 1 (December, 1847): 1–7.
———. "The Editors to the Reader." *The Dial* 1, no. 1 (July 1840): 1–4.
Empson, William. *Seven Types of Ambiguity.* New York: New Directions, 1966.
Engler, Bernd. "Literary Form as Aesthetic Program: The Envoy in English and American Literature." *REAL: The Yearbook of Research in English and American Literature* 7 (1990): 61–97.
Erkkila, Betsy. "Introduction: Breaking Bounds." In *Breaking Bounds: Whitman and American Cultural Studies,* edited by Betsy Erkkila and Jay Grossman, 3–20. Oxford: Oxford University Press, 1996.
———. *Whitman the Political Poet.* New York: Oxford University Press, 1989.
Esar, Evan. *The Humor of Humor.* New York: Horizon Press, 1952.
The Eye of the Poet: Studies in the Reciprocity of the Visual and Literary Arts from the Renaissance to the Present. Edited by Amy Golahny. Lewisburg: Bucknell University Press, 1996.
Facknitz, Mark A. R. "'The Calm,' 'A Small, Good Thing,' and 'Cathedral': Raymond Carver and the Rediscovery of Self Worth." *Studies in Short Fiction* 23 (1986): 287–97.

Felman, Shoshana. *The Literary Speech Act: Don Juan with J. L. Austin, or Seduction in Two Languages.* Translated by Catherine Porter. Ithaca, NY: Cornell University Press, 1983.

Fender, Stephen. *Sea Changes: British Emigration and American Literature.* Cambridge: Cambridge University Press, 1992.

Ferguson, Robert. *Reading the Early Republic.* Cambridge, MA: Harvard University Press, 2004.

———. "'We Hold These Truths: Strategies of Control in the Literature of the Founders.'" In *Reconstructing American Literary History,* edited by Sacvan Bercovitch, 1–28. Harvard English Studies 13. Cambridge, MA: Harvard University Press, 1986.

Fetterley, Judith. "Not in the Least American." In *Nineteenth-Century American Women Writers: A Critical Reader,* edited by Karen L. Kilcup, 15–32. Oxford: Blackwell Publishers, 1998.

Filreis, Alan. *Modernism from Right to Left: Wallace Stevens, the Thirties and Literary Radicalism.* Cambridge: Cambridge University Press, 1994.

———. "What's Historical about Historicism?" *The Wallace Stevens Journal* 28, no. 2 (October 2004): 210–18.

Finley, M. I. *The World of Odysseus.* London: Chatto & Windus, 1956.

Firda, Richard Arthur. "German Philosophy of History and Literature in the *North American Review: 1815–1860.*" *Journal in the History of Ideas* 32, no. 1 (January–March 1971): 133–42.

Fish, Stanley. "Authors-Readers: Jonson's Community of the Same." *Representations* 7 (Summer 1984): 26–58.

———. *Self-Consuming Artifacts: The Experience of Seventeenth-Century Literature.* Berkeley: University of California Press, 1972.

Fisher, Philip. *Still the New World: American Literature in a Culture of Creative Destruction.* Cambridge, MA: Harvard University Press, 1999.

Fishkin, Shelley Fisher. *From Fact to Fiction: Journalism & Imaginative Writing in America.* New York: Oxford University Press, 1985.

Fishwick, Marshall W. "*The Portico* and Literary Nationalism after the War of 1812." *The William and Mary Quarterly* 8, no. 2 (April 1951): 238–45.

Fliegelman, Jay. *Declaring Independence: Jefferson, Natural Language, and the Culture of Performance.* Stanford: Stanford University Press, 1993.

Foley, John Miles. "The Impossibility of Canon." In *Teaching Oral Traditions,* edited by John Miles Foley, 13–33. New York: Modern Language Association, 1998.

———. *The Singer of Tales in Performance.* Indianapolis: Indiana University Press, 1995.

———. *Teaching Oral Traditions.* Edited by John Miles Foley. New York: MLA, 1998.

Frank, Joseph. *The Idea of Spatial Form.* New Brunswick, NJ: Rutgers University Press, 1991.

Franklin, Benjamin. "Marginalia in a Pamphlet by Matthew Wheelock." In *The Papers of Benjamin Franklin,* edited by William B. Willcox, Dorothy W. Bridgwater, Mary L. Hart, Claude A. Lopez, C. A. Myrans, Catherine M. Prelinger, and G. B. Warden. Vol. 17. New Haven, CT: Yale University Press, 1973.

———. "Proposals and Queries to Be Asked the Junto." In *The Papers of Benjamin Franklin,* edited by Leonard W. Labaree, Whitfield J. Bell, Helen C. Boatfield, and Helene H. Fineman. Vol. 1. New Haven: Yale University Press, 1959.

Frederick, John T. "American Literary Nationalism: The Process of Definition, 1825–1850." *The Review of Politics* 21, no. 1, Twentieth Anniversary Issue (January 1959): 224–38.

Fredickson, Robert S. "Public Onanism: Whitman's Song of Himself." *Modern Language Quarterly* 46, no. 2 (1985): 143–60.

French, R. W. "Reading Whitman." *Essays in Literature* 10, no. 1 (April 1983): 71–80.

Fried, Michael. *Art and Objecthood: Essays and Reviews.* Chicago: University of Chicago Press, 1998.
Frost, Robert. *The Poetry of Robert Frost: The Collected Poems, Complete and Unabridged.* Edited by Edward Connery Lathem. New York: Henry Holt and Company, 1969.
Frye, Northrop. *Anatomy of Criticism.* Princeton, NJ: Princeton University Press, 1973.
Fuller, Margaret. "American Literature; Its Position in the Present Time, and Prospects for the Future." In *Papers on Literature and Art.* London: Wiley and Putnam, 1846, part 2, 121–65.
Furia, Philip, and Martin Roth. "Stevens' Fusky Alphabet." *PMLA* 93, no 1 (1978): 66–77.
Furnas, J. C. "Don't Laugh Now." *Esquire* (May 1937): 56, 236–37.
Fussell, Paul. *The Great War and Modern Memory.* New York: Oxford University Press, 2000.
"The Future is Better Than the Past." *The Dial* 2, no. 1 (July 1841): 57–58.
Garber, Marjorie. "'The Rest Is Silence': Ineffability and the 'Unscene' in Shakespeare's Plays." In Hawkins and Schotter, *Ineffability,* 35–50.
Gellner, Ernest. *Nations and Nationalism.* Oxford: Blackwell, 1983.
Gide, André. "The Value of Inconsistency." In *The Modern Tradition: Backgrounds of Modern Literature,* edited by Richard Ellmann and Charles Feidelson, Jr., 699–702. New York: Oxford University Press, 1965.
Gittes, Katherine. *Framing the Canterbury Tales: Chaucer and the Medieval Frame Narrative Tradition.* New York: Greenwood Press, 1991.
Glenn, Kathleen. "Gothic Indecipherability and Doubling in the Fiction of Cristina Fernández Cubas," *Monographic Review/Revista Monográfica* 8 (1992): 125–41.
Goodkin, Richard E. *The Symbolist Home and the Tragic Home: Mallarmé and Oedipus.* Amersterdam and Philadelphia: J. Benjamins Publishing Co., 1984.
Gordis, Lisa. *Opening Scripture: Bible Reading and Interpretive Authority in Puritan New England.* Chicago: University of Chicago Press, 2003.
Gore, Catherine. *Sketches of English Character.* London: Richard Bentley, 1846.
Graves, Robert. *Claudius the God: And His Wife Messalina.* New York: Vintage, 1989.
Gray, Douglas. "Sailing in Another Direction: Some Early New Zealand Writing." In Sampietro, *Declarations of Cultural Independence in the English-Speaking World,* 69–100.
Gray, Francis C. "An Address Pronounced Before the Society of Phi Beta Kappa." *North-American Review* 3, no. 9 (September 1816): 289–305.
Griswold, Rufus Wilmot, ed. *Poets and Poetry of America.* Philadelphia, 1842; 11th ed. 1851.
Gura, Philip. *A Glimpse of Sion's Glory: Puritan Radicalism in New England, 1620–1660.* Middletown, CT: Wesleyan University Press, 1984.
Gustafson, Thomas. *Representative Words: Politics, Literature, and the American Language, 1776–1865.* Cambridge: Cambridge University Press, 1992.
Hall, Stuart. "The Local and the Global: Globalization and Ethnicity." In *Culture, Globalization and the World-System: Contemporary Conditions for the Representation of Identity,* edited by A. D. King, 19–40. Minneapolis: University of Minnesota Press, 1997.
Halliday, Mark. *Stevens and the Interpersonal.* Princeton, NJ: Princeton University Press, 1991.
Hardwick, Elizabeth. "From Bartleby in Manhattan." In *Melville's Short Novels: Authoritative Texts, Contexts, Criticism,* edited by Dan McCall, 257–66. New York: W.W. Norton & Company, 2002.
Harries, Karsten. "Metaphors and Transcendence." In "Special Issue on Metaphor," *Critical Inquiry* 5, no. 1 (Autumn 1978): 71–88.
Harrison, Robert Pogue. "Not Ideas about the Thing but the Thing Itself." *New Literary History* 30, no. 3 (1999): 661–73.

Hartman, James D. *Providence Tales and the Birth of American Literature*. Baltimore: Johns Hopkins University Press, 1999.
Harvey, David. *The Condition of Postmodernity: An Enquiry into the Origins of Cultural Change*. Oxford: Blackwell, 1989.
Hathcock, Nelson. "'The Possibility of Resurrection': Re-Vision in Carver's 'Feathers' and 'Cathedral.'" *Studies in Short Fiction* 28 (1991): 31–39.
Hawkins, Peter S. "Dante's *Paradiso* and the Dialectic of Ineffability." In Hawkins and Schotter, *Ineffability*, 5–22.
Hawkins, Peter S., and Anne Howland Schotter, eds. *Ineffability: Naming the Unnamable from Dante to Beckett*. New York: AMS Press, 1984.
Hawthorne, Nathaniel. "Wakefield." In *Nathaniel Hawthorne: Tales and Sketches*, edited by Roy Harvey Pearce, 290–98. New York: The Library of America, 1982.
———. "A Select Party." *Democratic Review* XV (July 1844): 33–40.
Heimert, Alan, and Andrew Delbanco, eds. *The Puritans in America: A Narrative Anthology*. Cambridge, MA: Harvard University Press, 1985.
Heller, Michael. "Oppen and Stevens: Reflections on the Lyrical and Philosophical." *Sagetrieb* 12, no. 3 (1993): 13–32.
Hemingway, Ernest. *A Farewell to Arms*. London: Arrow, 1994.
———. *For Whom the Bell Tolls*. New York : Charles Scribner's Sons, 1940.
———. *Green Hills of Africa*. London: Vintage, 2004.
———. *The Sun Also Rises*. London : Jonathan Cape, 1927.
Herbert, George. *The Works of George Herbert*. Edited by F. E. Hutchinson. Oxford: Oxford University Press, 1941.
Hickey, Donald R. *The War of 1812: A Forgotten Conflict*. Chicago: University of Illinois Press, 1995.
Hindus, Milton, ed. *Leaves of Grass: One Hundred Years After*. Stanford: Stanford University Press, 1955.
Holland, Laurence B. *The Expense of Vision: Essays on the Craft of Henry James*. Baltimore: Johns Hopkins University Press, 1964.
Hosek, Chaviva M. "The Rhetoric of Whitman's 1855 Preface to *Leaves of Grass*." *Walt Whitman Review* 25 (1979): 163–73.
———. *Lyric Poetry: Beyond New Criticism*. Edited by Hosek and Patricia Parker. Ithaca: Cornell University Press, 1985.
Hulme, Peter. "Including America." *ARIEL: A Review of International English Literature* 26, no. 1 (1995): 117–23.
Hutcheon, Linda. "Response: Truth Telling." *Profession* (1992): Presidential Forum, 18–20.
Hutchinson, John, and Anthony D. Smith, eds. *Nationalism*. Oxford: Oxford University Press, 1994.
"Inchiquen's *Favourable View of the United States*." *Quarterly Review* 10, no. 20 (1814): 494–530.
Ineffability, Naming the Unnamable: From Dante to Beckett. Edited by Peter S. Hawkins and Anne Howland Schotter. New York: AMS Press, 1984.
Innes, Doreen. "Metaphor, Simile, and Allegory as Ornaments of Style." In *Metaphor, Allegory, and the Classical Tradition: Ancient Thought and Modern Revisions*, edited by G. R. Boys-Stones, 7–27. Oxford: Oxford University Press, 2003.
Irving, Pierre. *The Life and Letters of Washington Irving*. Vol. II. New York: G. P. Putnam, 1863.
Irving, Washington. "American Poetry." *The Knickerbocker Magazine* 12, no. 5 (November 1838): 383–88.
———. "Desultory Thoughts on Criticism." *The Knickerbocker Magazine* 14 (August 1839): 175–78.

Isenberg, Charles. *Telling Silence: Russian Frame Narratives of Renunciation.* Evanston, IL: Northwestern University Press, 1993.

James, Henry. *The Figure in the Carpet, and Other Stories.* Edited by Frank Kermode. London: Penguin, 1986.

———. *The American Scene.* Intro. Leon Edel. Bloomington: Indiana University Press, 1968.

James, William. *Principles of Psychology.* Vol. 1. New York: H. Holt and Company, 1890.

Jahn, Manfred. "Frames, Preferences, and the Reading of Third-Person Narratives: Towards a Cognitive Narratology." *Poetics Today* 18, no. 4 (Winter 1997): 441–68.

Jarrell, Randall. *The Woman in the Washington Zoo: Poems & Translations, Selected Poems: including The Woman at the Washington Zoo.* New York: Atheneum, 1966.

Jenkins, Richard. *Rethinking Ethnicity: Arguments and Explorations.* London: Sage, 1997.

Johnson, Barbara. "Melville's Fist: The Execution of *Billy Budd*." In *Deconstruction: Critical Concepts in Literary and Cultural Studies,* edited by Jonathan Culler, vol. 2, 213–43. London: Routledge, 2003.

Johnson, E. W. "American Letters: Their Character and Advancement." *The American Review: A Whig Journal of Politics, Literature, Art and Science* 1, no. 6 (June 1845): 575–80.

Jung, Jacqueline E. "Seeing through Screens: The Gothic Choir Enclosure as Frame." In *Thresholds of the Sacred: Architectural, Art Historical, Liturgical and Theological Perspectives on Religious Screens, East and West,* edited by Sharon Gerstel, 185–213. Washington, DC: Dumbarton Oaks Research Library and Collections, 2006. Distributed by Harvard University Press.

Kaplan, Amy. "'Left Alone with America': The Absence of Empire in the Study of American Culture." In *Cultures of United States Imperialism,* edited by Amy Kaplan and Donald E. Pease, 3–21. Durham, NC: Duke University Press, 1993.

Kaufmann, Eric P. *The Rise and Fall of Anglo-America.* Cambridge, MA: Harvard University Press, 2004.

Kelly, H. A. "*Occupatio* as Negative Narration: A Mistake for Occultatio/Praeteritio." *Modern Philology: A Journal Devoted to Research in Medieval and Modern Literature* 74, no. 3 (February 1977): 311–15.

Kibbey, Ann. *The Interpretation of Material Shapes in Puritanism: A Study of Rhetoric, Prejudice, and Violence.* Cambridge, Cambridge University Press, 1986.

Knight, Janice. *Orthodoxies in Massachusetts: Rereading American Puritanism.* Cambridge, MA: Harvard University Press, 1994.

Kolodny, Annette. *The Land before Her: Fantasy and Experience of the American Frontiers: 1630–1860.* Chapel Hill: University of North Carolina Press, 1984.

Kramer, Michael P. *Imagining Language in America: From the Revolution to the Civil War.* Princeton, NJ: Princeton University Press, 1992.

Kukla, André. *Ineffability and Philosophy.* Routledge Studies in Twentieth Century Philosophy 22. London: Routledge, 2005.

"Lack of Poetry in America." *Harper's New Monthly Magazine* 1 (August 1850): 403–4.

Lakoff, Robin Tolmach. "Some of My Favorite Writers Are Literate: The Mingling of Oral and Literate Strategies in Written Communication." In *Spoken and Written Language: Exploring Orality and Literacy,* edited by Deborah Tannen, 239–60. Advances in Discourse Processes 9. Norwood, NJ: Ablex, 1982.

Larson, Kerry C. *Whitman's Drama of Consensus.* Chicago: University of Chicago Press, 1988.

Leclerc, Georges-Louis, Comte de Buffon. *The Natural History of Animals, Vegetables, and Minerals; with the Theory of the Earth in General.* Translated by W. Kenrick, LL.D. and J. Murdoch. London: Printed for, and sold by, T. Bell, 1775–76.

Lenson, David. *Achilles' Choice: Examples of Modern Tragedy.* Princeton, NJ: Princeton University Press.

Lepore, Jill, *A Is for American: Letters and Other Characters in the Newly United States.* New York: Alfred A. Knopf, 2002.
Levenson, Michael H. *A Genealogy of Modernism: A Study of English Literary Doctrine 1908–1922.* Cambridge: Cambridge University Press, 1984.
Levett, Chistopher. *A Voyage into New England: Begun in 1623. and ended in 1624.* London: William Jones, 1624.
Lewis, C. S. *English Literature in the Sixteenth Century Excluding Drama.* Oxford: Oxford University Press, 1954.
Lloyd-Jones, Sir Hugh. *Greek Epic, Lyric, and Tragedy: The Academic Papers of Sir Hugh Lloyd-Jones.* Oxford: Clarendon Press, 1990.
Longfellow, Henry Wadsworth. "Our Native Writers." *Every Other Saturday* 1 (April 12, 1884): 116.
Longmore, Paul. *The Invention of George Washington.* Berkeley: University of California Press, 1988.
Looby, Christopher. *Voicing America: Language, Literary Form, and the Origins of the United States.* Chicago: University of Chicago Press, 1996.
Lowell, Amy. *Tendencies in Modern American Poetry.* New York: Macmillan, 1917.
Lowell, James Russell. "Nationality in Literature." *The North-American Review* 29, no. 144 (July 1849): 196–216.
Luckin, Bill. "Revisiting the idea of degeneration in urban Britain, 1830–1900." *Urban History* 33, no. 2 (2006): 234–52.
MacPhail, Scott. "Lyric Nationalism: Whitman, American Studies, and the New Criticism." *Texas Studies in Literature and Language* 44, no. 2 (Summer 2002): 133–60.
Mailloux, Steven. *Reception Histories: Rhetoric, Pragmatism, and American Cultural Politics.* Ithaca: Cornell University Press, 1998.
Mancini, Joseph, Jr. "A Hearing Aid for Berryman's *Dream Songs.*" *Modern Language Studies* 10, no. 1 (1979–80): 52–59.
Mariana, Paul L. *God and the Imagination: On Poets, Poetry, and the Ineffable.* Athens: University of Georgia Press, 2002.
Martin, Terence. "The Negative Structures of American Literature." *American Literature* 57, no. 1 (March 1985): 1–22.
———. "Reflections on Jürgen Wolter's 'Metafictional' Discourse in Early American Literature." *Connotations: A Journal for Critical Debate* 4.3 (1994/95): 280–82.
Mathews, Cornelius. "Our Forefathers." *The American Monthly Magazine* 7 (May 1836): 453–56.
———. "Nationality in Literature." *United States Magazine and Democratic Review* 20 (March 1847): 64–73.
McCall, Dan. *The Silence of Bartleby.* Ithaca: Cornell University Press, 1989.
McCloskey, John C. "The Campaign of Periodicals after the War of 1812 for National American Literature." *PMLA* 50, no. 1 (March 1935): 262–73.
McCullogh, David. *1776.* New York: Simon & Schuster, 2006.
McLaren, John. "The Australian Declaration of Independence." In Sampietro, *Declarations of Cultural Independence in the English-Speaking World,* 101–14.
Melville, Herman. "Hawthorne and His Mosses: By a Virginian Spending July in Vermont." *The Literary World: A Journal of Science, Literature and Art* 7 (July–December 1850): 125–27, 145–47.
———. *Moby-Dick.* New York: Macmillan, 1964.
———. *The Piazza Tales and Other Prose Pieces, 1839–1860.* Edited by Harrison Hayford. Chicago: Northwestern University Press, Newberry Library, 1987.
———. *Writings of Herman Melville 5.* Chicago: Northwestern University Press, 1970.
Mencken, H. L. *The American Language: An Inquiry into the Development of English in the United States.* New York: Knopf, 1967.

Miller, James E. *A Critical Guide to Leaves of Grass.* Chicago: University of Chicago Press, 1966.
Miller, Nancy K. "Facts, Pacts, Acts." *Profession* (1992): Presidential Forum, 10–14.
Miller, Perry. *The New England Mind: The Seventeenth Century.* Cambridge, MA: Harvard University Press, 1939.
Miller, Samuel. *A Brief Retrospect.* New York: Printed by T. and J. Swords, 1803.
———. "Nations Lately Become Literary." In *A Brief Retrospect of the Eighteenth Century. Part First; in Two Volumes: Containing a Sketch of the Revolutions and Improvements in Science, Arts, and Literature, during that Period.* Vol. 2 New York: T. and J. Swords, 1803 (1804): 394, 405.
Minter, David L. *The Interpreted Design as a Structural Principle in American Prose.* New Haven: Yale University Press, 1969.
The Mirth of a Nation: America's Great Dialect Humor. Edited by Walter Blair and Raven I. McDavid, Jr. Minneapolis: University of Minnesota Press, 1983.
Morgan, Edmund S. *The Genuine Article: A Historian Looks at Early America.* New York: W. W. Norton & Company, 2004.
Morris, Edmund. *The Rise of Theodore Roosevelt.* New York: Ballantine, 1979.
Morse, Samuel French. "Some Ideas about the Thing Itself." In *Critics on Wallace Stevens,* edited by Peter L. McNamara, 23–30. Coral Gables: University of Miami Press, 1972.
Nairn, Tom. *Faces of Nationalism: Janus Revisited.* London: Verso, 1997.
"National Literature." *The American Monthly Magazine* 1 (September 1829): 379–85.
"Nationality in Literature." *The Democratic Review* 20 (March 1847): 264–72.
Nelles, William. *Frameworks: Narrative Levels and Embedded Narrative.* New York: Peter Lang, 1997.
North-American Review 4, no. 10 (November 1816): 57–68.
Okereke, Augustine. "The Performance and the Text: Parameters for Understanding Oral Literary Performance." In *Across the Lines: Intertextuality and Transcultural Communication in the New Literatures in English,* edited by Wolfgang Klooss, 39–48. Amsterdam: Rodopi, 1998.
"Oldtown Folks." In *The Overland Monthly: Devoted to the Development of the Country,* Vol. III: 390. San Francisco: A. Roman & Company, 1869.
"Original Review." *Analectic Magazine* 1.1, 2nd ed. (1813): 208–26.
The Oxford Book of English Verse: 1250–1918. Edited by Arthur Quiller-Couch. Oxford: Clarendon Press, 1939.
The Oxford Book of Late Medieval Verse and Prose. Edited by Douglas Gray. Oxford: Clarendon Press, 1985.
The Panchatantra. Edited by Johannes Hertel. Cambridge, MA: Harvard University Press, 1908.
Parsons, Theophilus. "Comparative Merits of the Earlier and later English Writers." *The North American Review* 10, n.s. 1 (January 1820): 19–33.
Partridge, Eric. *The 'Shaggy Dog' Story: Its Origin, Development and Nature (with a few seemly examples).* Freeport, NY: Book for Libraries Press, 1953.
Pascal, Blaise. *Pensées.* Translated by W. F. Trotter. New York: P. F. Collier & Son, 1938.
Paton, Alan. *Too Late the Phalarope.* New York: Scribner, 1953.
Pease, Donald E. "New Perspectives on U.S. Culture and Imperialism." In *Cultures of United States Imperialism,* edited by Amy Kaplan and Donald E. Pease, 22–38. Durham, NC: Duke University Press, 1993.
"On Periodical Publications." *The Monthly Magazine and American Review* 1. no. 1 (April 1799): 1–3.
Perloff, Marjorie. "Irony in 'The Rock.'" In *Critics on Wallace Stevens,* edited by Peter L. McNamara, 101–12. Coral Gables: University of Miami Press, 1972.

Perspectives on the Jack Tales and Other North American Märchen. Edited by Carl Lindahl. Bloomington: Indiana University Press, 2002.

Pettit, Norman. "Subjects of the Crown: in Exile: Aliens in a Strange Land." In Sampietro, *Declarations of Cultural Independence in the English-Speaking World,* 23–36.

Pinsky, Robert. "Poetry and American Memory." *The Atlantic Monthly* (October 1999): 60–70.

"Pitkin's Stastical View" and "Pickering's Vocabulary." *North-American Review* 3, no. 9 (September 1816): 345–62.

Poe, Edgar Allan. "Critical Notices: Drake-Halleck." Review of *The Culprit Fay, and Other Poems* by Joseph Rodman Drake and *Alnwick Castle with Other Poems* by Fitz-Greene Halleck. *Southern Literary Messenger* 2, no. 5 (April 1836): 326–40.

———. *The Narrative of Arthur Gordon Pym of Nantucket.* New York: Harper and Brothers, 1838.

Poirier, Richard. *Poetry and Pragmatism.* Cambridge, MA: Harvard University Press, 1992.

The Port Folio, 3, no. 16 (18 April 1807): 241–67.

The Port Folio, n.s., 3, no. 25 (20 June 1807): 385–89.

The Port Folio 3, no. 26 (27 June 1807): 401–2.

The Port Folio, n.s., 4, no. 22 (28 November 1807): 342–46.

The Port Folio, n.s., 4, no. 23 (5 December 1807): 356–57.

Porter, N., Jr. "Prognostics of American Literature." *The American Biblical Repository and Classical Review,* 3rd ser., 3 (July 1847): 504–24.

Pound, Ezra. *Ezra Pound: Selected Poems, 1908–1959.* London: Faber and Faber, 1975.

Powell, Kirsten H. *Fables in Frames: La Fontaine and Visual Culture in Nineteenth-Century France.* New York: Peter Lang, 1997.

"Present American Literature." *The American Monthly Magazine* 1 (June 1829): 187–94.

Price, David A. *Love and Hate in Jamestown: John Smith, Pocahontas, and the Start of a New Nation.* New York: Vintage, 2003.

Price, Kenneth M., ed. *Walt Whitman: The Contemporary Reviews.* American Critical Archives 9. New York: Cambridge University Press, 1996.

"The Profession of Authorship." *The American Monthly Magazine* 1 (December 1829): 589–98.

Quilligan, Maureen. "Milton's Spenser: The Inheritance of Ineffability." In Hawkins and Schotter, *Ineffability,* 65–79.

Railton, Stephen. "The Address of *The Scarlet Letter.*" In *Readers in History: Nineteenth-Century American Literature and the Contexts of Response,* edited by James L. Machor, 138–63. Baltimore: Johns Hopkins University Press, 1993.

———. *Authorship and Audience: Literary Performance in the American Renaissance.* Princeton, NJ: Princeton University Press, 1991.

Read, Allen Walker. "British Recognition of American Speech in the Eighteenth Century." *Dialect Notes* 6, part 6 (1933): 313–34.

Readers in History: Nineteenth-Century American Literature and the Contexts of Response. Edited by James L. Machor. Baltimore: Johns Hopkins University Press, 1993.

Reaver, J. Russell. "From Reality to Fantasy: Opening-Closing Formulas in the Structures of American Tall Tales." *Southern Folklore Quarterly* 36, no. 4 (1972): 369–82.

Reid, Margaret. *Cultural Secrets as Narrative Form: Storytelling in Nineteenth-Century America.* Columbus: The Ohio State University Press, 2004.

Reynolds, David S. *Beneath the American Renaissance: The Subversive Imagination in the Age of Emerson and Melville.* Cambridge, MA: Harvard University Press, 1988.

Richards, Jeffrey. "Revolution, Domestic Life, and the End of 'Common Mercy' in Crèvecoeur's 'Landscapes.'" *William and Mary Quarterly,* 3rd ser., 55, no. 2 (April 1998): 281–96.

Ricoeur, Paul. *Time and Narrative.* Translated by Kathleen McLaughlin and David Pellauer. Chicago: University of Chicago Press, 1990.

Riddel, Joseph N. "The Contours of Stevens Criticism." In *The Act of the Mind: Essays on the Poetry of Wallace Stevens,* edited by J. Hillis Miller and Roy Harvey Pearce, 243–76. Baltimore: The Johns Hopkins Press, 1965.

Rigal, Laura. "In the Eye of the Pyramid: Geographic Enterprise from John Smith to America Incorporated." *American Literary History* 15, no. 4 (2003): 793–808.

Rourke, Constance. *American Humor: A Study of the National Character.* New York: Doubleday & Company, 1931.

Sampietro, Luigi, ed. *The Declarations of Cultural Independence in the English-Speaking World: A Symposium: Università degli Studi di Milano.* Novara, Italy: D'Imperio, 1989.

Scanlon, Larry. *Narrative, Authority, and Power: The Medieval Exemplum and the Chaucerian Tradition.* Cambridge: Cambridge University Press, 1994.

Scarry, Elaine. *The Body in Pain: The Making and Unmaking of the World.* New York: Oxford University Press, 1985.

Scharfstein, Ben-Ami. *Ineffability: The Failure of Words in Philosophy and Religion.* Albany: State University of New York, 1993.

Scheidley, Harlow W. "Passing the Federalist Torch." *The William and Mary Quarterly* 59, no. 4 (October 2002): 1034–36.

Schotter, Anne Howland. "Vernacular Style and the Word of God: The Incarnational Art of *Pearl.*" In Hawkins and Schotter, *Ineffability,* 23–34.

Schwarz, Daniel R. *Narrative and Representation in the Poetry of Wallace Stevens: 'A Tune beyond Us, Yet Ourselves.'* London: St. Martin's Press, 1993.

Schwenger, Peter. *Fantasm and Fiction: On Textual Envisioning.* Stanford: Stanford University Press, 1999.

"Sculpture and Sculptors in the United States." *The American Monthly Magazine* 1, no. 2 (May 1829): 124–31.

Shakespeare, William. *King Lear.* In *The Riverside Shakespeare.* Boston: Houghton Mifflin, 1974.

Shryock, Richard. *Tales of Storytelling: Embedded Narrative in Modern French Fiction.* New York: Peter Lang, 1993.

Sidewalks of America: Folklore, Legends, Sagas, Traditions, Customs, Songs, Stories and Sayings of City Folk. Edited by B. A. Botkin. New York: The Bobbs-Merrill Company, Inc., 1954.

Simpson, David. *The Politics of American English, 1776–1850.* New York: Oxford University Press, 1986.

Singer, Alan. *Aesthetic Reason: Artworks and the Deliberative Ethos.* University Park: Pennsylvania State University Press, 2003.

Singh, Amritjit, and Peter Schmidt. "On the Borders between U.S. Studies and Postcolonial Theory." In *Postcolonial Theory and the United States: Race, Ethnicity, and Literature,* edited by Amritjit Singh and Peter Schmidt, 3–69. Jackson: University Press of Mississippi, 2000.

Smith, Anthony D. *Nationalism and Modernism: A Critical Survey of Recent Theories of Nations and Nationality.* London: Routledge, 1998.

Smith, Ernest J. "John Berryman's 'Programmatic' for *The Dream Songs* and an Instance of Revision." *Journal of Modern Literature* 23, nos. 3–4 (Summer 2000): 429–39.

Smith, Sidney. "America." *Edinburgh Review* 33 (January 1820): 69–80.

Smith-Rosenberg, Carroll. "Surrogate Americans: Masculinity, Masquerade, and the Formation of a National Identity." *PMLA* 119, no. 5 (October 2004): 1325–35.

"Some Furthur Account of Peter Rugg The Missing Man Late of Boston, New-England," *New-England Galaxy* IX, no. 364 (Friday, September 1, 1826): 1–4.

Spencer, Benjamin T. "A National Literature, 1837–1855." *American Literature* 8, no. 2 (May 1936): 125–57.
Spencer, Philip, and Howard Wollman. *Nationalism: A Critical Introduction*. London: Sage, 2002.
Spengemann, William C. *A New World of Words: Redefining Early American Literature*. New Haven: Yale University Press, 1994.
Spenser, Edmund. *The Faerie Queene*. London: George Routledge, Ryder's Court, 1843.
Spurr, David. *Conflicts in Consciousness: T. S. Eliot's Poetry and Criticism*. Urbana: University of Illinois Press, 1984.
"A Statistical View of the Commerce of the United States of America." *North-American Review* 3, no. 9 (September 1816): 345–54.
Stein, Gertrude. *The Making of Americans: Being a History of a Family's Progress*. Normal, IL: Dalkey Archive Press, 1995.
Steiner George. *Language and Silence: Essays on Language, Literature, and the Inhuman*. New Haven: Yale University Press, 1998.
Stevens, Wallace. *The Collected Poems of Wallace Stevens*. New York: Vintage, 1982.
Streeter, Robert E. "Association Psychology and Literary Nationalism in the *North American Review*, 1815–1825." *American Literature* 17, no. 3 (November 1945): 243–54.
Swanson, Don R. "Toward a Psychology of Metaphor." In *On Metaphor*, edited by Sheldon Sacks, 161–64. Chicago: University of Chicago Press, 1979.
Symons, Dana M. "A Complaynte of a Lovers Lyfe." In *Chaucerian Dream Visions and Complaints*, edited by Dana M. Symons, 71–147. Kalamazoo, MI: Medieval Institute Publications, College of Arts & Sciences, Western Michigan University, 2004.
Tang, Edward. "Making Declarations of Her Own: Harriet Beecher Stowe as New England Historian." *The New England Quarterly* 71, no. 1 (March 1998): 77–96.
Tannen, Deborah, ed. *Coherence in Spoken and Written Discourse*. Advances in Discourse Processes 12. Norwood, NJ: Ablex, 1984.
Tanner, Tony. *City of Words: American Fiction 1950–1970*. London: Jonathan Cape, 1971.
Tompkins, Joanne. "'The Story of Rehearsal Never Ends': Rehearsal, Performance, Identity in Settler Culture Drama." *Canadian Literature* 144 (Spring 1995): 142–61.
Tonkin, Elizabeth. *Narrating Our Pasts: The Social Construction of Oral History*, Cambridge Studies in Oral and Literate Culture 22, edited by Peter Burke and Ruth Finnegan. Cambridge: Cambridge University Press, 1992.
Tucker, George. "On American Literature." In *Essays by a Citizen of Virginia: Essays on Various Subjects of Taste, Morals, and National Policy by a Citizen of Virginia*, 41–66. Georgetown, DC: Published by Joseph Milligan; Jacob Gideon, Junior, Printer, Washington, 1822.
———. "On the Future Destiny of the United States." In *Essays by a Citizen of Virginia: Essays on Various Subjects of Taste, Morals, and National Policy by a Citizen of Virginia*, 1–24.
Tyler, Royall. *The Algerian Captive, or, The Life and Adventures of Doctor Updike Underhill: Six Years a Prisoner Among the Algerine*. New York: Modern Library, 2002.
Vaughn, William. "Moving from Privacy: 'Bartleby' and Otherness." *Centennial Review* 43, no. 3 (1999): 535–64.
Vendler, Helen. *Poets Thinking: Pope, Whitman, Dickinson, Yeats*. Cambridge, MA: Harvard University Press, 2004.
———. "The Qualified Assertions of Wallace Stevens." In *The Act of the Mind: Essays on the Poetry of Wallace Stevens*, edited by J. Hillis Miller and Roy Harvey Pearce, 163–78. Baltimore: The Johns Hopkins Press, 1965.
Virtanen, Reino. "Tocqueville and William Ellery Channing." *American Literature* 22, no. 1 (March 1950): 21–28.
Wald, Priscilla. *Constituting Americas: Cultural Anxiety and Narrative Form*. Durham: Duke University Press, 1995.

Warren, James Perrin. *Walt Whitman's Language Experiment*. University Park: Pennsylvania State University Press, 1990.
Watts, Ann Chalmers. "*Pearl,* Inexpressibility, and Poems of Human Loss." *PMLA* 99, no. 1 (1984): 26–40.
Webster, Noah. *An American Dictionary of the English Language*. New York: Converse, 1828.
———. *Dissertations on the English Language with Notes, Historical and Critical, to Which Is Added, by way of Appendix, an Essay on a Reformed Mode of Spelling with Dr. Franklin's Arguments on that Subject*. Gainesville, FL: Scholars' Facsimiles and Reprints, 1951.
———. *Sketches of American Policy*. Hartford, CT: Hudson and Goodwin, 1785.
Weisbuch, Robert. *Atlantic Double Cross*. Chicago: University of Chicago Press, 1986.
Welsch, Roger L. "Of Light Bulbs and Shaggy Dogs." *Natural History* 102, no. 2 (1993): 20–25.
Welsh, Andrew. *Roots of Lyric: Primitive Poetry and Modern Poetics*. Princeton, NJ: Princeton University Press, 2978.
Wharton, G. M. "Literary Property." *The North American Review* 52, no. 111 (April 1841): 385–404.
Whitaker, Thomas R. "Some Reflections on 'Text' and 'Performance.'" *The Yale Journal of Criticism* 3, no. 1 (Fall 1989): 142–61.
Whitman, Walt. *Walt Whitman: Complete Poetry and Collected Prose*. New York: Library of America, 1982.
Wilde, Oscar. "The Gospel According to Walt Whitman." In Price, *Walt Whitman,* 318–21.
Willard, Sidney. "A Vocabulary, or Collection of Words and Phrases Which Have Been Supposed to Be Peculiar to the United States of America." Review of the book so entitled by John Pickering. *North-American Review* 3, no. 9 (September 1816): 355–62.
Williams, William Carlos. "An Essay on *Leaves of Grass.*" In *Leaves of Grass: One Hundred Years After,* edited by Milton Hindus, 21–31. Palo Alto, CA: Stanford University Press, 1955.
Willis, N. P. "To The Public (the Editor's Preface)." *American Monthly Magazine* 1 (1829): iii–iv.
Wolfreys, Julian, ed. *The J. Hillis Miller Reader*. Stanford: Stanford University Press, 2005.
Wolter, Jürgen. "'Novels are... the most dangerous kind of reading': Metafictional Discourse in Early American Literature." *Connotations: A Journal for Critical Debate* 4, nos. 1–2 (1994/95): 67–82.
Wonham, Henry B. *Mark Twain and the Art of the Tall Tale*. New York: Oxford University Press, 1993.
Wood, Gordon S. "Creating the Revolution." *The New York Review of Books* 50, no 2 (February 13, 2003): 38–41.
Wu, Duncan, ed. *Old and Middle English Poetry:* based on *Old and Middle English: An Anthology,* edited by Elaine Treharne. Oxford: Blackwell, 2002.
Xiques, Donez. "Whitman's Catalogues and the Preface to *Leaves of Grass.*" *Walt Whitman Review* 23 (1977): 68–76.
Yeats, W. B. *Mythologies*. London: Macmillan, 1959.

Index

A

Abrams, M. H.: inexpressible's spread into the absurd, 47
Adams, Henry: metaphor of a pencil or pen and, 48
Addison, Joseph: newer view of the ineffable and, 46
Adorno, Theodor W.: on Beckett's *Endgame,* 88
Alighieri, Dante: the topos and, 37; silences and, 136n14; truth outside human time and space, 40
The American Language (Mencken), 5
The American Review: measuring ourselves by ourselves and, 72; "a rock or two" and, 109; overlap of language and, 5; precise prophecy and, 63
The American Whig Review: on Nature, 117
American Monthly Magazine: equality with British magazines and, 74; on British personality, 79
American Review: on the task before America, 104
Ames, Fisher: achievement of "genius" and, 17; constrictions of imitation and, 25–26; despairing discourse of, 33; on aspects of genius and, 11, 18; rhetoric of "genius" and, 64
Anderson, Benedict: distinguishing communities and, 125n46; imagined community and, 70–71; language-of-power and, 14; linguistic action and founding of nation, 124n31
"The Ant and the Grasshopper" (Maugham), 101
Appleby, Joyce: importance of readers and, 14
Arabic framing, 134n1
Aristotle: definition of "character," 140n79

Astor, John Jacob, 99
Augustine, Saint, 87; intersection of the ineffable and religion and, 36; on fallen word and the ineffable, 52; truth outside human time and space, 40
"The Augustinian Strain of Piety" (Miller), 132n32
Austin, J. L.: doctrine of the performative/constative distinction, 138n50; Felman's work on, 62

B

Bailyn, Bernard: on re-formation of structure of public authority, 4
"Bartleby, the Scrivener" (Melville), 90–98; 101; 146n78; 147n91
"The Beast in the Jungle" (James), 50
Benjamin, Walter: "afterlife" and, 76–77
Bercovitch, Sacvan: Puritans' trust in a divine plan of progress, 41; rhetorical synthesis of man's time and God's, 41
Berryman, John: "damned serious humour" and, 76; dead serious humor and, 78
Bezeczky, Gabór: literal meaning and, 77
Bhabha, Homi: joining writing to an idea of nation, 14
Blair, Walter: shaggy dog stories and, 144n41
Bloom, Clive: the struggle with structure, 112
Bloom, Harold: Whitman as Center of the American Canon and, 19; commodity in which poets deal and, 117; essay on Whitman, 20; "Stevens antithetically completes Whitman" and, 118; strategies of reduction and, 117; tell-tale "self-consciousness" and, 116
Blunden, Edmund: World War I poet, 53
Booth, Stephen: human experience of "indefinition," 50
Borneman, Walter R.: on Battle of New Orleans, 12; on War of 1812, 12
Boucher, Jonathan: self-consciousness of American language and, 21
Bové, Paul A.: impossibility of defending 'truth' and, 112; Preface of 1855 and, 126n64, 126n68

Brackenridge, Hugh Henry: "ambiguous voice" and, 149n20; Modern Chivalry and, 107; "unmeaning phrases" and, 107, 119
Bradshaw, Henry: framing and, 50–51
Bradstreet, Anne: "America's first poet" and, 77
Breaking Bounds (Erkkila), 20
Britton, Celia: self-representation and, 26
Brogan, Jacqueline: on Stevens's "Thing Itself," 111
Brown, Charles Brockden: achievement of "genius" and, 17; defensiveness and, 63; footnotes, lengthy introductions and, 141n86; "incurable case of continuity" and, 117; interpretation of Rousseau and, 86; "The Rhapsodist" and, 67–69, 107; use of the word enlightened and, 16; verb tenses to represent an impasse and, 68
Brownson, Orestes A.: feelings of inferiority and, 23
Brunvand, Jan Harold: "insider" and "outsider" positions, 84–85; problematic nature of shaggy dog jokes, 147n104; shaggy dog stories, 85, 93, 129n90

C

Cahill, Edward: on Fisher Ames, 17; situation of Whigs and, 125n44
Camus, Albert: existential philosophy of, 47
"Can be hope a cloak?" (Berryman), 80, 82
Carne-Ross, Donald: notion of an original text and, 77
Carver, Raymond: "Cathedral" and, 88, 100, 101; nihilism and, 148n106
Channing, Edward: act of writing and, 30–31; notion of "imitation" and, 76–77; passage on rudeness and, 73, 76; plans to quash English influences and, 64
Channing, Walter: anxiety of, 70; discourse of, 33; doubling of English language and, 10; "incurable case of continuity" and, 117; literary originality and, 60, 62; literature as product of

national language, 19; on candidates for literary distinction, 61; on overlapping language, 6; 30; oral perspectives and inexpressibility and, 86; perceived inadequacy in expression and, 1; view of Indians and their language, 30–31

Channing, William Ellery: America's "moral and intellectual power" and, 21; on "condition of our literature," 130n2; on institutions and, 109

Chaucer, Geoffrey, 87; choral narrator and, 51–52; describing beauty in king's daughter, 34; dream visions and, 54; expressing God and, 33; trope of humility in *Troilus and Criseyde,* 37

choice: self-persuasion and, 2–4

The Christian Examiner: on institutions and, 109

Cobbett, William: on rudeness, 73–74

Cohen, Ted: dead metaphors and, 92; "shared awareness" among a "close community" and, 69; "special invitation" and, 29

Coles, Harry L.: on War of 1812, 123n25

Consolation of Philosophy (Boethius), 51

Cooper, James Fenimore: footnotes, lengthy introductions and, 141n86

Cotton, John: synthesis of time and, 41

Covici, Jr., Pascal: on writing humor, 78

Crane, Mary Thomas: history of "frame" in lyric, 127n71

Crawford, Robert: on poetry of Eliot and Pound, 107

"The Creations of Sound" (Stevens), 112

Cressy, David: American exceptionalism and, 5; colonists referring to themselves as "the English" and, 122n1; on controlling the flow of opinion, 15; readjustment of point of view and, 22–23; rhetoric of promotion and, 2; rhetoric of unreachable perfectibility, 148n4; state of insufficiency and, 137n39

Curtius, Ernst Robert: topos and, 35

D

Dana, Charles A.: on Whitman's message, 20

Dana, Sr., Richard Henry: on missing authors and false starts toward them, 42

Davidoff, Judith M.: framing fictions of the Middle Ages, 90, 134n1

Davidson, Cathy N.: postcolonialism in promoting American studies, 128n83, 130n100

Davis, Todd F.: reader as both participant and judge, 90–91

Day, Henry N.: on break with the classical, 14

dead metaphors: Bartleby and, 95–96; definition of, 92

defensive self-perception: self-same, English-language exclusion and, 136n21

Delbanco, Andrew: American exceptionalism and, 5

de Man, Paul: pulling back from narrative and, 97

The Democratic Review: on retaining language and, 59; self-conscious concern with progress and, 105

Dennie, Joseph; literary relations and, 63

Derrida, Jacques: on Declaration of Independence, 62

Desmarais, Jane: understanding of Bartleby and, 147n91

"Desultory Thoughts on Criticism" (Irving), 87

Dewey, Ariane: tall tales and, 94

The Dictionary of the American Language (Webster), 14

Dissertations on the English Language (Webster), 61

Donne, John: 1628 sermon and, 131n24

Donoghue, Denis: on Eliot and emotion, 106

The Dream Songs (Berryman), 79

Dryden, John: imitation and, 76–77

Dunlap, William: deviation from what audiences remember, 109; fear of "typing" and, 109; rhetorical patterns of framing and, 110

Duyckinck, Evert: on Author's employment, 84

E

Eliot, T. S., 87; "The Love Song of J.

Alfred Prufrock," 106; "The Waste Land" and, 105–6
Emerson, Ralph Waldo: territorial climate of lament and, 75
Endgame (Beckett), 88
Erkkila, Betsy: on Whitman's style, 20
"Essay on American Language and Literature" (Channing), 60
European Literature and the Latin Middle Ages (Curtius), 35
An Examination (Dennie), 63

F

The Faerie Queene (Spenser), 40
A Farewell to Arms (Hemingway), 130n7
Felman, Shoshana: work on J. L. Austin, 62
Fender, Stephen: American exceptionalism and, 5; "beneficent negative catalog" and, 137n39; cognitive work of metaphor, 29; literature of initiation and, 136n28; on rhetoric and choice, 3; on T. S. Eliot, 148n6; preoccupation with national character and, 127n76; self-debate and, 122n3; turning cultural loss to advantage, 18
Ferguson, Robert: style of foundational papers and, 21; substantiating forms and, 63; text-oriented cultures and, 129n97
Fetterley, Judith: act of naming and, 108
"The Figure in the Carpet" (James), 90
Filreis, Alan: pronouns in Stevens and, 112; on Stevens, 150n38
Fisher, Philip: description of Whitman and, 19; relating "Song of Myself" to Constitution, 125n53
Fish, Stanley: self-consuming artifacts" and, 38; Anglican sermons and, 131n30; on Donne's sermons, 39; on modes of action, 38–39; "self-identifying community" and, 70
Foley, John Miles: evocation of oral tradition and, 97; tradition of reception and, 102
framing: two parts and, 54–55; narrative and, 119; "improper naming" and, 92; ineffability topos and, 35; Middle Ages and, 52; "missing" authors and, 108; overview of, 49–50; "perfect" poet and, 55–56; preoccupation with originality and, 65; recasting and, 67–69; redirected time frames and, 58; search in frames for human wisdom, 134n1; Stevens and analogic world, 112; "thing itself" and, 106; topos of the inexpressible, 54; traditionally editorial use of, 136n19; Whitman's time frames and, 57; written discourse and, 76
Framing Authority (Crane), 136n19
Frankenstein (Shelley), 50
Frank, Joseph: on Eliot's *The Waste Land*, 105–6
Franklin, Benjamin: as printer-journalist, 14; perfection of oneself and, 46; unobtainable "perfection" and, 45
Fried, Michael, 105; "Authenticity" in the modern period, 105; "presentness" and, 91–92
Frost, Robert, 47–48, 110
Frye, Northrop: creative processes and, 99
Fuller, Margaret: on Great Britain's "insular position," 118
Furnas, J. C.: shaggy dog stories and, 127n78, 129n90

G

Garber, Marjorie: praise and wonder, 37; wonder and Shakespearean audience, 38
Gellner, Ernest: production or narration of nation, 15
Gide, André: "giving oneself away" and, 87; on inconsistency and, 87
"Good-bye, / Mrs. Pappadopoulos, and thanks" (Stevens), 116
Gore, Catherine: play with plurality and, 46
Graves, Robert: history surrounding the term "occupatio" and, 130n4
Gray, David: New Zealanders and, 122n4
Gray, Francis C.: unifies language with nation and, 13
Great Expectations (Dickens), 98
Green Hills of Africa (Hemingway), 137n38

INDEX

H

Hakluyts, Richard: promotional writings of, 18
Halliday, Mark: interactive power of Stevens and, 151n49
Hall, Stuart: production or narration of nation, 15
Hardwick, Elizabeth: on Bartleby and, 98
Harper's Monthly Magazine: American shortcomings and, 104; on Americans and poetry, 11
Harries, Karsten: refusal of metaphor and, 92
Harrison, Robert Pogue: craving for the thing itself and, 103; on Steven's poetry, 104; "Thing Itself" and, 103
Hawkins, Peter S.: on writings of St. Augustine, 36
Hawthorne, Nathaniel: formal labyrinths of, 101; narrator of "Wakefield" and, 68, 88, 90
Heller, Michael: critical reception of Stevens and, 150n38; on Stevens's poetry, 111
Hemingway, Ernest: *A Farewell to Arms,* 130n7; on English colonials, 61; topoi and, 35
Herbert, George: "The Flower" and, 40
Hickey, Donald R.: on gains made after war, 13; on War of 1812, 12
Histoire Naturelle (de Buffon), 30
Hobbes, Thomas: ordered language and ordered state and, 123n11
Hoccleve, Thomas, 54
Holocaust: topos of the inexpressible and, 5
"Homage to Mistress Bradstreet" (Berryman), 77–78, 80, 82, 101
Hulme, Peter: inclusion of America and "postcolonial," 128n83

I

"The Idea of Order at Key West" (Stevens), 112
Iliad: praising leaders or rulers and, 34
inexpressibility, 2, 6, 42; and Whitman's "imaginative literature," 43; attempts to ascertain the future and, 64; discourse of inadequacy and, 31; definition of adequacy and, 15–16; discourse of same-language and, 45; Donne's 1628 sermon and, 131n24; framing and, 49–50, 108; historical fissure of the ineffable, 42; historical genres and, 19; "just such" and, 73; *Life Illustrated* article, 20; of unsuitable sentences and, 45; perfectibility and, 70–71; propensity for hyperbole of discovery and, 3; Puritan perspectives and, 132n34; received languages and, 71; religious and choral roots of, 148n4; self-distancing English and, 47; shaggy dog dead-serious humor and, 86; spontaneous discourse and, 76; tall tales and, 84; time and, 24–25; topos of the inexpressible, 33, 47–48; verb tense and, 24–26
Innes, Doreen: dead metaphors and, 92; "safe" metaphors and, 145n67
Irving, Washington: patience and, 55; criticism of national literature, 87; framing and, 141n86; on absence of a national poetry, 22
Irwin, Bonnie D.: frame tales and, 102
Isenberg, Charles: framing and, 107, 110

J

Jackson, Andrew: Battle of New Orleans and, 12
Jahn, Manfred: frames and textual data, 58
James, Henry: "The Figure in the Carpet" and, 90; Roosevelt's reaction to, 10; "The Turn of the Screw" and, 101
James, William: nature of consciousness and, 105
Jan Brunvand: no-point shaggy dog stories, 28–29
Jarrell, Randall: choral figures and framing, 53
Jenkins, Richard: ethnicity and collective identity, 15
Johnson, Barbara: analysis of *Billy Budd,* 137n30; "irremediable human pluralism" and, 142n94; oscillations within text of *Billy Budd,* 141n92

Johnson, Richard M.: on ties to Great Britain, 13
Johnson, E. W.: on original literature, 60
"Jouga" (Stevens), 114
Judd, Sylvester: *Margaret: A Tale of the Real and the Ideal,* 94
Jung, Jacqueline E.: choral function and, 135n1

K

Kaplan, Amy: idea of empire and American studies, 128n83
Kibbey, Ann: Puritans' use of metaphor and, 132n34
The Knickerbocker Magazine: traditions and, 75; linking literature to intimations of the oral, 75; speaking the language of literature and, 61
Kolodny, Annette: fantasies of men and the New World, 138n39
Kramer, Michael P.: Whitman's denial as mode of contestation, 127n68
Kukla, André: "Bartleby" and, 97; category of ineffability and, 135n24; expressing an inexpressible and, 104; five categories of ineffability and, 133n38; inability of expression and, 99; intersection of mathematics and, 131n11; "new taxonomy" for the ineffable and, 42–43; new strategies and, 42–44; new taxonomy of, 45; power of language, 36; "unselectability" and, 56

L

Lakoff, Robin Tolmach: written frames and, 74–75
Leaves of Grass: final design and desire of (Erkkila), 20
Leaves of Grass (Whitman), 6, 89–90, 126n64
Lenson, David: choral roots and, 51
Levenson, Michael: humanism in modernist thought, 105
Levett, Christopher: observations of bounty and, 2
Lewis, C. S., 35; on rhetoric, 35
Life Illustrated: inexpressibility and, 20

Longfellow, Henry Wadsworth: dead end of originality and, 66; on poetry, 62
Longmore, Paul: Washington's self-conscious development and English ideals, 124n35
Looby, Christopher: sense of nation fabrication and, 30
"The Love Song of J. Alfred Prufrock" (Eliot), 106–7
Lowell, Amy: universalism and, 118; on sudden change and, 119
Lowell, James Russell: America's "social organization" and, 81; call for a new language and, 73; possibility of exclusion and, 81
Luckin, Bill: "racially tinged urban tribalism" and, 129n95

M

Madison, James: on War of 1812, 12
Major André (Dunlap), 110
The Making of Americans (Stein), 110
"Man Carrying Thing" (Stevens), 115
Mancini, Jr., Joseph: on Berryman's poetry, 82
Margaret (Judd), 94
Martin, Terence: "The Negative Structures of American Literature" (Martin), 94; rhetorical achievement of "absence" and, 94
The Massachusetts Quarterly Review: on material organizations and, 88
Maugham, Somerset: "The Ant and the Grasshopper," 101
McCloskey, John C.: on triumphs in War of 1812, 12
McLaren, John: "The Australian Declaration of Independence," 122n4
Melville, Herman: "Bartleby" and, 90–91; lengthy introductions and, 141n86; future animating the present and, 63; imported influence and, 65; national dare and, 79–80; on being finite on infinite subjects, 6; rhetoric of the inexpressible frames and, 110
Mencken, H. L.: popular speech and Whitman, 129n89; "surviving differences," 121n8 and; *The American Language* and, 5

metaphor: "improper naming" and, 92
Miller, Nancy K.: autobiographical impulse and, 144n48; "truth effect" and, 39
Miller, Perry: on space between revelation and inconceivable, 42; Puritan perspectives on inexpressibility, 132n34; reaching truth through language, 41
Miller, Samuel: ingenuity of America and, 63; progress of American Literature and, 109; rhetoric of insufficiency and, 61; want of leisure and, 67
Milton, John: concern for the audience's role and, 38
Minter, David L.: work on "interpreted design," 127n75
Modern Chivalry (Brackenridge), 107
The Monthly Magazine and American Review: letter to editor, 16
Morgan, Edmund S.: on George Washington, 14–15; quest for originality and, 140n72
Morris, Edmund: on Roosevelt's reaction to James, 10
Morse, Samuel French: on Stevens's poetry, 150n46

N

Nairn, Tom: production or narration of nation and, 15
naturalists: degeneration and relocation, 129n95
"The Negative Structures of American Literature" (Martin), 94
The New American Review: perceived deficiencies of originality and, 60
New England, or a Briefe Enarration of the Ayre (Morrell), 23
Norman, Liane: reader as both participant and judge, 90–91
The North American Review: national self-consciousness and, 105; on American letters, 137n37; entitlement and, 13; origin of poetry and, 75; review of Pickering's book, 10; use of the word "character" and, 140n79
'Not Ideas about the Thing but the Thing Itself' (Stevens), 111–12

O

"Ode to a Nightingale" (Keats), 47
Okereke, Augustine: indisputable "communicative competence," 95; oral performance and, 89
On Christian Doctrine (St. Augustine), 52
"The Oven Bird" (Frost), 47–48
Owen, Wilfred: World War I poet, 53

P

Paradise Lost (Milton), 38
Paradiso (Alighieri), 37
Parsons, Theophilus: comments on best authors, 64; creating a national literature and, 57–58; oral perspectives and inexpressibility and, 86
Partridge, Eric: "cosy human" touches and shaggy dogs, 95, 100, 115; non sequitur and Bartleby, 93; tall tales and, 86
Pascal, Blaise: intellect and, 63
Paton, Alan: *Too Late the Phalarope,* 101
Pettit, Norman: on emerging American "voices" and, 122n1; on founders of New England and, 9
Pickering, John: book review in *North American Review,* 10
Pilgrim's Progress: binary frames and, 52
Pilgrim's Progress (Bunyan), 35
Pinsky, Robert: on acting together, 15
Poe, Edgar Allan: subserviency and, 68
"The Poem That Took the Place of a Mountain" (Stevens), 112–13, 115
poetry: original expression and, 61–62; commodity and, 117; "The Future is Better Than the Past," 102; implicit narratives and, 113; National Poetic Literature and, 110; native American poets and, 69; on Eliot and Pound, 107; origin of, 75; self-reflexive poems and, 114; strategies of reduction and, 117
Poets Thinking: Vendler on Whitman, 20
Poirier, Richard: "Emersonian pragmatism" and, 149n15; studies on the "vague" and, 144n51; transparency and, 47
The Port Folio: rhetorical question and, 128n85; fear of naming wrong author

176   INDEX

and, 108; focus on youth and, 27; intimate connection with Europe and, 89; literary criticism and, 120; national literary journal, 14; on American mannerlessness, 73; on being latecomers and, 104; rhetoric twists and, 26; classical learning and, 139n64; "character" and, 140n79

Porter, Jr., N.: dream of the American language, 61

The Portico: literary journal, 14

Pound, Ezra: Crawford's writing on, 107; topos of the inexpressible and, 104

Powell, Kirsten H.: visual frames for literary texts and, 135n1

Preface of 1855: adaptation in, 49–50; defensive posturing in, 28–29; "double" voicing and, 33; disclaimers in, 30; point of view and, 29; recasts leisure to advantage and, 67; resonances of youth and, 27. See also Whitman, Walt

public authority: anxiety of separation and, 4–5; re-formation of the structure of, 4–5

Q

Quilligan, Maureen: *Paradise Lost* and, 38

R

Railton, Stephen: "rhetorical stance and strategy" and, 69

"Re-Statement of Romance" (Stevens), 114

Reaver, J. Russell: vertical vertigo of story structure and, 94

recasting: strategies of, 67–69

Reynolds, David S.: plot in "Bartleby" and, 146n78

Richards, Jeffrey: personal and familial independence and, 133n41

Riddel, Joseph: on Stevens's poetry, 110–11

"The Rime of the Ancient Mariner" (Coleridge), 50

Roosevelt, Theodore: denunciation of writers and, 10

Rosenberg, Isaac: World War I poet, 53

Rousseau, Jean-Jacques: Brown and, 86

rudeness: asset of character and, 76; "just such" and, 76; overview of, 73–74

S

Sartre, Jean-Paul: existential philosophy of, 47

Sassoon, Siegfried: World War I poet, 53

The Scarlet Letter: as "rhetorical project," 69

Scarry, Elaine: "The Inexpressibility of Physical Pain," 52

Scharfstein, Ben-Ami: on Buddhist philosophy and, 36

Schotter, Anne Howland: action of admonishing and, 36; human capacities to express wonder and, 37; Pearl-poet and, 37

Schwarz, Daniel R.: implicit narrative and poetry, 113

"Seeing through Screens" (Jung), 135n1

self-persuasion: as matter of perception and opportunism, 4

sermons: truth in language and, 40–41; Donne's 1628 sermon, 131n24; prevailing pattern or strategy of, 39–40

shaggy dog stories: 98, 127n78, 129n90; performance and, 100–101; "dialect humor" and, 143n41; generating consensus and, 86; humor in Stevens's poems and, 115; oral strategies of framing and, 119; origins of, 147n104; overview of, 84; types of, 144n44; typical story and, 95

Shryock, Richard: embedded narratives and, 27; essential role of a frame and, 54

Simpson, David: language as national argument, 11

Singer, Alan: regarding character and, 146n78

"Siren Song" (Atwood), 53

Sketches of English Character (Gore), 46

Smith-Rosenberg, Carroll: "overdetermined ways" and national identities, 137n35

"So-And-So Reclining on Her Couch" (Stevens), 114–15

Spencer, Benjamin T.: patriotic exultation and War of 1812, 13; self-confidence after war of 1812, 74
Spencer, Philip: on spread of written vernacular, 14; written code of the Bible and, 15
Spengemann, William C.: American literature placed in context and, 132n34
Spenser, Edmund: concern for audience's role and, 38; inexpressible's humility and, 40; methods for representing the unreadable and, 131n29
Spurr, David: on "The Love Song of J. Alfred Prufrock," 106
"St. Armorer's Church from the Outside" (Stevens), 103
St. John de Crèvecoeur, J. Hector: soil as metaphor and, 44; temporary impediment of language and, 48; whig practices defeating whig principles and, 133n41; words uttered in name of God or country and, 44; voice of American farmer and, 45
Steiner, George: language and frontiers and, 140n78; on German and French philosophical despair, 46; origins of topos looking to God, 67; search for primordial unity and, 134n47; topos of the inexpressible, 5
Stein, Gertrude: *The Making of Americans* and, 110
Stevens, Wallace: Bloom's comparison to Whitman and, 118; critical reception and historicism, 150n38; formalizing the frame and, 8; framing and, 110; "Good-bye, / Mrs. Pappadopoulos, and thanks," 116; "thing itself" and, 71; interactive power of, 151n49; "Jouga" and, 114; lack of assertion and, 111; "Man Carrying Thing," 115; "Not Ideas about the Thing but the Thing Itself," 103, 111; "The Poem That Took the Place of a Mountain," 115; "The Poem That Took the Place of a Mountain," 112–13; poetics of inexpressibility and, 116; "Re-statement of Romance," 114; "So-And-So Reclining on Her Couch," 114–15; "Thinking of a Relation between the Images of Metaphors," 114

Symons, Dana M.: on medieval English poetry, 135n9

T

tall tales, 101; alienating an audience and, 86; humor in Stevens's poems and, 115; oral strategies of framing and, 119; overview of, 83–85
Tannen, Deborah: "structures of expectations" and, 74, 101
Tanner, Tony: "foregrounding" in American narrative, 129n87
The Dial: "The Future is Better Than the Past," 102
The Scarlet Letter: as "rhetorical project," 69
"thing itself": framing and, 106; overview of, 103–5
"Thinking of a Relation between the Images of Metaphors" (Stevens), 114
Tonkin, Elizabeth, 95; "oral narrative's character of time unfinished" and, 95
Too Late the Phalarope (Paton), 101
topos: definition of, 35; medieval writers and, 37; styles and modes of representation and, 35; unavailability of human language and, 48
Troilus and Criseyde (Chaucer), 37, 51
Tucker, George: comparing the "individuals of the two continents," 27; fate of exclusion from "genius" and, 22; preoccupation with originality and, 65; rhetoric of insufficiency and, 61
"The Turn of the Screw" (James), 101
Tyler, Royall: habits of a strange country and, 27

U

unabducible: definition of, 44
United States Review: on Whitman's style, 20

V

Vaughan, Henry, 54

Vendler, Helen: descriptions of Whitman's "reprise-poem," 125n54; on Stevens's prevalent voice of hesitation, 111; on Whitman's intellectual capacity, 20; theological possibilities for conveying the ineffable and, 150n39

A Vocabulary, or Collection of Words (Pickering), 10

W

Waiting for Godot: human and choral fallibility and, 53
"Wakefield" (Hawthorne), 88, 90, 101
Washington, George: quest for originality in life of, 140n72; reputation of, 14; honor and, 15
The Waste Land (Eliot), 88, 106
Watts, Ann Chalmers: inexpressibility topos and, 143n26; struggle between word and not-word, 87
Weber, Max: belief in common ancestry, 15
Webster, Noah: championing American words and, 45; complex politics of, 123n16; on American language, 61; on sameness of expression, 11
Weisbuch, Robert: "actualism" and, 127n77
Welsch, Roger L.: *Bartleby* and, 93; shaggy dog stories and, 84
Wharton, G. M.: Indians' "mystery" and, 75
Wheelock, Matthew: expecting perfection in human institutions and, 46
Whitman, Walt: 1856 letter to Emerson and, 22; 1876 Preface and, 29–30, 89–90; as-yet unnameable "poet" and, 107; Bloom's comparison to Stevens and, 118; concerns with his language and, 19; expressing the inexpressible and, 32–33; on "first-class song" and, 108; forging a language and, 8; historic importance of Preface of 1855 and, 18; inexpressibility and "imaginative literature," 43; *Leaves of Grass* and, 6, 20, 89–90, 126n64; English language and, 86; American National Literature and, 28; Preface of 1855, 5–6, 9, 16–21, 33, 49–50, 56–58, 67–69, 89, 120; rhetoric of a national "birthmark," 108; "the signs are effectual" and, 17; temporal dare of "probably" and, 16; the words "I say" and, 29–30
Wiesel, Elie: topos of the inexpressible and, 5
Wilde, Oscar: on Whitman's style, 20
Willard, Sidney: views on Pickering and, 10
Williams, William Carlos: on Whitman's style, 20
Winthrop, John: synthesis of man's time and God's and, 41
Wollman, Howard: on spread of written vernacular, 14; written code of the Bible and, 15
Wolter, Jürgen: anticipatory complexity of frames, 146n89
"The Woman at the Washington Zoo" (Jarrell), 53
Wonham, Henry B.: "collaborative games" and, 95; oral discourse and, 83–84; "invitation for collusive agreement" and, 84; multiple verbal meanings and, 100; tall tales and, 86, 89
Wood, Gordon: practice of recasting and, 140n72

Y

Yeats, W. B.: exploiting rhetorical confusion and, 71; nationalist rhetoric and Celtic folklore and, 75

www.ingramcontent.com/pod-product-compliance
Lightning Source LLC
Chambersburg PA
CBHW031629160426
43196CB00006B/341